D0875778

# FINAL JUDGMENTS

# FINAL
# JUDGMENTS

## DUTY AND EMOTION
## IN ROMAN WILLS,
### 200 B.C.—A.D. 250

Edward Champlin

University of California Press
*Berkeley · Los Angeles · Oxford*

University of California Press
Berkeley and Los Angeles, California

University of California Press, Ltd.
Oxford, England

© 1991 by
The Regents of the University of California

**Library of Congress Cataloging-in-Publication Data**

Champlin, Edward, 1948–
  Final judgments: duty and emotion in Roman wills, 200 B.C.–A.D.
250 / Edward Champlin
      p. cm.
  Includes bibliographical references and index.
  ISBN 0-520-07103-4
  1. Rome—Social conditions.  2. Social structure—Rome.  3. Wills
(Roman law).  I. Title.
HN10.R7C43 1991
306'.0945'632–dc20                                        90-38795
                                                                    CIP

Printed in the United States of America

9  8  7  6  5  4  3  2  1

The paper used in this publication meets the minimum requirements of
American National Standard for Information Sciences—Permanence of Paper
for Printed Library Materials, ANSI Z39.48–1984. ∞

*Parentibus Optimis*

# Contents

# Acknowledgments

This book was begun in the lively and hospitable environment of the Seminar für Alte Geschichte at the University of Heidelberg, during the academic year 1984/85. My first debt is to my host during that year, Géza Alföldy, for his initial invitation, his unstinting personal kindness, and his generous scholarly support: to him my warmest thanks, with the realization that this book is but small repayment of what I owe him. Special thanks, also, to Johannes Hahn, whose innumerable acts of friendship during the year are fondly remembered. And I am deeply grateful for the generosity of the Alexander von Humboldt-Stiftung and of Princeton University, which made my stay in Heidelberg possible.

Since then, several scholars have given much needed help at various stages. I am grateful first to the small band of highly critical students who endured an early draft of much of this material during weekly seminars in the spring of 1988: Jane Chaplin, Craige Champion, Drew Keller, and Sara Maxwell. Bob Connor and Bruce Frier provided much guidance to an early version of chapter 1. And my greatest debt is to four friendly critics who generously read the entire manuscript: David Johnston, Jim Luce, Richard Saller, and Richard Talbert. To them, and again to Caroline for all her help, my deepest thanks.

# Note on Abbreviations

For abbreviations readers are directed to the following standard works.

Classical authors and texts: *The Oxford Classical Dictionary*, 2d ed. (Oxford, 1970).
Learned journals: *L'Année philologique.*
Papyri: J. F. Oates, R. S. Bagnall, W. H. Willis, and K. A. Worp, *Checklist of Editions of Greek Papyri and Ostraca*, 3d ed. (Atlanta, 1985).
Inscriptions: I. Calabi Limentani, *Epigrafia Latina* (Milan, 1968); A. G. Woodhead, *The Study of Greek Inscriptions*, 2d ed. (Cambridge, 1981).

The following collections of inscriptions and papyri are particularly important:

| | |
|---|---|
| *Chrest. Mitt.* | L. Mitteis and U. Wilcken, *Grundzüge und Chrestomathie der Papyruskunde*. Vol. 2, *Juristischer Teil*. Pt. 2. *Chrestomathie*. Leipzig and Berlin, 1912. |
| D'Ors | A. D'Ors. *Epigraphía jurídica de la España romana*. Madrid, 1953. |
| *FIRA* | V. Arangio-Ruiz. *Fontes iuris romani anteiustiniani.* Vol. 3, *Negotia*. 2d ed. Florence, 1972. |
| Laum | B. Laum. *Stiftungen in der griechischen und römischen Antike*. Vol. 2. Leipzig, 1914. |

# Introduction

In the second century A.D., the historian Florus wrote that the testament of Julius Caesar was the prime cause of the great civil war which broke out after his murder: his substitute heir (*secundus heres*), Mark Antony, was furious that Caesar had preferred Octavian to him.[1] None of us would accept this as a serious explanation, but did Florus' own audience also pass over his claim with a smile? Or would they have understood him somewhat differently?

This book finds its origin in two sharply contrasting but similar ancient beliefs. One, recorded by the younger Pliny, was the popular saying that a person's will was the mirror of his or her character; the other, attributed by Lucian to a professional Greek philosopher, was that the Romans told the truth but once in their lives, when writing their wills. Valid or not, both suggest that their last wills and testaments may open an extraordinary window into the Roman mind.

My purpose is to draw a map of the universe of the individual Roman testator as he or she contemplated personal extinction, to describe what mattered to them and why. To do this we must first consider testators' motives in making a will at all, a complicated interaction of personal wishes and external pressures,[2] and then attempt a sketchy profile—in terms of gender, status, wealth, age, and family situation—of those likely to leave a will under Roman law. Then we must consider the act of testation itself, the possibilities and constraints of the situation: at what point in the course of a lifetime a testator was likely to make a will, who actually composed and drafted the document, how witnesses were selected; and then the dark side, the deep-rooted fears of forgery and

---

1. Florus *Epit.* 2.15: *Prima civilium motum causa testamentum Caesaris fuit, cuius secundus heres Antonius, praelatum sibi Octavium furens, inexpiabile contra adoptionem acerrimi iuvenis susceperat bellum.*
2. An earlier version of chapter 1 appeared in *Classical Philology* 84 (1989).

inheritance hunting, and their effect on the act of testation. Next we must place the testator, *ego*, within a ring of concentric circles, to search for patterns and intentions in the posthumous treatment of the people who meant something to him or her in life: the immediate family and close kin; servants and friends; and at the furthest remove, social groups and the community at large. And finally, returning to the testator at the center, and to the motives for leaving a will at all, we must peer into a vague and uncertain afterlife.

Several assumptions, prejudices, or limitations inherent in the study should be registered here. One is that this is not a work of Roman law or legal history, though I hope that much in it will be of interest to students of Roman law. Romanists are particularly concerned with what happened after death, with the solution of legal problems and the application of rules, or with the history of the law of succession. My concern here is with what happened before death, if not immediately before death then at least in contemplation of it, and with the very human testator. It is not with the infinite legal problems which arise after death, but with the pressures moral and social on testators, the options available to them, and the strategies they adopted to achieve their wishes posthumously.

I have limited myself to Roman law wills. This excludes non-Roman practices coexisting within the same empire, the same province, even the same village; it excludes parallel but nontestamentary acts such as gifts made in life to take effect after death, *donationes mortis causa*; and it doubtless excludes too many relevant nonlegal acts and opinions. All of these certainly affected Roman testation. The reason for their exclusion is the singularity of the Roman will. Lawyers and custom imposed a strict formality on the document, certain forms and certain actions were expected by law and society, and since ignorance or inattention could so easily overturn them at law, the testator must express his last wishes with exceptional care. Hence the document imposed an invaluable uniformity, one which bound emperor and commoner, from Spain to Syria.[3] The great bulk of the human race under

---

3. Neatly captured by J. Crook, *Law and Life of Rome* (Ithaca, N.Y., 1967), 130: "Most impressive and significant, however are two wills of very ordinary men

the Roman empire did not leave Roman law wills; but those who did wrote them with care, identifying themselves (whether consciously or not) in the face of death, and subscribing to a whole code of conduct becoming to a Roman citizen. Hence, whatever the vagaries and disparities of our evidence, of geography and chronology, and of the idiosyncrasies of individual men and women, we can legitimately attempt to identify patterns in the options available to and actions taken by those who left Roman wills.

The study will impinge on a variety of important wider topics, from inheritance hunting to the structure of the family, from public philanthropy to views of the afterlife, from slavery to political loyalty. It cannot begin to explore many of these. For the sake of classicists and ancient historians, I do hope that it has collected and interpreted what Roman testators have to tell us about some of the basic customs and institutions of the world which they took for granted.

Finally, the terminal dates of this study are circa 200 B.C. and circa A.D. 250, although I have arbitrarily incorporated evidence from the period down to the death of Constantine (A.D. 337) and even after. These dates correspond roughly at the one extreme with the beginning of Latin literature and at the other with the end of classical jurisprudence; moreover, no individual wills are attested before the second century B.C., while the number of known testators drops off dramatically with the virtual disappearance of juristic literature in the later third century A.D. At the same time, the period is bounded by important legislation. Its beginning corresponds with the first major testamentary laws, the Lex Furia testamentaria (204/169 B.C.) and the Lex Voconia (169), while its end is marked by two imperial constitutions which profoundly affected the character of Roman law testation, that is, the Constitutio Antoniniana (c. A.D. 212), which granted citizenship to most inhabitants of the empire, and that constitution of Severus Alexander (emperor 222–235), which allowed Roman wills

---

indeed, a private soldier and a veteran, preserved by the sands of Egypt—significant precisely because they are no botch jobs or humble scraps, but dispose of their little patrimonies with all the formality of the testament *per aes et libram* exactly as the emperor did."

to be writted in Greek. Whether historical and legal changes within these five centuries significantly alter any conclusions is for the reader to judge.

One theme, about which much could be said, I have all but ignored. That is the economic importance of wills. Inheritance was a major mode for the transfer of wealth in the ancient world, hence the fascination with wills which pervades Roman literature, and the intense concern of family and friends in daily life: for most people, inheritance was the only real chance they had of becoming significantly richer. But I wish to concentrate on the testator, for whom the value of the estate was not a primary motivation, beyond the common understanding that if you had something of value you should direct the disposition of it in a will.

Rather, another theme will receive repeated attention here, a theme which divides with particular sharpness Roman testators from their modern counterparts. In his classic *Ancient Law*, Sir Henry Maine observed that the Romans had a "horror of Intestacy." The phrase is too dramatic; it demands qualification. It is better to assert that among those Romans who had property worth leaving and who subscribed to traditional Roman values as they perceived them, there flourished a strong duty of testation, a duty owed to oneself, one's family, one's servants, one's friends, and one's society. If we accept the existence of that duty, it must have had a profound effect on all aspects of making a will.

# 1

# Motives

> There is dispute over inheritance from the dead, until the testament is produced in public. And when the testament has been produced in public, everyone is silent so that the tablets may be opened and read. The judge listens intently, the lawyers fall silent, the heralds enforce silence, the entire populace hangs in suspense, so that the words of a dead man may be read out, the words of one lying senseless in a tomb. He lies senseless in a tomb, and his words have power.[1]

Augustine's arresting tableau, sketched shortly before the collapse of the central Roman power in the West, touches on two emotional commitments that can be traced back through the history of Rome: an intense public interest in the last will and testament of the individual; and the unshaken acceptance by both society and the law (in principle, at least) of the fundamental paradox that the wishes of an individual who had ceased to exist, ceased to have a "will," should be held valid.[2] At the beginning and the end of its existence—when it was sealed and when it was opened—the Roman will was a very public document. Its earliest form was indeed a public ceremony, a declaration made before the *comitia calata*, called specifically for that purpose (and others) twice a year.[3] And the form standard throughout the classical period, the *testamentum per aes et libram*, was in essence an oral ceremony before witnesses, although the mere written record in

---

1. Augustine. *Enarr. in ps.* 21 2.30: *Tamdiu contenditur de hereditate mortuorum, quamdiu testamentum proferatur in publicum; et cum testamentum prolatum fuerit in publicum, tacent omnes, ut tabulae aperiantur et recitentur; iudex intentus audit, advocati silent, praecones silentium faciunt, universus populus suspensus est, ut legantur verba mortui, non sentientis in monumento. Ille sine sensu iacet in monumento, et valent verba ipsius.*
2. The younger Pliny took pride in allowing even his slaves to make *quasi testamenta,* valid within his household: *Ep.* 8.16.1–2.
3. Gaius *Inst.* 2.101.

time displaced the act.[4] Similarly, at the other end of its existence, writing of the formal public opening of the will Ulpian could remark that the tablets of a will were a document belonging not to one person, the heir, but to all those to whom something was assigned therein, indeed that they were a public document (hence the public interest in the opening so vividly described by Augustine and others).[5] Inevitably this strong social dimension affected the will itself. What is for us a very personal document was for the Romans much more consciously the product of a tension between private hopes and social expectations.

Certain elements of Roman society—that is, the propertied and the educated—were obsessed with the making of wills, both their own and others', to a degree and for reasons which may be hard to grasp today.[6] True, some with higher concerns could profess incomprehension of an individual's interest in a world left behind. The Christian Augustine naturally made much of the care expended on the earthly testament to the neglect of God's. You will certainly die, he thundered in one sermon, and be quite unaware of what goes on in your house, yet you want your will to have effect there, you pass on the buildings to your sons, and if you know that they will divide them otherwise you mourn. What care, what anxiety over a mere house, a roof doomed to collapse! How you resist to the limit raging fevers, pressing illness, the onset of death itself, gasping out your last words so that you can finish your testament. Similarly, more than two centuries earlier, Lucian's Platonist friend Nigrinus poured scorn on the Romans' concern with last wills and with life after their own deaths, on their testamentary outspoken-

4. Briefly, M. Kaser, *Das römische Privatrecht*, vol. 1, *Das altrömische, das vorklassische und klassische Recht*[2] (Munich, 1971), 678–80.

5. *Tabularum testamenti instrumentum non est unius hominis, hoc est heredis, sed universorum quibus quid illic adscriptum est: quin potius publicum est instrumentum:* Dig. 29.3.2 pr. On the meaning of "public," cf. P. Leuregans, "Testamenti factio non privati sed publici iuris est," *RHDFE*[4] 53 (1975): 225–57, discussing an assertion of Papinian (*Dig.* 28.1.3). He traces a shift in thought from emphasis on the *voluntas defuncti* to concern for the common good. Augustine's tableau can be matched by one in Lucian (*Timon* 21, Loeb translation, A. M. Harmon: "Wealth" is speaking): "The dead man is laid out in a dark corner of the house with an old sheet over his knees, to be fought for by the weasels, while those who have expectations wait for me in the public square with their mouths open."

6. That we are dealing only with a minority must be understood; cf. the ironical reminder of D. Daube, *Roman Law: Linguistic, Social and Philosophical Aspects* (Edinburgh, 1969), 71–75.

ness after a lifetime of careful repression ("The Romans tell the truth only once in their lives, in their will") and on the vanity of their desire to burn favorite clothing at the funeral, to have servants tend their tombs, or to strew the grave with flowers: they remain foolish, he said, even on their deathbeds.[7]

Although philosophical minds might rise above such folly, Augustine and Nigrinus were clearly criticizing something that they and their audiences considered to be a fact of daily life and an act of great importance. Thus, to Pliny, the normal daily round in Rome included the witnessing of wills, and for Seneca the active life consisted of appearing as a lawyer, witnessing wills, and supporting candidates for election; indeed most Roman writers betray a keen interest in the composition and contents of wills.[8] And for once we can be sure that the writers reflect something of the larger world for, insofar as we can measure it, some 60 to 70 percent of all Roman civil litigation seems to have arisen over problems connected with succession on death.[9]

Despite such general interest, no extended meditation on the fundamental question "Why does a person leave a will?" has survived; the loss of Galen's *On Making Wills*, listed among his works on moral philosophy, is particularly sad.[10] The closest thing to such a meditation comes, not surprisingly, in Seneca's treatise *On Benefits*:[11]

> And tell me, when we have reached the very end of life, and are drawing up our will, do we not dispense benefits that will yield us nothing? How much time is spent, how long do we debate with ourselves to whom and how much we shall give! For what difference does it make to whom we give since no one will make us any return? Yet never are we more careful in our giving, never do we wrestle more in making decisions.... We search for those who are most worthy to inherit our possessions, and there is nothing that we arrange with more scrupulous care than this which is of no concern to ourselves. Yet, heavens! the great pleasure [*voluptas*] that comes as we

7. Augustine *Serm.* 47.22; Lucian *Nigr.* 30.
8. Pliny *Ep.* 1.9.2; Seneca *Ep.* 8.6.
9. The calculations are those of J. M. Kelly, *Studies in the Civil Judicature of the Roman Republic* (Oxford, 1976), 71–92 ("The Statistics of Litigation"). For a sociological explanation of the phenomenon: B. W. Frier, *The Rise of the Roman Jurists* (Princeton, 1985), 37–38.
10. *Libr. propr.* 13 (19.46 K).
11. *Ben.* 4.11.4–6; from the Loeb translation of J. W. Basore, slightly modified.

think: "Through me this man will become richer, and I, by increasing his wealth, shall add new luster to his high position." If we give only when we may expect some return, we ought to die intestate!

Although he considers only one aspect of the will, Seneca here touches upon several elements worth consideration, and one of his observations, however casual, deserves repetition: people simply derive present pleasure (*voluptas*) from making wills, they enjoy what might otherwise seem a morbid or a futile act. If nothing else, in the words of pseudo-Quintilian, making a will was a *solacium*, a comfort, in the face of death.[12]

It is the interaction of this private pleasure in testation with an intense public interest in it that gives the Roman will a character markedly different from its modern counterpart. The motives of the Roman testator in making a will are fundamental to all that follows.[13]

Wills are, most obviously, expressions of emotion: *testamenta, quibus omnem adfectum fateremur.*[14] Fundamentally, and implicitly, they offer a simple index of likes and dislikes, and particularly of concern for the future happiness and well-being of loved ones when the testator is no longer there to care for them. The law of intestacy imposed a standardized pattern of succession on all citizens: in the late republic (for instance) *sui heredes, proximus agnatus, gentiles*, in that order—that is (roughly speaking), heirs in the testator's power (*patriapotestas*) at the time of death, male relatives on the father's side, and members of the same clan (*gens*). The will is in essence a vehicle for moderated deviance from the rules of intestacy, deviance moderated both by law and by custom, as (broadly speaking) most wills name children or very near rela-

---

12. [Quintilian] *Declam.* 308.1. Hence perhaps the slip on the part of stonecutters who wrote forms of *voluptas* (pleasure) for *voluntas* (will): *CIL* 5.4488 (Brixia), 3.4282 = *RIU* 690 (Civitas Azaliorum), *ex voluptate testamenti*. On the other hand, receiving an inheritance was no solace for the loss of the testator: *P. Bon.* 5.

13. Among works on social aspects of the will in general, the following are particularly useful: E. Wistrand, *Arv och testamenten i romarnas sociala liv*, vol. 22 of *Studia graeca et latina Gothoburgensia* (Göteborg, 1966); L. Boyer, "La fonction sociale des legs d'après la jurisprudence classique," *RHDFE*⁴ 43 (1965), 333–408; K. Hopkins, *Death and Renewal* (Cambridge, 1983), 235–47; M. Corbier, "Idéologie et pratique de l'héritage (Ier s. av. J-C – IIe s. ap. J-C)," *Index* 13 (1985): 501–28 (mainly on Pliny the Younger).

14. [Quintilian] *Declam.* 332.4.

tives as heirs. But so simple are the nature and intent of the law of intestate succession that it cannot possibly answer the needs of most people who have something to leave. To assign a larger share of the inheritance to one child than to another; to disinherit a third; to nominate guardians; to subtract from the estate legacies of varied nature and value for different friends and relations; to manumit slaves: all of these acts are impossible under intestate succession in the classical law, and all can be read with caution as indications of the individual testator's emotions, his or her concern to protect, to reward, and to punish. They were indeed commonly read as such—witness the testator who carefully explained to his dearest daughter in his will that her brother would be getting a larger share of the estate than she because, as she knew, her brother's expenses would be great and he would be responsible for payment of the legacies.[15]

What naturally catch the eye are the explicit expressions of emotion: the dearest, most affectionate, most pious (or most ungrateful) of children, the rarest (or most obnoxious) of friends, the most (or least) deserving of slaves, the most beloved of fatherlands.[16] Seldom do the actual documents that survive at any length omit some overt indication of the testator's feelings. Hope, fear, anger, doubt, delight, satisfaction, and disappointment—*furor, foedis adulatio, lamentationes*—can visibly tumble over each other in the succeeding paragraphs of a single will, all tremendously compressed by the nature of the document and normally presented as the explanation of an action or an instruction: "I beg you, my dearest wife, not to leave anything to your brothers when you die: you have your sisters' sons to whom you may leave things. You know that one of your brothers killed our son while robbing him: and another did even worse things to me."[17]

What distinguishes such expressions of emotion is how the Romans perceived them. According to the unfriendly critic Nigrinus, only once in life did the Romans speak without reserve, in their wills—so that they might not be harmed by the truth they

15. *Dig.* 31.34.6.
16. E.g., *FIRA* 48.3 (*amicus rarissimus*), 7 (*filia pientissima*), 92 (a slave *pessime de me merito*); 53 (*patriae meae amantissimae*); 55b (*municipes carissimi*); *CPL* 222 (*uxori quam dilego*).
17. *Dig.* 31.88.16.

spoke. And, whatever the reality, it is abundantly clear that the will was indeed perceived as a vessel of truth, a document carefully weighed and written free of ordinary constraints and without fear or favor, since it became public knowledge only when its author was past caring. Such, for instance, was Seneca's point in speaking of one's freedom in the will from the hopes, fears, and desires that compromise daily judgment; and it is one aspect of the popular saying recorded by the younger Pliny: "creditur vulgo testamenta hominum speculum esse morum"—that is, testaments reveal people's true nature.[18]

Two particularly dramatic examples illustrate both the public's interest in the will and its perception of the will as the vessel of truth. Valerius Maximus tells of a late republican Pompeius Reginus whose brother had passed over him in silence in his will. To show the iniquity of this act, Reginus took his own will to the assembly and opened it there before a large number of senators and knights in order to demonstrate that, if he had died first, he would have left his brother as his major heir: there could be no stronger evidence for his own proper conduct.[19]

Equally instructive here is a crucial incident in Octavian's propaganda campaign against his rival and former colleague Mark Antony, the seizing and reading of Antony's will in 32 B.C. When deserters from Antony's party told him where to find it, Octavian took the testament from the temple of Vesta, where it had been deposited with the Vestal Virgins, and read it out in senate and assembly to reveal Antony's infatuation with Cleopatra, his royal treatment of their children, and his wish to be buried with her in Egypt, at Alexandria. This is instructive not only because great scandal was raised by the terrible act of reproaching a man with what were to be his private and posthumous wishes, but also because on this grave occasion Octavian was held to be excused by the very nature of those wishes, for here was proof positive that Antony was no longer acting as a Roman citizen.[20] Antony himself could not deny the contents. In one's will one said, at last, exactly what one felt.

18. *Ep.* 8.18.1.
19. Valerius Maximus 7.8.4.
20. Plutarch *Ant.* 58.4–8 (scandal); Dio 50.3.4 (excuse); Suetonius *Aug.* 17.1 (proof). There has been considerable debate over the document, most recently: J. Crook, "A Legal Point about Mark Antony's Will," *JRS* 47 (1957): 36–38; J. R.

This perception of freedom from restraint in the testament is central to the Roman point of view. Obviously life was led, at least by the will-making classes, in the midst of considerable social restraint. There were correct Roman ways to act toward parents and children, toward brothers and sisters, toward relatives and friends, toward patrons and clients and servants: *amicitia*, for instance, suggests a whole code of behavior corresponding only in part to modern notions of emotional friendship.[21] But after death everything changed, and testators' freedom of expression depended not so much on their lack of posthumous accountability as on their reasonable certainty that society would sanction their carefully considered last wishes, within the confines of the law. There was, in brief, a commonly recognized *licentia testamentorum*.[22] The Romans accepted this license of testators to say what they wished because it was felt to be the truth, confirmed or revealed; one could be sure of what another person thought only after he or she had laid aside the mask of daily life.

The importance of this final revelation of a testator's true feelings is strikingly illustrated in Suetonius' account of a man who probably inherited more than any other Roman from his duly grateful friends: the first citizen, Augustus. It was the emperor's habit to weigh the final judgments of friends with obsessive anxiety. Economic advantage was the least of his concerns, as Suetonius claims and as we can well believe. What he demanded from his friends after their deaths was the same goodwill, *benivolentia*, that they had shown him in life. If they left him too little or failed to praise him enough, he was visibly upset, but he was delighted if they spoke of him *grate pieque*.[23] The last wishes of the dead were also a last—and therefore true—judgment, *supremum iudicium*, and that judgment mattered terribly to the living.

Johnson, "The Authenticity and Validity of Antony's Will," *AC* 47 (1978): 494–503, with earlier bibliography; F. A. Sirianni, "Was Antony's Will Partially Forged?" *AC* 53 (1984): 236–41; J. Crook, "A Negative Point about Mark Antony's Will," *AC* 58 (1989): 221–23. The matter is not relevant here, but I see no reason to doubt the will's authenticity.

21. P. A. Brunt, " 'Amicitia' in the Late Roman Republic," *PCPS* 11 (1963): 1–20 = (revised) *The Fall of the Roman Republic and Related Essays* (Oxford, 1988), 351–81, at 351–61.

22. Which Augustus refused to curtail: Suetonius *Aug.* 56.1.

23. Suetonius *Aug.* 66.4.

A flowery parody of the designation of an heir reads: "Let P. Novanius Gallio—to whom as my benefactor I will and owe all that is good, in return for the great affection which he has borne me [then follow other details]—be my heir."[24] There is an appropriate technical term for just such an explicit last judgment: *elogium*. The word is defined generally as a clause added to wills; yet it is not just any clause but one that sums up the character of (normally) the heir. Thus, a man designates an heir and adds the *elogium* "I found her chaste"; or "they recited the wills of his *saltuarii* [his rural laborers] in which Trimalchio was disinherited *cum elogio*."[25] More often the judgment is negative, and the original idea, connected with dedicatory inscriptions, is transmuted into the reason for disinheritance, as in Augustine's remark that a man disinherited his two children, one with praise, the other with *elogium*, "that is, with vituperation."[26]

Most commonly, of course, by the simple choice of heirs, legatees, and slaves to be freed, a will indicated positive judgments: one could even speak of the *honos iudici*.[27] Naturally the greatest honor (*honos*), and the greatest burden, lay in being instituted an heir, particularly if one was not a *suus heres*.[28] However, the choice of an heir was determined by a number of external factors. Much greater freedom of expression or judgment lay in the assignment of legacies, which also allowed a more precise evaluation of the testator's relations with others. Again, family affection was to a large extent expected to dictate action: "He distinguished his grandchildren with many most pleasing legacies," or "I have treated my grandson honorably."[29]

Such affection aside for the moment, by one standard a legacy

24. Quintilian *Inst.* 9.2.35, Loeb translation of H. E. Butler, modified.

25. Seneca *Controv.* 2.7; Petronius *Sat.* 53.8 (clearly reversing the norm for comic effect).

26. *Sermo* 355.2: *ambos exheredavit: illam cum laude, istum cum elogio, id est, cum vituperatione.* Cf. [Quintilian] *Declam.* 2.15; Apuleius *Apol.* 99; Cicero *Cluent.* 135; *Dig.* 28.2.14.2, 37.10.1.9; *CJ* 6.55.9; Fulgentius *Sermones* 54.

27. As does the *laudator Murdiae* (*FIRA* 70): *Viro certam pecuniam legavit, ut ius dotis honore iudici augeretur.* In *ILS* 8261 (Puteoli) the writer reserves his tomb for himself, his wife, the freedmen and freedwomen "whom I have honored in my will" (*quos tabulis honoravi*), and their descendants.

28. See Cicero *Quinct.* 14; cf. Ulpian *Dig.* 37.5.5.6, and F. von Woess, *Das römische Erbrecht und die Erbanwärter* (Berlin, 1911), 138–51, on the primacy of the *honos institutionis*.

29. Pliny *Ep.* 8.18.2; Cicero *Att.* 2.18a.2. See further, chapters 6 and 7 below.

was simply a mark of honor, inevitably intended and understood as a reward for friendship and its services; and the receipt of a legacy was a matter of pride: "He was approved by the *iudicia* of many *cognati* and *propinqui*," or "Curianus has left me a legacy, and marked out my deed with a notable honor," or "How reverently and faithfully he served his friends you may learn from the last wishes of many," or "He showed his gratitude to all of his relatives for the services of each," or "In that recent testament of his he remembered me most dutifully and most honorably."[30] In Martial's words on a dying testator, "Dead already to himself, he yet lived for his dear friends."[31] For the *amicus legato honoratus*—the friend honored by a legacy—its economic value was professedly immaterial;[32] and all our sources, literary and documentary alike, suggest that at all levels of society most legacies outside the family were little more than keepsakes when measured against the total wealth of the testator and the legatee.[33] The honor for the legatee rested on the simple theory that merit was being publicly rewarded—real merit, since the bestower of the honor could expect nothing in return.[34] Cicero was particularly proud that friends continued to remember him in their wills when he was in exile.[35]

More arresting to modern sensibilities is the common indulgence by Roman testators in negative *iudicia*. Such condemnations were expressed in three different ways: through omission, disinheritance, and abuse.

30. *CIL* 2.3504; Pliny *Ep.* 5.1.1, 7.31.5, 8.18.7; Apuleius *Apol.* 92.2.
31. 4.73.5: *iam sibi defunctus, caris dum vivit amicis.*
32. "Modest but extremely gratifying" (Fronto *M. Caes.* 1.6.6); "some small amount *honoris gratia*" (Apuleius *Apol.* 100.2).
33. Further below, pp. 142–50. E.g., the will of Antonius Silvanus, *FIRA* 47, with fifty denarii to the procurator of the estate and fifty to his commanding officer; or the so-called *testamentum Dasumianum, FIRA* 48.15–26, single pounds of gold and silver; Martial 2.76.
34. See von Woess, *Erbrecht,* 149, for references to *merita* rewarded. Cf. the institution of an *extraneus* as heir at Quintilian *Inst.* 9.2.35 (quoted above); Nepos *Att.* 21.1, *multas enim hereditates nulla alia re quam bonitate consecutus.* Pliny professed shock at Regulus' acceptance of inheritances and legacies *quasi mereatur* (*Ep.* 2.20.11); Apuleius spoke of *immeritae hereditates* (*Apol.* 23.7). The form letters of *P. Bon.* 5, demonstrating how to congratulate a friend on an inheritance won, or to commiserate with him on receiving too little, speak repeatedly of *obsequia* or *merita* being rewarded: col. 3.15, 3.20, 5.15, 9.9–10, 9.22.
35. *Dom.* 85. See S. L. Mohler, "Cicero's Legacies," *TAPA* 63 (1932): 73–87, with I. Shatzman, *Senatorial Wealth and Roman Politics* (Brussels, 1975), 409–12. It should be noted that the 20 million sesterces inherited by Cicero and flaunted by him before Antony were explicitly inheritances, not legacies: *Phil.* 2.40–41.

The most dramatic of omissions marked the will of the ancient and wealthy Iunia, sister of Brutus and widow of Cassius. This document named almost every leading citizen of Rome with honor, but pointedly passed over the emperor Tiberius; this was the topic of much popular discussion, according to Tacitus, but Tiberius did, and could do, nothing. Here Iunia followed the dictator Sulla one hundred years earlier, who had named all but one of his friends as legatees or as guardians for his son, pointedly ignoring the young Pompey.[36] And should that prove too subtle, there was a useful variant on the insult: one could leave a trifling sum to someone who might expect much more, so that (in the words of Apuleius) it would be clear that the testator had judged the legatee in anger rather than passed him over in absence of mind.[37]

The key element here is publicity: the insult is intended less to upset its recipient than to damage his or her reputation. Such omission from the wills of one's nearest and dearest was a joy to one's enemies,[38] and Valerius Maximus devotes a lively and highly disapproving section to a series of bad examples—testators who should have rewarded a relative or a friend or a patron, yet who shocked society by ignoring them in their wills.[39] Antony's taunt, that Cicero had never received any inheritances, stung the orator into calculating in public exactly how much he had inherited.[40]

Disinheritance, potentially far more damaging, is accordingly more restricted. The law required that disinheritance of a *suus heres* be explicit, and that the person be specifically named if he was a son in his father's power. But, in Seneca's words, what sane person would disinherit his own son, save for great and repeated

---

36. Tacitus *Ann.* 3.76; Plutarch *Sulla* 38.2, *Pompeius* 15.3; cf. the insult at Horace *Serm.* 2.5.62–69. Further pointed omissions at Cicero *Att.* 1.16.10; *Dom.* 49; *Sest.* 111.

37. Apuleius *Apol.* 97.5; cf. Cicero *Caec.* 17 (an heir to 1/72); Valerius Maximus 8.8.2. Suetonius considered even the HS 800,000 legacy left to his great-nephew Claudius by Augustus to be inadequate (*Claud.* 4.7). The biographer had seen the will, and knew the vast size of the emperor's fortune: cf. Champlin, "The Testament of Augustus," *RhM* 132 (1989): 162.

38. Cicero *Dom.* 49, *Sest.* 111, *Att.* 1.16.10, and below; cf. Petronius *Sat.* 43.5: *et ille stips, dum fratri irascitur, nescio qui terrae filio patrimonium elegavit.*

39. 7.9.1–5: one was an ungrateful client of that careful reader of wills, Augustus.

40. *Phil.* 2.40.

offense?[41] At the least, there was a strong notion throughout Roman history of the natural right of family members to family property; indeed the jurist Paul (and others) could write that when *sui heredes* succeeded to property, there was no inheritance since they were already in a sense owners (*quodammodo domini*).[42] Society and the law took a dim view of the upsetting of natural affection and of the transfer of property away from those who had a natural claim on it. Thus there is a real tone of experienced disapproval in the observation of the jurist Gaius that "we must not approve of parents who injure their own children in their wills, which many do, ill-naturedly passing judgment on their own blood, corrupted by the wiles and incitements of stepmothers." From the last century of the republic children who were disinherited or otherwise un-fairly treated might appeal in an action known as the *querela inofficiosi testamenti*, the complaint of the unduteous will, the basis of which was that the testator had offended against the duty to respect the family, the *officium pietatis*.[43] Moreover, disinheritance, if upheld, was a stigma, and it might be grounds for abuse of pro-spective heirs by their enemies if it were even contemplated.[44] Therefore, to avoid successful challenge to the will, to show that one was both sane and justified, it was essential to give a reason: my son was bribed while acting as a judge, he fell in love with a harlot, he is not my son, and so forth.[45] But disinheritance out of anger is rarely recorded. A *suus heres* had, by definition, a right to the inheritance; posterity had to be persuaded by the testator that the prospective heir had forfeited that right.

41. *Clem.* 1.14.1; cf. Apuleius' struggle with his wife over her son: *ne hunc ob tot insignis contumelias, ob tot iniurias exheredaret* (*Apol.* 99).

42. *Dig.* 28.2.11. Cf. Pliny *Pan.* 37.2: *quae sanguine gentilitate sacrorum denique societate meruissent, quaeque numquam ut aliena et speranda sed ut sua semperque possessa ac deinceps proximo cuique transmittenda cepissent.*

43. Gaius *Dig.* 5.2.4; see Pliny *Ep.* 6.33 for precisely such *novercalia delenimenta.* Cf. Scaevola *Dig.* 28.2.43.19: *exheredationes autem non essent adiuvandae.* E. Renier, *Étude sur l'histoire de la querela inofficiosi en droit romain* (Liège, 1942), 39–124, esp. 65–76, on the *officium pietatis.* (The *color insaniae*, the argument that the testator must have been ipso facto insane, is a rhetorical embellishment and a much later addition. However, any reasonable testator could harm his or her children while staying comfortably within the law.)

44. Cicero *Caec.* 17, *Rosc.* 52–53, *Phil.* 2.42; Pliny *Ep.* 6.33.6; Tertullian *De praescr. haeret.* 37.

45. See Cicero *Cluent.* 135; Quintilian *Inst.* 7.4.20; *Dig.* 28.2.14.2, 15. For a very different view of disinheritance, see below, pp. 107–11.

Not so with explicit abuse of people who did not stand to gain from the will: they posed no threat to its validity, and the testator could express himself freely, thus causing immense discomfort to those left behind. The testator might urge that certain obnoxious slaves never be manumitted, that ungrateful freedmen and freed-women or offensive relatives be denied access to house or tomb.[46] Indeed, there seems to have been a commonplace that malefactors in general should receive as a bequest a rope (with or without a nail) to hang themselves.[47] Historically notorious, and to Tacitus worth recording, were the wills of Fulcinius Trio, which flung accusations of senility at Tiberius and of terrible crimes at the praetorian prefect Macro and the imperial freedmen; of Petronius, which set out a list of Nero's debaucheries; and of Annaeus Mela, whose testamentary charges led to a man's suicide.[48] A real appreciation of the problems for the living caused by the adverse judgment of the dead can be gained from the letters of the orator Cornelius Fronto in the mid-second century. Fronto was acutely embarrassed by a friend who, after naming him part heir in an otherwise blameless testament, had proceeded to vilify a third person in unmeasured terms. But there was more than just embarrassment, for the testator was a former imperial procurator, and his victim was the prefect of the praetorian guard himself, M. Gavius Maximus, a man, says Fronto, "whom I must treat with respect." Here the judgment of a dead man forced the living heir into a difficult choice between his duty to a friend and the displeasure of a powerful man—and delicately-phrased letters to the emperor, to the emperor's son, and to Gavius Maximus himself set out the orator's position.[49]

To repeat: the testator's last judgment mattered terribly to the living. Accordingly the concept of the *supremum iudicium* pervades both Latin literature and Latin epitaphs; and, most importantly,

46. E.g., the so-called *testamentum Dasumii, FIRA* 48.82, 92, 109; *P. Berl.* inv. 7124; *Dig.* 34.4.29; *P. Lips.* 29.
47. Martial 4.70; *CIL* 6.12649 (apparently in earnest); cf. 6.20905 = *CLE* 95 (not a will). There is a variation in the *Testamentum Porcelli,* the *popia et pistillum* to be hung from the neck of the unmentionable cook who is about to slay the piglet-testator: F. Buecheler, ed., *Petronii Saturae*[8] (Berlin, 1963), 346–47.
48. Respectively *Ann.* 6.38, cf. Dio 58.25.2; 16.17.7; 16.19.5.
49. *Ant. Pium* 3, 7, 4; for exegesis of the affair, see E. Champlin, *Fronto and Antonine Rome* (Cambridge, Mass., 1980), 100–101.

the metaphor was accepted and very heavily used by the jurists who dealt so often with inheritance disputes: *testamentum* and *supremum iudicium* were synonymous.[50]

The attention devoted by Roman testators to explicit and implicit judgments of the living in their wills is striking. Why did they feel impelled to deliver them? A clue is offered in the sometimes mechanical nature of the honor accorded to heirs and legatees by the testator's supposedly free last judgment. Take for instance the dozens of scrupulously equal keepsakes bequeathed to friends and recorded in the so-called testament of Dasumius. These bequests occupy some fifteen lines of a huge inscription and appear in what might be taken as a position of honor, immediately after the institution of heirs; but they are an undifferentiated lump—"to the friends listed below"—in sharp contrast to the subsequent sixty lines of detailed bequests to individuals. A pleased remark by Pliny in a letter to Tacitus is directly relevant: "You must have observed how in testaments, unless the testator is a very close friend (*amicissimus*) of one or the other of us, we both receive legacies of the same kind and value."[51] That is, outside of the circle of close friends, there were others who merely had to be remembered.

The last judgment at Rome was tempered with a strong sense of duty, mixed with self-esteem. The Junia who so pointedly omitted Tiberius from her will named almost every other leading citizen *cum honore*. Caesar listed "the greater part of his [future] assassins" as tutors to his son, if one should be born. Augustus, too, named the *primores civitatis* as his heirs in the third degree; many of them he detested, Tacitus noted, but by naming them he would increase his own glory.[52]

50. *Thesaurus linguae latinae* 7.2.610, s.v. "iudicium," cites authors from Cicero to Ammianus (e.g., Pliny *Ep.* 10.94, *iudicia amicorum*). Some ninety instances in the Digest are to be found in the *Vocabularium iurisprudentiae romanae (VIR)* 3. 1376–78, s.v. "iudicium" 2. B (and cf. *ultimum, postremum, novissimum*). Also in *CIL* 2. 3504 (cited above at n. 30) and *FIRA* 70 (the word appears twice in the fragment of the *laudatio Murdiae*). The *iudicia* of *CLE* 999, 1000, and 2091 do not refer to wills. By the third century, the *praetor fideicommissarius* was known as the *praetor supremar(um): ILS* 1168, 8978. In the formula letters of *P. Bon.* 5, *suppremum* has also become a substantive: col. 3.11, 5.1, 5.21, 9.2.
51. *Ep.* 7.20.6, *quin etiam in testamentis adnotasse: nisi quis forte alterutri nostrum amicissimus, eadem legata et quidem pariter accipimus.*
52. Suetonius *Iul.* 83.2, *plerosque percussorum,* cf. Dio 44.35.2; Tacitus *Ann.* 1.8.2.

Augustus' choice uncovers a real conflict for normal citizens: philosophers and popular perception to the contrary, even in their wills Romans could not speak without reserve. They might have to mask or to exaggerate their feelings in order to ensure that beneficiaries complied with their wishes, and particularly to avoid giving grounds for challenge in court.[53] Notoriously, under certain emperors it might be necessary for prominent citizens to flatter the prince with words or bequests in order to safeguard part of the property for the heirs.[54] And less dramatically, even while contemplating their own extinction testators might temper their freedom of expression by an inclination to tell people what they wanted to hear, so as to leave a good memory behind.

Inevitably, people talked about wills: "I hear that Sextus is dead. Let me know who is his heir and when his testament will be opened."[55] Cicero in particular not only was interested in wills in which he had no concern—"I want to know who the secondary heirs are and the date of the testament," "I desire earnestly to know what Hortensius has done," "Let me know what Mundus has done in his will (for I'm curious)"—he also passed judgment on them: "I'm delighted that Macula has done his duty," "I learned of Calva's will, an odious and sordid character."[56] A whole series of letters shows his concern that his estranged wife, Terentia, "give enough to those she ought to" in her will; and to her complaints about his own testament he replies that he has treated their grandson with honor and will give his will to be read by anyone who wishes to see it.[57] Similarly Pliny, whose correspondence betrays throughout an avid interest in matters of inheritance and a detailed knowledge of other people's wills, can remark with satisfaction that "she died with a most respectable will, leaving her grandchildren heirs," or that "his will is all the more praiseworthy since he wrote it with duty, honesty, and propriety."[58] Epistolog-

53. What precisely were the emotions of the man who made Aurelius Claudius his heir, "if he can prove to a judge that he is my son" (*Dig.* 35.1.83)?

54. See below, chapter 7.

55. *P. Mich.* 8.475 (Karanis): Papirius Apollinarius to the veteran Claudius Terentianus, early second century A.D.

56. *Att.* 15.2.4; 7.2.7, cf. 7.3.9; 15.26.5; *Fam.* 6.19.1; *Att.* 15.3.1.

57. *Att.* 11.16, 25, 23, 24, 22; 12.18a.2. On reading the testament in the testator's lifetime, see below, p. 24.

58. *Ep.* 7.24.2, 8.18.1.

raphers less gifted than a Cicero or a Pliny might even consult a sort of etiquette book, which offered them samples of letters they might send to friends who had profited by a good will or suffered from a bad one.[59]

The *honestum testamentum* was cause for satisfaction, a will that not only conferred honor but was also considered praiseworthy in itself.[60] It is very clear that a sense of duty was a strong motivation for the Roman testator: he or she was obliged to do the proper thing, to repay favors, to honor friends.[61] Cicero, in the *De finibus* (3.64–65), attributes to the younger Cato a revealing explanation of wills: People were born for society and social intercourse, wills and last wishes were born of patriotism and care for posterity. Therefore one's final judgment not only attracted great interest, it was itself the subject of judgment—it was praised or blamed as the final mirror of one's character. This is strikingly conveyed in the funeral laudation of the otherwise unknown Murdia, preserved in part on stone, which devotes ten lines to praising the testamentary dispositions of the speaker's mother. Not only are their contents sketched, each is interpreted as an expression of virtue: maternal love, honor to a second husband, loyalty to the memory of the first.[62]

The more prominent the testator, the wider the comment, as with the testament of Junia—*multo apud vulgum rumore*. The whole city, reports Pliny, was filled with debate over the will of the wealthy Domitius Tullus: some blamed him for hypocritically encouraging inheritance hunters, other praised him for frustrating them by leaving his wealth to his family. Inheritance lawsuits

59. So I interpret *P. Bon.* 5 of the late third or early fourth century, a bilingual document which has aroused no interest since its publication (I am grateful to Peter Parsons for pointing it out to me). The date of the text itself, and how widely available it may have been, are not known. It also contains samples of other types of letters, including two congratulating slaves on their manumission.

60. Fronto *Ant. Pium* 4.1, *testamento cetera honesto;* Apuleius *Apol.* 92.2, *honestissime meminuit;* 97.5, *honesto legato;* cf. *HA Pius* 12.8, *legatis idoneis.* For Cicero (*Off.* 3.74), inheritances won by captation were *hereditates non honestae.* Cf. *Nov. Marc.* 5 (A.D. 455): a disputed will is confirmed because it remembered all who deserved remembering.

61. Cf. R. P. Saller's observation that "legacies constituted the final gifts in exchange relationships": *Personal Patronage under the Early Empire* (Cambridge, 1982), 124, cf. 71–73—penultimate gifts in some cases, cf. pp. 162–80.

62. *FIRA* 70. 4–13.

aroused intense public interest, if we can trust Pliny's vivid description of a packed courtroom eagerly following the case against her stepmother by a woman who had been disinherited by her aged father.[63] And if one did not do what the public judged the proper thing, there was always the terrible fate of the wealthy knight Q. Caecilius of the late republic, who owed everything, rank and fortune, to the patronage of the great general Lucullus, and who constantly proclaimed that Lucullus would be his heir, even passing to him his ring on his deathbed. Despite these protestations, he left his property in the end to his nephew, Cicero's friend Atticus. Lucullus had no recourse at law, but the outraged people of Rome dragged Caecilius' corpse through the streets with a rope around its neck, and the horrible man (says the moralist) got the heir he wanted but the funeral he deserved. The social climate that could produce such a public reaction is difficult to appreciate. It does not matter much whether the story is true or not—it was true enough for Valerius Maximus' purpose; and Mark Antony's will was certainly used to rouse public fury, indeed civil war, against him.[64]

The strong interest shown in wills by those who did not stand to gain, the influence of this widespread interest on testators, above all their sense of duty to others and their concern for their own memory among posterity: all lead to a central problem. In his classic work *Ancient Law*, Sir Henry Maine observed almost in passing that the Romans had a "passion for Testacy" or, more dramatically, a "horror of Intestacy," and the phrase has become ingrained in legal literature.[65] The notion has recently been powerfully attacked and powerfully defended; it should still stand, though in a slightly modified form.[66]

63. *Ep.* 8.18.2, *varii tota civitate sermones,* 6.33. Cf. Tacitus, *Dial.* 38.2, *causae centumvirales, quae nunc primum obtinent locum:* the greatest prestige for an orator was to be won in the centumviral court from the time of Augustus on.

64. Valerius Maximus 7.8.5, part of his outrage against bad wills. (The anecdote is not to be found in Cicero's letters to Atticus or in Nepos' biography.)

65. H. Maine, *Ancient Law* (New York, 1864), 216 (chapter 7).

66. The first and salutary criticism of Maine's dictum came from D. Daube, "The Predominance of Intestacy at Rome," *Tulane Law Review* 39 (1964/65): 253–62; repeated in his *Roman Law,* 71–75, and extended by A. Watson, *The Law of Succession in the Late Roman Republic* (Oxford, 1971), 175–76. A convincing defense was mounted by J. Crook, "Intestacy in Roman Society," *PCPS* 19 (1973), 38–44. Further arguments can be added, but one of Daube's major points must be

Indeed, one should go further. The observable interest of the public in wills and the testator's sense of duty offer strong confirmation: the horror of intestacy, or at least deep distaste, is essentially a reflection of the social responsibility of the individual citizen. It is a communal, not an individual emotion. The law of intestacy took care of property only. The making of a proper will was an actual duty, designed to honor or rebuke family, friends, and servants as they deserved. If this *officium* was properly fulfilled, the testator was praised.[67] If it was done improperly, from the time of the late republic certain close relatives were allowed legal recourse with the *querela inofficiosi testamenti*, the complaint of the unduteous will.[68] But if the *officium* was not performed at all, if you died intestate, you risked having (in Juvenal's blunt formulation) a lot of angry friends at your funeral; if, at the other extreme, you wrote your will with such care that it could not be broken, you might be praised by posterity.[69] Cato's notorious regret, that he had lived one day without a will, reflected the proper attitude.[70] There was, in short, among those who had something to leave, a duty of testacy.[71]

What did the testator gain by properly fulfilling this duty, beyond the pleasure and comfort derived from treating others well? The blend of individual emotion and judgment with social pressure, of personal with communal needs, brought to the testator a present sense of future security, security both before and after death. In Rome, that sense of security had three distinct aspects, each shaped by a reciprocity between the individual and

---

correct, that the "horror" was confined only to that small minority of Roman citizens who had the ability to make a will and who had some property worth leaving. These will-making classes are the subject here. See further below, chapter 3.

67. E.g., Cicero *Fam.* 6.19.1, *Maculam officio functum esse gaudeo, Att.* 3.20.1, *avunculum tuum functum esse officio vehementer probo; CJ* 9.23.1 (A.D. 212) *functus dulci officio* (of a father naming his son in his will).

68. Principles and bibliography at Kaser, *Privatrecht,* 709–13.

69. Juvenal 1.144; *CIL* 12.4036 = *CLE* 112 (Nemausus).

70. Plutarch *Cato* 9.9. The meaning of the passage and of *adiathetos* in it is debated by Daube and Crook.

71. Thus, it was vitally important to keep the will up-to-date, by adding codicils or by completely replacing it: see further pp. 64–70. What other society would account it a tremendous virtue when a dying man begged time of the Fates that he might be allowed to divide his property among his friends (Martial 4.73)?

the society: first, a real security for oneself while still alive; second, a security in the foreknowledge that one's family would continue after one's death; and third, a security in the feeling that one would be remembered after one's death.[72] All three aspects are notably pragmatic, with relatively little of altruism or religious sentiment; all are concerned to some extent with individual survival.

The most striking of these is the measure of security afforded a testator in his or her lifetime, not merely the mental tranquillity resulting from a proper and dutiful will, but simple physical security in old age. The will is an instrument of control. Power over the future devolution of property, when combined with the ability to change one's mind, gives the testator present influence over those who might expect to benefit. In theory, such control could be passive or active: passively, the very secrecy of the document might ensure the good behavior of potential beneficiaries; but actively, the testator was always free to go further, to promise or to threaten. Most commonly, the will reinforces a father's control over mature children in his power, with its potent double effect on the child's future wealth and reputation, its mixing of praise or blame with the distribution of property.[73] On the other hand, where no children existed, one could in effect buy the solicitude for one's old age that children might be expected to provide, through indicating to *extranei*—that is, people *not* in the testator's powers—what they could anticipate by way of inheritance or legacy.[74] Built on these basic

72. One testator, uncertain of the future, could even speak of his will as a *pignus*, literally a pledge or security: Tacitus *Dial.* 13.5. The formulation may be recognized as that of J. Goody, "Strategies of Heirship," in his *Production and Reproduction* (Cambridge, 1976), 87, although he uses it there in a different and much broader sense. He goes on to illustrate how difficult it is "for individuals in advanced industrial economies to understand the importance of such security in other societies and other sectors." The last two aspects of security could be combined into a general regulation of the world after death.

73. For a reevaluation of the practical effect of *patriapotestas*, see R. P. Saller, "*Patria potestas* and the Stereotype of the Roman Family," *Continuity and Change* 1 (1986): 7–22, with bibliography.

74. Not just security for old age. An honored place in the annals of testation should go to Artorius, a soldier in Titus's army at the siege of Jerusalem: Josephus *BJ* 6.188–89. Trapped on a burning portico of the temple in August A.D. 70, he shouted down to his comrade and tent-mate Lucius that he would leave him his possessions if he caught him. Lucius ran up to help, Artorius jumped and was saved, but Lucius was killed by the impact. The formulation of the promise—not "I will reward you handsomely," but "I will make you my heir"—is remarkable.

premises are three particularly Roman practices that attracted the notice of historians and satirists; all are extreme, or at least prominent, manifestations of the underlying phenomenon.

First, it was a common and accepted practice for testators to talk openly about their intentions, despite the privacy of the will: "You swear by your *sacra* and your head, Garrica, that you have made me your heir to one quarter, and I believe you," says Martial.[75] The evidence for this is particularly striking in those notorious cases where the living testator, taking advantage of the privacy of the will, lied. The anecdotes are improving: Caecilius, who constantly asserted that Lucullus was his sole heir; Marius of Urbinum, who told Augustus up to the day before he died how he owed everything to him and yet did not so much as mention his name in his will; Barrus, who on his deathbed gave Lentulus Spinther his ring and called him his only heir; Rubrius of Casinum, who always openly called his good friend Fufius his heir.[76] As a supposedly wiser Martial put it later, "You say that I am your heir, Catullus. I won't believe it until I read it."[77]

The most obvious heir or legatee was the emperor, patron of all, and a patriotic citizen might not only leave him something but might boast about it.[78] Again, the best evidence is negative; not the immense amount in inheritances that we know to have come to the emperor as heir or coheir, but the amount that did not. Caligula and Domitian even raised money by taking advantage of this custom, confiscating the estates of those who were said to have claimed that the emperor was their heir, but did not in the event name him as such; and we can judge how seriously such loyal promises were taken from the sympathetic notice by the jurist Paul in his *Sententiae*: "The property of one who boasted that he would make the emperor his heir is not to be taken over by the treasury."[79]

75. Martial 9.48.1–3, cf. 11.67, 12.40; Lucian *Dial. mort.* 19(9).3. From Cicero *Att.* 14.3.2 and 14.5, E. Wistrand suggested that in the uncertain days after Caesar's assassination, some of his followers tried to win Cicero's favor by naming him in their wills and informing him of this through Atticus: *The Policy of Brutus* (1981), 37, n. 81.
76. Valerius Maximus 7.8.5, 6, 8; Cicero *Phil.* 2.41.
77. 12.73.
78. See below, chapter 7.
79. Suetonius *Gaius* 38.2, *Dom.* 12.2; *Dig.* 28.1.31.

More dramatic than proclaiming who the heir would be was the actual recitation from a copy of the will, or at least the offer to read the will or to have it read, to prove what one's intentions were. By such means the man ignored in his brother's testament showed by his own how generous he would have been to that brother; persons on trial showed that the emperor was heir to half; others offered to demonstrate that a son or grandson or friend was honorably treated; the first emperor wanted to prove that he had left no successor to the empire.[80] Thus, the will could be an instrument of defense for the living testator, protecting both person and reputation. The classic example is found in a parody, the will ascribed in the *Satyricon* to Trimalchio: not content with discussing certain legacies and announcing at dinner that his wife is to be his heir, Trimalchio orders a copy of the document to be brought in and reads it out complete, from the first paragraph to the last, accompanied by the groans of his servants.[81] His motives are clearly demonstrated by Petronius: self-glorification, the approval of his friends, and the present assurance that he will be mourned after his death. The satire may be gross, but it surely reflects a wider reality. Beyond any desire for financial or physical advantage, a testator might also publicize his will in his lifetime to win the affection of those around him.

The practice of announcing or reciting the contents of a will plays a considerable part in the third and most difficult aspect of personal security, *captatio*. Captation, or inheritance hunting, is such a commonplace among ancient writers that it is important first to remember that it is precisely that, a literary commonplace. *Captatio* was a matter of immense interest to satirists and philosophers, but there are distressingly few historical instances among the scores of ancient notices, and the few that do exist are heavily distorted by literary stereotype or personal animus.[82]

The interesting figure here, historical or not, is the quarry, the testator who submits to and encourages the attentions of *captatores*, even to the point of simulating illness. The quarry in literature— there is no Latin word for such a person—is invariably old (or very

80. Valerius Maximus 7.8.4; Dio 58.4.5, cf. 55.9.8; Suetonius *Vit.* 14.2, cf. *Iul.* 83.1; Apuleius *Apol.* 100.2; Cicero *Att.* 12.18a.2; Dio 53.31.1.
81. *Sat.* 71.
82. See further, chapter 5.

ill), childless (or pretending to dislike his or her children), and rich. But the quarry is not a victim. As early as the bachelor Miles Gloriosus, in Plautus's play of that name, around 200 B.C., the advantages of being courted and sacrificed for, of receiving meals and gifts, have become obvious; and according to caustic observers the quarry might win anything from sexual favors to free advocacy in court to ostentatious naming in the wills of the *captatores* themselves. Childlessness in Roman society, so the consensus held, visibly brought power, authority, rewards.[83] The ability to leave property worth having thus gave to some a measure of security in their lifetime.

Security after death is more difficult to arrange, and nowhere is the social nature of the will more evident than in testators' attempts to continue their existence in the world of the living, specifically to live on in their families. Cicero touches on the matter in a curious passage in the *Tusculan Disputations*. The greatest proof of the immortality of the soul is that Nature herself implants human anxiety over life after death. "Why," he asks, "do we have children, why continue our name, why adopt sons, why take care over our wills, why take care over eulogies and the monuments of tombs? We are thinking of the future."[84] Personal immortality is conceived not in terms of an afterlife but as an extension of existence by various means on this earth. Whether or not this is a good argument for the immortality of the soul (as it is intended to be), the concept is by no means unfamiliar. One clear example is the bond between family affection and the idea of the family as a continuation of the self, as one lives on in one's descendants. The huge majority of known Roman testators with surviving children designated all or some of them as heirs or major legatees, and where a spouse survived as well there was a strong urge to keep the family unit together.[85] Hence most testators took great care in the division of their estates among the

83. Cicero *Parad.* 39, *quem nutum locupletis orbi senis non observat?* References below, pp. 87–102.
84. *Disp. Tusc.* 1.31.
85. E.g., O. Montevecchi, "Ricerche di sociologia nei documenti dell'Egitto greco-romano: I. I testamenti," *Aegyptus* 15 (1935): 67–121, at 100–105. This is not to deny the importance of legacies to *extranei*, on which see Hopkins, *Death and Renewal*, 237–38. The important factor is the existence or nonexistence of spouse and children: below, chapters 6 and 7.

survivors. Relevant also, where the testator was childless, is the practice in the upper classes of the late republic and early empire known as "testamentary adoption," probably no legal adoption at all, but the institution of an *extraneus* as heir on the condition that he take the testator's name.[86] And most significant, from the time of Augustus on, is the use of the *fideicommissum* in the attempt to entail property; for example, "I commit it to the faith of my heirs, that they not alienate the *fundus Tusculanus* and that it not leave the family of my name."[87] The breakup of property risked the breakup of the family, and hence the passing of the testator from memory.

For the Roman testator, personal immortality was survival in the memory of others. The will was not the place for reflections on the afterlife or for those measures to ensure the welfare of the soul familiar from medieval and early modern wills; it was the place to strike bargains with posterity. All wills are effectually tacit pacts for remembrance with the heirs instituted, the legatees honored, the slaves manumitted: at the least those who have profited should make the funeral a memorable occasion.[88] But several of those who left some wealth behind made explicit arrangement for the use of a part of the estate in visible preservation of their memory, in two main ways.[89]

The first was the establishment of a tomb, with instructions that ranged from simple assignment of money for an epitaph to long and elaborate blueprints. Such arrangements were standardized, and they are well illustrated in the longest surviving blueprint, the testament of an anonymous Gallo-Roman aristocrat of the second century. This testament includes instructions for a chapel with a seated statue of the deceased, furnishings, and altar; careful orders for its maintenance and protection, with anxious concern for ensuring future generations of caretakers; equally detailed care that no one use the burial place save the testator and his *familia* (household); and instructions for sacrifice to

86. Below, pp. 144–46.
87. *Dig.* 31.77.11. On the mechanisms available, see D. Johnston, "Prohibitions and Perpetuities: Family Settlements in Roman Law," *ZSS* 102 (1985): 220–90; and below, pp. 176–80.
88. Dionysius Hal. 4.24.6 (a reason for freeing slaves by testament), and cf. esp. Trimalchio at Petronius *Sat.* 71.
89. Cf. Hopkins, *Death and Renewal*, 247–55.

the testator's memory at six specified times in the year.[90] With variations and omissions, these same four elements are the main concern of testators in scores of inscriptions: the establishment of a physical memorial, care for that memorial, exclusion of others from it, and sacrifice for the occupant. All fostered and protected the memory of the dead in the minds of the living.

The second method for preserving memory is through non-funerary foundations, devised for a myriad of purposes: the distribution of money or food, the erection of buildings for public use, the staging of games, the endowment of alimentary schemes.[91] An example is the elaborate provisions by a Greek woman for her hometown of Gytheion, the Laconian port, in A.D. 41/42.[92] Money left for the purpose was to be lent out by the magistrates, with land given as security; the interest on these loans was to supply the people of Gytheion with oil forever, and even slaves were to share in the distribution of the oil three times yearly. What is striking is the insistence on eternity: the elaborate moral and legal sanctions against the magistrates if they ever allowed the gift to lapse; the request that the terms of the bequest be set out on three marble pillars in specified public places; and the frank admission that the purpose of her philanthropy was "to achieve immortality." Not so explicit but equally clear are the scores of other foundations entrusted to communities or their magistrates, to professional or religious colleges, or to the order of Augustales, the guild of leading freedmen organized around the imperial cult: as long as the group benefits, the memory of the founder is preserved, and there is a strong tendency to direct that annual celebrations or distributions of largesse take place on the testator's birthday.[93] In a world with only vague or uncomforting views of an afterlife, the simple urge to be remembered is for some people one of the strongest motives for writing a will.

The four cardinal elements in the making of a Roman will were

90. *FIRA* 49; cf. Petronius *Sat.* 71, or Lucian *Nig.* 30. A most elaborate program of sacrifices is laid down (e.g.) in *CIL* 6.10248. Cf. below, pp. 171–75.

91. See further chapter 8, with bibliography.

92. *SEG* 13.258 (reproducing a much improved reading by A. Wilhelm of *IG* 5.1.1208).

93. E.g., *FIRA* 55a, *ILS* 6468; below, p. 159–68.

the license of the testator to speak the truth, the document's
privileged status as a last judgment, its role in fulfilling a duty,
and the measure of security it afforded. The combination makes
Roman wills somewhat unusual. In the heat of the French Revolu-
tion, Mirabeau argued passionately for the abolition of wills in
favor of intestate succession: "What is a testament? It is the expression of the will of a man who no longer has any will, respect-
ing property which is no longer his property. It is the action of a
man no longer accountable for his actions to mankind. It is an
absurdity, and an absurdity ought not to have the force of
law."[94] The emotion and the logic are powerful, but the argument
is valid only for a society where individual caprice operates un-
checked. That was not the case at Rome. The Roman will was
indeed an expression of deepest emotion, particularly of affection in the form of concern for the future happiness or security of
family and friends. But it was also a solemn evaluation of the
surrounding world, one prompted by a deep sense of obligation,
of the need for reciprocity, and it was an insurance that the individual would be remembered by others both in life and in death.
At all points the testator's motives intersected with the needs or
expectations of other people, from those benefited explicitly in
the will to the community interested in the proper fulfillment of
the testator's duty to it. Hence it was that "he lies senseless in a
tomb, and his words have power."

94. Quoted by B. Nicholas, *An Introduction to Roman Law* (Oxford, 1962), 252
(not attributed), and by F. Bresler, *Second Best Bed* (London, 1983), 22. I have not
been able to track down the source of this. It does not appear in the *Discours de M.
Mirabeau l'aîné sur les héritages et sur l'égalité des successions en ligne directe, par
l'abolition des testaments* (Paris, 1791), but that speech, delivered posthumously to
the assembly by Talleyrand, is packed with similar sentiments.

# 2

## Sources
### *Literary—Legal—*
### *Papyrological—Epigraphical*

No complete Roman will in its original form survives from the classical period of Roman law.[1] The dramatic effect of this is slightly exaggerated, as among the papyri alone we find the almost completely preserved testament of Antonius Silvanus, for instance, or the Greek version, lacunose but perfectly recoverable, of that of Longinus Castor.[2] However it does point up the central problem, that we have the more or less complete contents of only a handful of wills. All of our sources are interested only in certain limited aspects of wills: in their revelation of character, in their instructions for monuments, in the disputes which arose over them, in their effect on the person recording them. Thus, in the literature, there is much talk by lawyers, historians, poets, and orators about wills, but little desire to record their contents. For those we must turn to the chance survival on papyrus of Roman law wills—original, in translation, or embedded in the protocol of a formal opening—and to the unusual instance of a testator ordering the inscription on stone of provisions from his or her will.

The limitations and possibilities of our evidence are best seen in the disparate natures of the sources. For convenience, if not with taxonomic precision, they can be divided into four very different groups: literary, legal, papyrological, and epigraphical.

### LITERARY SOURCES

Wills and succession are topics of interest for every writer of Latin prose and for many of the poets, and from the mass of classical

---

1. The earliest complete Roman law will is that of St. Gregory Nazianzus (329–389) from A.D. 381: I. B. Pitra, *Iuris ecclesiastici graecorum historia et monumenta* (Rome, 1868), vol. 2, *A VI ad IX saeculum*, 153–60.
2. *FIRA* 47, 50.

29

literature, both Latin and Greek, can be extracted a wealth of detail.[3] For present, numerical, purposes, only "real" testaments will be considered; the legendary (such as that of Acca Larentia, in the days of Romulus), the fictional (such as Trimalchio's, in the *Satyricon* of Petronius), the literary (such as the mathematical puzzle presented in *Anthologia Graeca* 14.123[4]), and the completely un-Roman are excluded, informative as they may be. Likewise codicils written by sons still under their father's power, *patriapotestas,* (such as the poet Lucan) are here set aside. The wills of individual anonymi are included where we know something of their historical circumstances, but nameless groups (such as the soldiers of Caesar or of Otho, writing their wills before battle) are excluded. As to intestacy, those who died without wills are of course not counted, but those whose wills were successfully challenged at law or illegally suppressed are considered to be testators: our concern is with the situation before death, regardless of what may have followed.

What we are left with, after these subtractions, is 227 mentions of historical testators (23 of them anonymous), plus one group (the 40 martyrs of Sebaste), of whose wills we know something, however slight. In the cases of Augustus and Vergil we can be reasonably certain that we have all of the salient items, thanks to their biographer Suetonius; but it is normally only the isolated fact that survives—the name of an heir, the value of a legacy, the nature of a command or a condition.

The strong and obvious bias of the literary evidence can be quickly summed up: it is elitist, written by, for, and about the ruling classes, particularly the two highest social orders. Almost all of the writers who preserve information on wills and whose rank is known were senators or equites;[5] at least half and probably many more of the testators whose acts they record belong to the

3. Full references will be found in appendix I.
4. Considered in the Conclusion.
5. Not to mention two or more bishops. Sources (cited in appendix I) include Appian, Apuleius, Caesar, Cicero, Cyprian, Cassius Dio, Eusebius, the *Historia Augusta,* Josephus, Livy, Lucilius, Macrobius, Nepos, Nicolaus of Damascus, Philostratus, Pliny the Elder, Pliny the Younger, Plutarch, Polybius, Quintilian, Scribonius Largus, Seneca the Elder, Seneca, Suetonius, Tacitus, and Valerius Maximus. I exclude the numerous writers who mention only the wills of Caesar, Augustus, Vergil or Constantine; all poets save Lucilius; and testators themselves, such as Augustus.

same upper 2 or 3 percent of society. Moreover, Rome and Italy naturally received far more attention than the rest of the empire.

The chronological limits and emphases of the evidence are likewise clear. Despite the very early legal recognition of testation, no authentic Roman will from before the year 200 B.C. is on literary record, while the second century yields only 13. The first century B.C., on the other hand, offers almost half the examples, with about 107, followed by 64 in the first century after Christ, 39 in the second century, and a scant 5 in the years between A.D. 200 and 337.[6]

Obviously these numbers have no relevance to any patterns of testation: they reflect the survival of literary works and the interests of their authors. Thus, of some twenty-seven prose writers represented, six are the primary sources for our knowledge of over 70 percent of the testators, 163 out of 228: Cicero (60), Pliny the Younger (31), Suetonius and works derived from him (23), Tacitus (20), Valerius Maximus (17), and Pliny the Elder (12).[7] Had the third century produced a Cicero or a Pliny, there would have been more than enough wills for him to discuss; witness the voluminous writings of the last generations of classical lawyers. As it is, half of the testators mentioned in literature antedate those known from the other sources, legal, epigraphical, and papyrological—a discrepancy to be borne in mind. However, despite the various changes in the law over the centuries, the chronological discrepancies will prove less significant than others.

### LEGAL SOURCES

Of the legal literature, the imperial constitutions and codifications, particularly the *Codex* of Justinian, are useful; but they are far less important than the writings of the jurists, primarily those excerpted in the *Digesta* of Justinian, but also several important works, such as the *Sententiae Pauli* and the *Fragmenta Vaticana*,

6. The numbers are only approximate, as a few testaments cannot be closely dated. The last five include the wills of an emperor and his mother, an item in Cyprian, a notice in the *Historia Augusta*'s Life of Gordian III, and the so-called testament of the 40 martyrs of Sebaste: not a typical sample for any period.

7. The figures are again approximate, since several wills are referred to by more than one author: each is assigned to the author who provides most detail.

which have survived separately.[8] Easily the best way of approaching these is through the *Palingenesia Iuris Civilis* of Otto Lenel, which reconstitutes from the Digest and the independent fragments the original works of each jurist, as far as is possible.[9] The advantage of a palingenesia is immediately clear. From the different kinds of juristic composition we can easily separate those most relevant to daily practice; that is, those which are classified as "problematic," such as *digesta, responsa, quaestiones,* and *disputationes.*[10] Such works pose three related problems to the historian.

The first problem is that, for purposes of discussion, the jurists strip away much or all of the mundane detail irrelevant to the legal issue at hand. Thus, while they offer an immense amount of information about much-loved topics, such as the *querela inofficiosi testamenti* or the *fideicommissum,* they tell us disappointingly little about the status, age, or family of the testator in the case; indeed, with a writer as succinct as Papinian it is often impossible to determine the sex of the testator.[11]

Second, the writings of the jurists may represent everyday reality no more than does any other literary genre: to a man, where they can be identified, they too belong to the senatorial or equestrian orders, and those whose work has survived represent the leaders of Roman jurisprudence.[12] Operating as the advisers of emperors and magistrates, or as judges and magistrates themselves, or as private consultants, how often did they come into contact with, let alone interest themselves in, the ordinary concerns of ordinary citizens, in a judicial system which heavily favored the economically privileged? Moreover, even if the average citizen is somehow represented in the Digest, it may be a heavily one-sided representation, in that jurists were most concerned with problems.

8. Most of them are collected in *FIRA*[2] 2 (Florence, 1940).

9. Published Leipzig, 1889, republished 1960 with a 23-page *Supplementum* by L. E. Sierl, adding papyrus discoveries.

10. F. Schulz, *History of Roman Legal Science*[2] (Oxford), 1953), 223–26.

11. Cf. Schulz, *History,* 236, on Papinian: "At times the brevity of expression borders on the baroque." The problem is vastly worsened by the compilers' responsibility for deleting proper names and replacing them with stock names such as Seius, Titius, Maevius: the process can actually be seen at *Dig.* 14.3.20 or 33.1.21.3

12. W. Kunkel, *Herkunft und soziale Stellung der römischen Juristen*[2] (Graz, Vienna, and Cologne, 1967), esp. 38–61, 271–317.

The third and most important question likewise turns on the relationship of the Digest with reality. At one extreme, much of the writings of the jurists is clearly hypothetical; at the other, much of it explicitly reports the actual events of an imperial hearing or a private consultation. A vast amount, however, occupies the indeterminate middle ground. The danger of using the Digest may then lie in taking as a reflection of reality what are in fact the musings of a jurist intent on working out in his study or classroom the remotest implications of a point of law uncommon or unimportant in daily life. However, this danger—the most difficult of the three problems, in that it involves not bias but fact—is not insurmountable, and there are defences against it.

Two are particularly attractive. First, L. Boyer boldly assumed that jurists who were constantly advising on the making and interpretation of wills must have been affected by daily practice and their historical context. Through examination of the legacies mentioned in the Digest, regardless of historicity, Boyer succeeded in analyzing their function in Roman society: statistics he could not offer, but certainly convincing trends.[13] Second, for his study of the inheritance expectations of wives and daughters, F. von Woess sensibly took a large sample of evidence from those individual works of the jurists which observably contained a striking proportion of real cases; that is, from certain of their casuistic or problematic writings.[14] The outstanding examples of these—obvious from even the most cursory glance at the Digest or, better, the Palingenesia—are the *Digesta* and *Responsa* of Cervidius Scaevola who, far more than any other jurist, retained juristically unnecessary but historically useful details, details ranging from personal and geographical names to documentary quotation.[15] In addition to Scaevola, von Woess examined the *Quaestiones* and *Responsa* of Papinian; the *Decreta*,[16] *Quaestiones,* and *Responsa* of

13. Boyer, "Fonction sociale," 335–37.

14. Von Woess, *Erbrecht,* 42–44.

15. The two works are closely interrelated. F. Schulz argued that both are derived from a posthumous, third-century publication of Scaevola's *responsa* entitled *Digesta:* "Überlieferungsgeschichte der *Responsa* des Cervidius Scaevola," *Symbolae Friburgenses in honorem Ottonis Lenel* (Leipzig, 1931), 143–244.

16. A unique and invaluable collection of imperial court decisions in which Paul had participated. Together with six books of *Imperiales sententiae in cognitionibus prolatae,* it is derived from a single work, now lost: C. Sanfilippo, *Pauli decretorum libri tres* (Milan, 1938).

Paul; and the *Responsa* of Modestinus. Together these works certainly contain the great majority of factual cases recorded in the Digest and the other surviving fragments of classical jurisprudence.

For the immediate purpose of describing the Roman testator I have selected from the eight works just mentioned the instances where there seemed a reasonable likelihood that a real case was being considered, as signalled by: the use of the indicative mood; the mention of real names (as distinct from the omnipresent juristic pseudonyms, such as Titius, Seius, and Maevius); the apparent quotation from real documents (particularly in Greek); and the employment of such phrases as "the emperor said" or "I replied." Such a selection is, in every case, highly subjective, and the twin dangers will always remain, that one may be dealing with hypothesis disguised as fact, or fact as hypothesis.[17] Nevertheless, the attempt is worth making and the result seems to be a fair approximation, if not of reality, at least of that part of it raising questions which attracted the attention of certain jurists at a certain time. The sources are the following.

Scaevola's *Digesta* in forty books (dealing primarily with cases from the reign of Marcus Aurelius) yields 217 apparently authentic testators, his *Responsa* in six books (with cases from the time of Marcus to Septimius Severus) some 122. Papinian's *Quaestiones*, published in thirty-seven books, offer 22 (most from Severus); his *Responsa* in nineteen books (Severus and Caracalla) some 227. Paul includes 16 in his *Decreta* (three books, Severus and Caracalla), 16 in his *Quaestiones* (twenty-six books, the same emperors), and 30 in his *Responsa* (twenty-three books from Severus to Severus Alexander). And Modestinus refers to some 37 in his *Responsa* (nineteen books, Alexander). The great advantage of the 687 testators selected here is their contemporaneity, all of them being discussed, and most of them probably dying, in a period of some seven decades in the later second and early third centuries A.D.[18]

17. Yet another problem appears in the recurrence of the same case. Where I have noticed it, like von Woess, I have counted it as one; the number of these is not great.

18. Most but by no means all dying in that period: thus Papinian under Septimius Severus refers back to cases from the time of Commodus (*Dig.* 22.3.26), Marcus Aurelius (34.9.12, 34.9.16.2), Antoninus Pius (35.1.77 pr.), and Hadrian (36.1.52, 36.1.60.3).

This sample is by no means intended to exclude testators recorded elsewhere in the Digest or the Code, some of whom will turn up
later.

PAPYRI

The papyrological evidence for wills has been conveniently gathered and thoroughly examined by M. Amelotti in his indispen-
sable *Il testamento romano attraverso la prassi documentale* (1966), of
which it forms the backbone. Two of his items are ignored here,
one being a formulary, the other probably not a will, while several
wills or references to wills have turned up in the last two decades.[19]
Some 79 testators are to be considered, and here the sample can
claim to represent the great majority of known Roman law testators in Egypt from Augustus to Constantine.[20] The nature of the
evidence and its state of preservation vary widely. At least six
different testators appear to be involved in one document, a
group of receipts from legatees acknowledging payment of their
legacies from funds which the deceased had held in the camp
treasury.[21] The remaining 73 wills attested fall into two distinct
categories. In 35 cases, the actual text of the document survives in
some form—whether in the rare Latin version, in Greek translation or original, in an abstract, or as part of an official record—
and in a state of preservation ranging from nearly perfect to all
but unintelligible. The remaining documents embrace references
to wills which range in nature from a passing mention to a more or
less elaborate record of judicial proceedings.

The special character of the papyrological evidence is self-evi-
dent: it is Egyptian.[22] That is to say, it all comes from a single,

19. Papyri are listed in appendix II. Excluded are Amelotti's Oriental 44 (*P. Hamb.* 72) and 68 (*P. Mich.* 453).

20. New material continues to accrue, most notably *P. Oxy.* 54 (1987) 3756. 4–6, and 3758. 134–55, 181–213, all from A.D. 325. These and others arrived too late to be taken into account here.

21. *P. Mich.* 435 + 440 = *CPL* 219 + 190 = (best) Fink, *Roman Military Records* no. 77.

22. And has therefore been much considered. See especially V. Arangio-Ruiz, *La successione testamentaria secondo i papiri greco-egizi* (Palermo, 1906); H. Kreller, *Erbrechtliche Untersuchungen auf Grund der graeco-aegyptischen Papyrusurkunden* (Leipzig, 1919); Montevecchi, "Ricerche"; R. Taubenschlag, *The Law of Greco-Roman Egypt in the Light of the Papyri (332 B.C. – 640 A.D.)*[2] (Warsaw, 1955), 181–222.

non-Latin-speaking eastern province, where Roman citizens were for long a minority—immigrants or members of the elite or both. The implications of being a Roman citizen in a mass of non-Romans must be borne in mind. One is immediately obvious in the crucial chronological division imposed on the evidence by the joint impact of Caracalla's massive extension of Roman citizenship through the Constitutio Antoniniana and Severus Alexander's concession that wills could be written in Greek. In the early third century, a mass of potential Roman testators was created, unfamiliar with Roman culture and the rigid legal formalisms of the Roman will; they worked profound changes on the nature of the will itself, as Amelotti has demonstrated.[23] Thus the papyrological evidence falls into two clear periods: one of stability, the other of gradual but profound change, corresponding essentially to the second and third centuries after Christ, respectively. Little survives from before that time: a stray reference as early as 14 B.C. to what appears to be the will of a Roman businessman,[24] then 4 wills from the first century A.D., plus another uncertainly assigned to the first or second century. Then about 35 from the second century, plus 4 uncertainly second or third, to which can be added one that certainly preceded the Constitutio Antoniniana.[25] And, markedly different in tone and substance, about 28 from the period down to 337 (of which only 3 postdate the year 300).

## INSCRIPTIONS

Finally, the epigraphical evidence, which covers a period of about 300 years, from the mid-first century B.C. to the mid-third century A.D. This can be divided into two types.

First are those relatively rare inscriptions that actually quote or paraphrase significant portions of a will. Again, definition of these individually important texts is highly subjective. Amelotti selected some 35, of which three-fourths come from the western half of the empire; to these we can easily add another 30.[26] Out-

23. *Testamento* 217–50.
24. *BGU* 1113.
25. *P. Coll. Youtie* 64.
26. Listed in appendix III.

standing among them, is the only will known to have been inscribed in toto, the so-called *testamentum Dasumii,* which records
the last wishes of a wealthy senator in the year 108, and exists
today only in a narrow central fragment extending to some 133
lines.[27] All of the other inscriptions preserve particular *capita*
from wills, and are limited in scope, without exception, to those
legacies and *fideicommissa* (trusts) that cover funerary arrangements and various kinds of foundations. That is to say, for all the
richness of the information which they contain, they are confined
to one aspect of testation, the implicit or explicit assurance that
the testator will be remembered. Indeed, in that assurance they
are joined by the *testamentum Dasumii,* which the testator had ordered to be inscribed and attached to his tomb. Thus, the individually important inscriptions are, like the mass of inscriptions in
general, exclusively memorial in nature, and in this they differ
sharply from our other sources.

Around this small core lie the thousands of inscriptions, almost
all funerary and undated, which attest the existence of a will. Most
of these are very brief and follow a relatively standardized form,
indicating that the deceased left a testament which had ordered
the heirs to erect a memorial (of whatever kind) to himself or
herself and (possibly) to close relatives and freed slaves. However,
many give considerably more than this, and even if the content of
such memorials is rigidly restricted to one particular item of the
will, there are often indications of the testator's family situation,
sex, age, status, and wealth. Faced with the great variety in quality
and extent of epigraphical publications, for present purposes I
have sampled four small but relatively homogeneous selections of
inscriptions.

The first and largest embraces all inscriptions from the city of
Rome in the *Corpus Inscriptionum Latinarum* (*CIL*) volume 6 (bar-
ring those too fragmentary to use) which indicate the existence of
a will.[28] The more elaborate texts which quote or refer to wills
naturally include such words as *testamentum, legatum, tabulae, iussi,
do lego,* and so forth. Many more are recognizable by such simple

27. *CIL* 6.10229, to which add the important new fragment as restored by W.
Eck at *ZPE* 30 (1978): 277–95.
28. A selection greatly facilitated by the existence of a complete word-index
for the volumes, *CIL* 6.7.

standard phrases, usually abbreviated, as *t(estamento) p(oni) i(ussit)*, *t(estamento) f(ieri) i(ussit)*, *ex voluntate*, and *e(x) t(estamento)*. Where no such clues exist, the words *heres* and *heredes*, used alone or in a variety of phrases such as *h(eres) e(ius) f(ecit)* or *h(eres) b(ene) m(erenti) f(ecit)*, pose a problem: without further information I can see no sound means of determining whether the heir involved was testamentary or *ab intestato*, nor was the heir under any obligation to give this information. I have therefore included such inscriptions as indicate explicitly or implicitly that the heirs had *not* inherited on intestacy, that is, those signaled as *liberti* (freedmen) and *libertae* (freedwomen), friends, fellow townspeople, fellow soldiers, *alumni* and *alumnae* (foster children), relatives by marriage (including spouses), and (though with misgivings in several cases, particularly where there is a female testator) those with different family names. Moreover, I have excluded all those heirs who might have inherited on intestacy—children, siblings, and the rare uncle or cousin—unless a will is explicitly recorded or they appear as heirs in the company of one of the above categories, most commonly of freed slaves. The resulting sample, embracing 223 testators, is therefore undoubtedly biased against the nuclear family, but the alternative—that we exclude the many instances where a will might be inferred from the appearance of *extranei* as heirs—seems unacceptable.[29] Of all areas in the empire, the city of Rome contains by far the largest collection of inscriptions, and it offers one supreme advantage, unmatchable by the inscriptions of any other region in the empire, let alone by the literary, legal, or papyrological evidence: we can observe here, however dimly, the testament of the person in the street.

Second, of the 30,000 to 40,000 inscriptions in *CIL* 6, I have excluded one category from the above count, the collected epitaphs of serving and sometimes veteran members of the armed forces (praetorian guards, urban cohorts, *statores Augusti*, *vigiles*, and so forth), though the stray soldier's memorial which turns up

---

29. I have also ignored for these purposes any new texts or corrections to old texts not included within *CIL* 6 itself. The only comparable study to this is K. Visky's paper on the law of succession in inscriptions, *Iura* 13 (1962): 110–32, which assumes far too high an incidence of intestacy, to the point that *manus* marriage is seen as common in Pannonia because so many wives appear as heirs (and hence were as daughters to their husbands).

elsewhere in these volumes has been included. The reasons for this exclusion are several: most of these had, as serving soldiers, left wills subject to quite different rules from those governing ordinary citizens; most of them were, or intended to be, transient, coming from outside the capital and (witness the small number of veterans here and the considerable numbers elsewhere) not meaning to stay there; all of them were male; and most of them were unmarried (by law under the principate before Septimius Severus, but also observably by custom throughout the period). Thus they correspond to no norms in the civilian world of Rome, and should be kept separate. That is not to say that they are to be ignored, not least because the incidence of attested testation is strikingly higher than that found among civilians.[30] Thus, looking at the first and largest of the military groups in *CIL* 6, the praetorian guards, one can find no fewer than 115 testaments represented. This group is here taken as a separate sample.

The third and fourth groups are based on the lists of epigraphically attested African and Italian costs compiled by R. P. Duncan-Jones.[31] The bias here is toward wealth, particularly in the erection of buildings, the establishment of perpetual foundations, and the funding of feasts, games, and handouts: even the relatively modest outlays at the bottom end of the scale, for tomb costs, are considerably higher than the burial grants made to members of various societies (*collegia*).[32] However the economic bias ought not to be overestimated. Clearly the vast majority of people did not, could not, bequeath several hundred sesterces for burial and a modest epitaph, let alone several thousands for an alimentary foundation or annual games. Yet the question must be, for our purposes, how many of those people left wills; that is, what is the correlation between wealth and testacy?[33] While not pretending

30. See below, pp. 56–58.
31. *The Economy of the Roman Empire*[2] (Cambridge, 1982), 89–119, with 378, and 156–237, with 379–80. Most of the testamentary outlays are marked in his lists by one or three asterisks.
32. Duncan-Jones, *Economy*, 131.
33. More specifically, how far does the evidence which happens to record specific sums left in wills from the African provinces and from Italy outside of Rome correspond to what can be gleaned from the inscriptions of Rome generally and from the other, noninscriptional evidence, about the social and economic status of the Roman testator?

to be complete, the samples based on Duncan-Jones's lists include 60 items from Africa and 115 from Italy. One element worth noting is the slightly different chronological emphases, the African inscriptions, as one might expect, coming primarily from the second and early third centuries, the Italian from the first and second.

With the limits and limitations—chronological, geographical, social, and intellectual—of our various kinds of sources in mind, we can turn to a portrait of the Roman testator.

# 3

## Testators

*Intestacy—Gender—*
*Rank and Wealth—Family and Age*

A celebrated passage in Plutarch has immortalized Cato's regret that he had passed through one day in his life intestate (*adiathetos*), that is, without a will, or (more likely) with one that had been for some reason invalidated.[1] In so doing, he had certainly failed to act as a Roman citizen should; yet how typical was this particular sentiment, expressed as it was by a man who has been accurately characterized as a "cranky insider"?[2] That is, was Cato, who strove always to set an ostentatiously Roman example, expressing the profoundly held beliefs of his contemporaries, or was he chiding them for their departure in practice from those beliefs? It is impossible to say how many Romans made wills and how many did not, nor can we tell whether the incidence of testacy was greater or less in one era than another. Nevertheless, a rough sketch can be attempted of that portion of humanity living in the Roman world between 200 B.C. and A.D. 300 which made a Roman will and, closely connected with this, we can also attempt some definition of the Roman testator in terms of sex, age, health, status or occupation, wealth, and family situation, all important factors which combine in other societies to determine the likelihood of an individual leaving a will. The process of defining the Roman testator is inevitably reductive, and one broad and unsurprising conclusion can be stated quickly, that whatever its impact on society at large, the Roman will was of crucial significance to a small and easily definable section of it, for whom Cato may be taken as a fitting spokesman.

1. *Cato* 9.9.
2. In the excellent analysis of Cato's remark by J. Crook, "Intestacy," 39–41.

• • •

The population of the Roman empire at the time of the death of Augustus was, on an explicitly conservative estimate, about 54 million; at the same time, the number of Roman citizens was, on a most liberal estimate, 5 to 6 million.[3] That is, in the early years of the empire at least 90 percent of its inhabitants had, as noncitizens, no capability (or necessarily even desire) to make a Roman law will, and down to the Constitutio Antoniniana of the early third century Roman citizens must have remained a clear minority.

Moreover, within the citizen body several groups were debarred from making wills for all or most of our period: all those who were *alieni iuris* (that is, commonly, children in the power of their father; with a partial exception made, from the time of Augustus, for serving soldiers) and all those *sui iuris* but under age, the insane, interdicted prodigals, the deaf and dumb, Junian Latins, some condemned criminals, and (until the time of Hadrian, who changed the law) all women who had not undergone *capitis deminutio*.[4] Moreover, women with (male) tutors could at no time make a valid will without the tutor's consent, unless they had won exemption; and freed slaves were obliged in many cases to leave a part of their property to their patrons, according to the size of their estate and the number of children they had.[5] In short, large parts even of the citizen body were also unable to make, or were seriously restricted in making, a will under Roman law.[6]

Technically, most people died "intestate" as far as Roman law was concerned. How then can one claim that the Romans had a

---

3. K. J. Beloch, *Die Bevölkerung der griechischen und römischen Welt* (Leipzig, 1886), 507; P. A. Brunt, *Italian Manpower* (Oxford, 1971), 113–20.

4. *Capitis deminutio:* roughly speaking, loss of family ties through marriage or emancipation. Kaser, *Privatrecht,* 682f.; on women also A. Watson, *The Law of Persons in the Late Roman Republic* 152–154. Criminals: Dio 57.22.5, cf. *Dig.* 28.1.8.1–4.

5. A woman did not need the tutor's consent if she possessed the *ius liberorum,* a much-prized privilege which deserves further attention; for the Egyptian evidence, see P. J. Sijpesteijn, *Aegyptus* 45 (1965): 171–89. The privilege was also useful in circumventing the Augustan law limiting inheritance by the childless. The tutor's *auctoritas,* it should be noted, apparently governed the making of the will alone, not the determination of its contents: Gaius 2.112, Ulpian *Epit.* 20.15. Freed slaves: Gaius 3.39–76, Ulpian *Epit.* 20.10; cf. Kaser, *Privatrecht,* 708f., Watson, *Persons,* 231f.

6. Moreoever, any failure to comply with these restrictions might damage or invalidate the will, as would naming as heirs any of a variety of disallowed persons.

"horror of intestacy"? The question here, as before, is one of attitude rather than of practice; but there is also a problem of definition.[7] "Intestacy" certainly covers most of humanity, embracing not merely those unable to leave a Roman law will, but also the citizen masses who could make a will but who had nothing to leave—or so little to leave that they and their heirs took as little interest in the workings of the law as the law took in them—and it even includes the considerable numbers of would-be testators whose wills were technically voided, or were successfully challenged posthumously, or simply lapsed for want of a willing or living heir.[8] Yet the question should be not "how frequent was intestacy?" but much more narrowly, "how frequently did people who had the capacity to make a will, and who had something to leave, nevertheless die without a will?"—not "without a valid will" (which might be called technical intestacy) but "without a will" (which might be called real intestacy).[9] Horror of intestacy implies the obverse, a duty of testacy: the problem is to define who felt such a duty and who did not, and why.

The evidence for intestacy needs careful handling. Intestate succession was clearly important, indeed preponderant, in the Roman world; but that this can be demonstrated from the sources is dubious. Thus, it has been supported by the assertion "that in Cicero's writings alone we meet as many as seven separate factual instances where a Roman citizen who had property did not leave a will."[10] The details need further attention, but the force of this is greatly vitiated when we consider the sixty and more wills mentioned by Cicero: are we to assume from this that the ratio of testacy to intestacy in Cicero's world was nine to one? Moreover, the force of the argument is further reduced by the observation that there seems to be only one other instance in all the nonlegal literature outside of Cicero of a propertied citizen not leaving a will.[11] Eight cases are not enough, and without details it is hard to

7. Bibliography above, p. 20n. 66.
8. A point made by Watson, *Succession,* 176.
9. Even then it may be necessary to distinguish, theoretically at least, between those who consciously chose to die intestate and those who were somehow prevented from making a will.
10. Watson, *Succession,* 175, with references in n. 3.
11. Tacitus *Ann.* 2.48.1.

say whether they suggest a rule or are the individual results of special conditions.[12]

The other evidence for intestacy is remarkably slender and its interpretation dubious. *Heredes ab intestato* do occasionally appear as such on inscriptions, but that is no guarantee that everyone else named simply as *heres* succeeded by a testament. Indeed, the emphasis of such phrases as "heres institutus" or "testamentari heredes"[13] might even suggest that some of the colorless "heredes" were not instituted or testamentary heirs, but heirs by intestacy. On the other hand, most inscriptions are epitaphs, and heirs by intestacy may have felt less obligation to commemorate the deceased.

The legal evidence seems more promising. Very few cases turning on the fact of intestacy are reported; in the jurists surveyed, some 15 intestacies appear, as against 687 wills. But that is no index of the frequency of intestacy in society, since the rules of intestate succession, involving as they do questions not of human behavior but of personal status, afford little room for debate and few points of interest for the jurist, beyond questions of their fundamental validity.[14] Yet the promise of the Digest may be fulfilled by the papyri, which do reflect real life with less distortion. The word *adiathetos* occurs, on one survey, some twenty-six times in the papyri from the Roman period; not one instance concerns a Roman citizen before the Constitutio Antoniniana.[15] Is there perhaps a cultural difference at issue here? The point of the exercise is not just that intestate succession is relatively rarely recorded, but that we should look beyond that fact, to the circumstances.

Take, for example, the 15 instances in the Digest.[16] Most strik-

12. Quickly dismissed as the latter by Crook, "Intestacy," 42.
13. *CIL* 3.9802, 10561, 12091; 12.3538. Intestacy explicitly at (e.g.) 6.3180 (a soldier), 10322 (a freedman), and 2.4143 (a soldier).
14. Again, a point made by Watson.
15. *P. Amh.* 72; *Chrest.* 2.200; *BGU* 19. 2.7; *P. Flor.* 68, 86, 97; *P. Tebt.* 320; *P. Oxy.* 105, 490, 1114, 1121, 1201; *P. Lond.* 1164; *P. Stras.* 29; *P. Ryl.* 117; *PSI* 1102; *P. Oxy.* 2133; *Stud.* 22.55; *P. Harr.* 68; *P. Oxy.* 2431, 2474; *P. Vindob. Boswinkel* 37: from Preisigke's *Wörterbuch* 1 (1925) through Supplement 1 (1969). A check on the Ibycus computer adds *BGU* 2097, 2100; *CPR* 5.9; *P. Mert.* 121; *P. Oxy. Hels.* 44; *P. Stras.* 555; *P. Wisc.* 1.13. (Several of these appear merely within formal conditions on dying childless and intestate.)
16. *Dig.* 46.3.88 pr.; 36.1.80; 41.4.14; 41.9.3; 10.2.39.1; 38.8.10; 37.6.9; 29.1.36.3; 31.77.26; 31.77.26; 31.77.29; 38.12.2; 36.1.76.1; 29.2.92; 31.34.2; 38.8.8.

ing is the fact that in 8 of the 15 cases the intestate was a woman—pure chance perhaps but remarkable when compared with the proportion of known testators who were women. Again, two or possibly three of the 15 intestates were unmarried and childless, and two more apparently left underage children. One naturally begins to wonder: were certain groups in society—women, single people, younger people—less likely to leave a will than others? Comparison with those who did leave wills is necessary.

The cases in literature are all from a much earlier period. In the few instances where some detail is known, we can observe a common element, namely their relative obscurity or, more positively, their marginality: one of those who died intestate came from a recently enfranchised region of Italy, one was Spanish, one was the son of a freedman, one was a freedwoman married to an Asian Greek, and two others were almost certainly freedmen.[17] The main significance of intestacy thus lies in the questions it raises about testacy: who were more likely to make a will, men or women, young or old, freed or freeborn, Italian or provincials, rich or poor, and why?

The duty of testacy is clearly a relative concept. The masses who had little or nothing to leave would not be troubled by it, whereas it fits neatly into the thick texture of an aristocratic code. Cato was, after all, speaking as an ex-consul, and by no means prescribing for everyone; while Fronto's passionate plea three centuries later that Marcus Aurelius take up an inheritance, so as not to create a posthumous intestacy, was entered on behalf of "a most noble lady, of the highest birth and the greatest wealth."[18] Particularly interesting here is the Lex Voconia of 169 B.C., which barred testators in the first class of wealth from instituting women as heirs. The great loophole, observed by moderns and surely evident to the legislator, is that many of the women prevented from succeeding under a will—precisely, daughters still in their fathers' legal power (*in potestate*), wives in their husbands' power (*in manu*), and sisters—could still succeed to vast property *ab intes-*

17. Cicero *Cluent.* 165; *De Orat.* 1.183; 1.176; *Pro Flacco* 84, with A. J. Marshall *CQ* 25 (1975): 82–87 and S. Mitchell, *AS* 29 (1979): 13–22; Tacitus *Ann.* 2.48.1; Cicero *De Orat.* 2.283. Another case is almost certainly that of Pompeius Vindillus at *Att.* 6.1.25, again most probably a freedman.

18. *Ant. Imp.* 2.1, discussed by Crook, "Intestacy," 42f.

*tato.* The only feasible explanation is that intestacy was of no real significance in the Rome of Cato's day.[19] Of no significance, that is, among the wealthiest class at Rome; we cannot yet generalize downward from a very restricted group, any more than we can from the fact that, against the scores of prominent senators known to have left wills, we know of not one who, having the legal capacity to make a Roman will (*testamenti factio*), died intestate.[20]

Who left a will? The most striking characteristic of recorded testators is that the overwhelming majority were men. Some rough figures are indicative. The gender of some 214 of the testators known from classical literature is recorded: 181 were male (about 85 percent), 33 (15 percent) female.[21] Gender is less easily determined in the juristic sources, being more often than not of no particular interest to the legal issue: of the approximately 468 determinable cases, 371 (79 percent) were male, 97 (21 percent) female.[22] In the papyri we can on a conservative estimate identify the sex of 62 testators: 51 (82 percent) were male, 11 (18 percent) female. Of the epigraphically attested wills sampled, those of the praetorians are naturally to be set aside. The city of Rome otherwise yields about 214 inscriptions where the testator's sex can be determined: about 159 (74 percent) were men, about 55 (26 percent) women. The Italian inscriptions fall yet again into the same rough pattern: of 107 instances where sex is determinable, 87 (81 percent) were male, 20 (19 percent) female.[23] Only the African inscriptions are wildly out of line, in part affected (but not explicable) by the number of soldiers' or veterans' memorials: of 58 determinable cases, 56 (97 percent) were men, only 2 (3 percent) women.

19. So Crook, "Intestacy," 43f., based essentially on von Woess, *Erbrecht,* esp. 65–121. See now S. Dixon, *Adelaide Law Review* 9 (1985): 519–34.
20. Suggestive here are some of the 15 instances of intestacy noted in the Digest. Although legally intestate, at least 5 of the 15 (and conceivably more) left instructions to their heirs via codicil, letter, or *fideicommissum;* that is, their last wishes were presumably not complicated and they placed absolute faith in their nearest relatives, rather than in the law. In other words, at least one-third of those who wittingly died intestate left a de facto will. It would be very hard to say whether they did, or did not, have a horror of intestacy.
21. The sex of 10 of the 23 anonymi can be inferred. I exclude the 40 martyrs of Sebaste here.
22. Scaevola 169 (75%) and 56 (25%); Papinian 132 (83%) and 28 (17%); Paul 44 (83%) and 9 (17%); Modestinus 26 (87%) and 4 (13%).
23. 105 inscriptions: two were joint bequests.

First, what do these figures signify? They certainly cannot pretend to be precise. They rest necessarily on a foundation built from scores of individual decisions—selecting sources, evaluating context, determining relevance—and may well show omissions, errors, and prejudices. Certainly close study of the mass of inscriptions that mention wills would bring out regional and chronological variations. Nevertheless the figures are strikingly consistent in suggesting that roughly four out of every five wills were written by men.

But, a more troublesome question, how representative are the sources from which such figures derive? The answer is by no means clear. Literature was after all written mainly by and about men, and certainly the small proportion of women on written record in no way corresponds to their numbers, roughly equal to men, in real life. That the actions of men were considered more worthy of commemoration need not imply that their possessions were any greater. Juristic writers, however, are quite uninterested in the gender of the testator, and there is no need to see their selection of cases as anything but sex-blind. It might be objected that men were more litigious than women (which is by no means clear); but then perhaps they had more to be litigious over. And with the collection of Roman wills on Egyptian papyri and on the inscriptions from Rome itself, we have quite another story, for they are the product of random survival, and they too suggest that at best only one out of every four or five wills was that of a woman.

This is not surprising when compared with the very few other similar figures that have been compiled from the Roman world. In a pioneering paper published over fifty years ago, O. Montevecchi collected all of the then known wills and gifts in contemplation of death (*donationes mortis causa*) on papyrus, including both Roman and Greco-Egyptian, and covering a millenium, from the third century before Christ to the eighth after: of the 119 wills, 52 fall within the period 30 B.C. to A.D. 337, and some 8 of the 14 *donationes*.[24] Of the 124 testators and donors whose sex was known, 100 (81 percent) were men, 24 (19 percent) women.[25]

24. Montevecchi, "Ricerche."
25. Montevecchi, "Ricerche," 8of. More recently, D. Hobson, *TAPA* 113 (1983): 311–21, has found some 96 wills and *donationes* from the Roman period, of which 63 (66%) are men's, 33 (34%) women's. This is roughly the same 2:1 proportion she finds among property owners at Socnopaiou Nesos.

One could also compare this ratio with the results of J. Andreau's more recent study of private foundations in Italy (the majority of them testamentary) from the first to the third centuries A.D. Of 144 foundations, 104 were begun by men, 18 by women, 6 by men and women, and 16 by people whose sex is unknown. Thus of 134 known donors, 110 (82 percent) were male, 24 (18 percent) female.[26] Such figures suggest then that the samples presented above are indeed a fair approximation of the ratio of male to female Roman law testators.

But what do the figures imply? It appears that very roughly one-fifth of those who left wills were women; that is, many more women than men must have died intestate. This can hardly be ascribed to that *infirmitas* of women which (in later interpretation) supposedly led in archaic times to their perpetual guardianship; nor can one seriously entertain a mass reluctance on the part of tutors to grant their authority—a recalcitrance which has left no historical trace and which could in any event have been easily circumvented at law by the women concerned.[27] It might be nearer the mark to suggest that some, but not all, women were much more accustomed than men to a role of passivity, and more content or resigned to allow their property to pass back to the family from which they came—the rules of intestate succession did not embrace their own children until a very late date (A.D. 178). But the more obvious explanation is that most testators were male because most of the property at Rome was held by men.[28]

Such an assertion may require modification. The independent economic power of women certainly existed and was recognized. Women of property had wide discretion over it by the time of the late republic, and hence had an economic and social power exceptional for a traditional agrarian society. In other words, the quantity of property held by women may be less remarkable, in context, than the quality of their control over it. Nevertheless the rough ratio of four to one in the ownership of property, if correct, remains a figure of fundamental importance.

26. *Ktema* 2 (1977): 157–209, esp. 189ff.
27. S. Dixon, "Infirmitas Sexus: Womanly Weakness in Roman Law," *TvR* 52 (1984): 343–71, demonstrates convincingly the late importation of the idea of womanly weakness into Roman legal vocabulary, an idea at odds with common custom.
28. Von Woess, *Erbrecht,* 106.

There is also a corollary worth noting. In the matter of inheritance, law and custom are widely separated; not in the sense that the law always lagged behind social change, as one normally expects, but in the unexpected sense that the law constantly strove to liberalize a conservative society. The culprit at Rome is the very early recognition of freedom of testation, and the emphasis on this basic freedom and the individual's duty to exercise it is constant throughout Roman history.[29] Liberal notions as to natural affection or the possible unduteousness of a will, not to mention the basic principle of intestacy that sons and daughters are to be treated equally, are juristic inventions. Do they correspond to a perception of reality or to ideals of justice? Left to their own devices, would the Roman testator or testatrix favor not merely one child over another but, in general, sons over daughters? The answer is already implicit in the ratio between the sexes of those leaving wills: if women held proportionately much less property than men, they must have inherited proportionately less, since for women, far more even than for men, inheritance must have been the major means of acquiring property. That is, sexual inequality in testation reflects inequality in inheritance.[30]

That men outnumber women by three or four to one is the only sure observation to be made about testators. Beyond that, there are more hints and possibilities than certainties. Three areas can be explored, to identify the testator further: the social, the familial, and the physical, the first being easily the most important.

We would naturally want to know the rank, occupation, wealth, education, race, and origin of every Roman testator, but the information is seldom there. The central question to be posed, then, is a general one: "How far down in Roman society are we likely to find wills?" The upper and lower extremes are obvious. A very rich person of the senatorial or equestrian order, educated, literate, and urban, could confidently be expected to leave a will. At the other end, the impoverished peasant or indigent laborer, the ignorant and perhaps non-Roman provincial, could not. The

---

29. The ideas here are essentially those of von Woess, *Erbrecht*, 279–309.
30. Discussion of gender and inheritance is postponed to chapter 6, below.

problem is to define the middle ground and to assess the extent of testation there.[31]

Take first the related matters of rank and occupation. Here the literary and legal sources are the least helpful. The literary suffer from a double bias: not only do they concentrate quite disproportionately on the senatorial and equestrian orders, but of those testators whose status is not indicated we can, using other evidence, most easily identify the senators and knights. Thus, of 228 testators, not all of whom can be assigned to a social class, some 139 are certainly or probably senators or knights. Moreover, another 31 can be identified as municipal magnates, that is, of curial (and perhaps often equestrian) rank; and of yet another 22 or so the only clue we have about them is that they moved in senatorial or equestrian circles. Otherwise, some 4 or 5 freedmen and freedwomen can be identified. Where professions are mentioned, we find 2 doctors, 4 or 5 bankers and businessmen, 1 contractor, 1 architect, 1 philosopher, 1 poet, 1 rhetor, and 1 courtesan (Hispala Faecenia)—soldiers occur only once, in the very late and quite anomalous testament of the 40 martyrs of Sebaste. In short, the testators of literature are heavily upper-class, roughly the *honestiores* of the high empire, with a sprinkling of professional men and successful *liberti*.

The legal evidence, while perhaps sharing this bias to some extent, is even more hampered by simple lack of information about the testators: the contents of the will and the situation of the survivors were of far greater interest to the jurists.[32] Nevertheless, something of interest does emerge from the roughly 41 cases (or about 6 percent of the 687 testators surveyed). Somewhat surprisingly, only 3 senators, 1 knight, and 1 woman of high rank (*honestissima femina*) are explicitly identified as such, while there are some 9 *liberti* or *libertae*.[33] And two groups virtually ignored by the

---

31. In some comparable preindustrial societies, the incidence of intestacy has been seen as much lower than at Rome. S. Epstein, *Wills and Wealth in Medieval Genoa, 1150–1250* (Cambridge, Mass., 1984), 38–45, suggests that anyone who could afford the small notary's fee and had any property at all would leave a will. Cf. R. S. Gottfried, *Epidemic Disease in Fifteenth Century England* (New Brunswick, N.J., 1978), 22, on East Anglia in the later fifteenth century.

32. Cf. Boyer, "Fonction sociale," 341.

33. *Dig.* 5.3.58; 33.7.12.40; 34.9.16.1; 29.1.43; 32.37.6. One more at least (32.27.1) is recognizable as a senator from other sources. *Liberti:* 32.35 pr; 32.38.1; 33.2.36; 36.3.18; 31.89.6; 28.5.93?; 31.83; 36.1.62.

literary sources dominate: the military (1 prefect of a legion, 3 first centurions, 4 centurions, 11 soldiers, 1 veteran), and the commercial (1 businesswoman, 1 banker, 1 moneylender, 1 procurator, one man whose interests included money changing, and one who employed slave agents in commerce).[34] It should be clear that the legal sources are much more representative than the literary of the world at large, the legal interest of their cases, rather than the rank of the participants, being the prime motive for selection.

The papyri, again, tell a different story: no senators, no knights and only two men and one woman of curial rank, all from the later third century; and only two freedmen explicitly identified as such. The most important character in the papyri is the soldier. One-third of the Roman wills from Egypt (26 out of 79) are those of veterans or serving soldiers, indeed they account for one-half of the surviving wills written before the Constitutio Antoniniana. That could mean one of two things: first, that military men were more likely to leave wills than civilians;[35] and second, that for a long time Roman citizens unconnected with the military were indeed a very small portion of the populace, hence that mere citizenship can be taken as a sign of membership in the elite.

Finally, the inscriptions, specifically those from the city of Rome. The majority of the 223 give no indication of rank or occupation. Among the identifiable freeborn are 15 senators and knights, and 16 men are of the apparitorial class; 4 soldiers of different ranks (not included in the separate categories), 2 doctors, 1 professor, 1 teacher of rhetoric, 1 banker, 1 surveyor, 2 businessmen, and an organizer of the Green circus faction. Particularly striking is the number of freedmen, some 55 (25 percent), of whom 12 are imperial freedmen, *liberti Augusti*. The few jobs indicated include imperial accountant, centurions' butler, announcer in the census office, and subprefect in the Alexandrian fleet, among the imperial freedmen; and grain merchant, prima donna (*archimima*), and attendant at the temple of Venus in the Sallustian gardens, among the rest.[36] Noteworthy also are some 37

---

34. Military: 26.7.47.4; 32.38.4; 34.2.32.3; 34.4.23; 26.7.40; 29.1.27; 28.6.15; 40.4.51; 29.1.12; 29.1.36 pr; 29.1.36.1; 29.1.36.2; 29.1.36.4; 31.75 pr; 35.2.18; 40.4.52; 29.1.40 pr; 29.1.40.1; 29.2.90.1. Commerce: 34.2.32.4; 40.7.40.8; 33.7.12.43; 18.5.8; 31.77.16; 26.7.58 pr.

35. See below, pp. 56–58.

36. *CIL* 6.8427, 8938, 33131, 9427, 10107, 32468.

other testators, another 17 percent, for whom neither rank nor occupation is attested, but whose names include a non-Roman—in all cases Greek—element: many will have been the near descendants of former slaves.

Before we consider the implications of these numbers, a word about the closely related question of wealth, which lies at the heart of the matter. Did testators always own "a house or something of comparable value," or did their ranks include many "little people" who "had a bit of this and a bit of that to leave"?[37] Thus has the debate been framed, and it is difficult to be any more precise, as again the sources diverge widely, and nothing approaching statistics can be offered.

Literature affords examples of vast fortunes being transferred or dispersed, either without figures (testators who were wealthy, extremely rich, and so forth), or with values as great as 60 or 70 million sesterces,[38] and legacies ranging from public games to artistic masterpieces. The lowest figures for legacies in all of the literature are 20,000 sesterces to a daughter (considered an insult: she should have inherited half of the estate) and 30,000 to a friend. These are arresting reminders of how much the writers assume: there are few real poor people in literature.[39] Indeed, the record of the private estate which we know best from literature is preserved precisely because of its extraordinary size; that of the freedman Caecilius Isidorus who, in 8 B.C., despite great losses in the civil war, nevertheless left 4116 slaves, 7200 oxen, 257,000 other cattle, 60 million sesterces in cash, and orders to spend one million on his funeral.[40]

The other three sources share one feature, despite their diverse natures: none has any reason to give the value of an estate. Inscriptions, for instance, are concerned almost exclusively with the funeral or memorial of the testator and with commemorative foundations. Figures for the latter range from two to seven digits,

37. The formulations are those of, respectively, Daube, "Predominance," and Crook, "Intestacy," 39. I can find no other considerations of the general wealth of testators in the Roman world.
38. Caecilius Isidorus and Pompey: appendix I.
39. Valerius Maximus 7.8.2; Cicero *Cluent.* 162.
40. Pliny *HN* 33.135, on which see P. A. Brunt, *Latomus* 34 (1975): 624ff. Value of estates mentioned on tombs: Horace *Serm.* 2.3.84; *CIL* 11.5400.

but they tell us nothing about the fortune of the donor, except that he or she must have possessed much more.[41] Similarly the legal sources, when they consider property at all, concentrate normally on a single *legatum* or *fideicommissum,* to the exclusion of the rest of the will, material information being at best incidental to discussions of definition and interpretation. To observe that 133, or about one-fifth, of the references in the four jurists indicate that the testator owned land in some form is not to say that the other four-fifths were or were not landowners. At best we can see that the testators all left property of value (slaves, lands, equipment, jewelry)—which doesn't get us much further.

The papyri offer the closest we will get to a picture of any estate, and what little has been said about testators' wealth has been based on them: that most Roman and Greco-Egyptian testators in Egypt owned land or a house (or part of a house), or both; that they do not frequently mention slaves and animals; that no large fortunes are discernible; and that the two largest landowners known from papyri were Roman citizens.[42] But the nature of the estate is more important than its (usually unknown) size: did it normally include a house or something similar, or could it run merely to a bit of this and a bit of that? The answer is unambiguous.

Of the 35 Roman wills extant on papyrus, 18 are too fragmentary to allow us to be sure whether the testator did or did not leave land; but of the remaining 17, no fewer than 13 explicitly indicate rural or urban landed property owned or bequeathed by the testator.[43]

The remaining four testators require brief attention. One of them, the cavalry centurion Valerius Aion, actually lists all of his

41. Duncan-Jones, *Economy,* 129–131, attempted to relate size of outlay on memorials by soldiers to known rates of pay, concluding only that the wealthier spent proportionately more of their annual income. See below for some attempt to relate size of inheritance to size of gifts away from it. Extensive lands and chattels aside, Caecilius Isidorus directed that 1 million of 60 million sesterces be expended on his funeral. Cf. Conclusion: in a fictional will, about 5% of the estate is spent on funeral and tomb, 9/10 of it on the funeral.

42. Montevecchi, "Ricerche," 89–100.

43. *BGU* 326, 1655, 1696, *P. Berol.* inv. 7124, *P. Coll. Youtie* 64, *P. Laur.* 1.4, *P. Lips.* 29, *P. NYU* inv. 2.15, *P. Oxy.* 907, 2474, *P. Princ.* 38, *PSI* 1325, *P. Select.* 1.14. Two of these, *PSI* 1325 and *BGU* 326, were noted by Montevecchi, "Ricerche," 95, as the two richest landowners found in the testaments. Seven of the 13 also mention slaves or freed slaves.

property owned and owing in A.D. 320; since he begins with 8 gold solidi and 199½ silver talents, he was clearly not a poor man. Similarly a Julius, who had a son and at least two daughters, left the following individual legacies away from the family: two of 1 talent; one of 600 drachmae; three of 200 drachmae; and two of unknown value. In A.D. 142 the cavalryman Antonius Silvanus left legacies totaling 1350 denarii, along with freedom to a slave and the payment of the manumission tax. And in 134, the freedman Ti. Claudius Alexander left two legacies totaling a mere 300 drachmae and instructions that not less than 100 be spent on his funeral, a sum which is comparatively low.[44] In short, on the very lowest reckoning we can see that most of the testators owned or could have owned land. The significant point is that this reckoning must be extremely low, and it is of little use in estimating the size of personal fortunes; as a general rule, we must assume that most Roman heirs inherited the bulk of the estate (even if, in many cases, to hand much or most of it on by way of *fideicommissum*), and that legacies seldom intentionally drained away anything approaching the three-quarters allowed by the Lex Falcidia.

Take the situations of the two "poorest" of the testators. The heir of Antonius Silvanus was to be his son, M. Antonius Satrianus; his brother Antonius R... was to be substitute heir or to receive a legacy of 750 denarii, and the "mother of his heir" Antonia Thermutha was to have 500 denarii and control of his military estate (*bona castrensia*).[45] The heir of Claudius Alexander was to be his fellow freed slave (*colliberta*) Claudia Theanous, while her son was to be substitute (with no mention of a legacy): as the editors suggest, these are surely the testator's concubine and son. Outside of the family, Silvanus left only 100 denarii in legacies, Alexander 200; surely we should assume that the great bulk of the estate—of unknown size in both cases, and perhaps including land—stayed tacitly (no need to spell out a division) with the single heir from the nuclear family. In the other testaments in the papyri (excluding those of Valerius Aion and Iulius) landed property is mentioned in the form of legacies subtracted from the estate; the

44. *P. Col.* 188, *CPR* 6.2.76, *CPL* 221, *P. Oxy.* 2857. Other burial costs in the wills: 200 (*BGU* 1695, A.D. 157), 300 (*P. Lips.* 30, third century), 500 (*P. Oxy.* 2348, A.D. 224), and 800 (*P. Select.* 14, A.D. 127/148).
45. *CPL* 221.

identifiable legatees were an illegitimate daughter (two concubines being the heirs[46]), a daughter (sons heirs), substitute heirs (heirs unknown), a wife (brother heir), a wife (sons heirs), and a husband (mother heir)—that is, members of the nuclear family. No suggestion is given of the size of the estate.[47] In sum, the papyri give little hint of testators who were not landowners and people of some substance, and there is no evidence for "little people."[48]

The conclusion must be that testation in Roman society was even less common than might be surmised. One takes its existence for granted among the more or less wealthy political elite—senators, knights, and decurions. Equally, one does not expect to find the wills of miners or of itinerant farm workers on daily wages. What is striking is the very restricted area of the middle ground. Moneylenders, merchants, doctors, architects, imperial servants, even a contractor (*conductor*) or an *archimima,* all had opportunities for accumulating capital. But there is very little hint of the ordinary man or woman leaving a will, the cobbler, the tavern keeper, the wage laborer, the porter, the sailor, the tenant farmer or smallholder. Much is known of their existence; they must have owned something, yet documents do not link them with leaving a will and there is no reason to assume that they shared any sense of a duty of testation.[49] Studies of wills in the United States have amply demonstrated that capital is the major element determining

46. Concubinage was a form of respectable second-class marriage where a formal Roman marriage (*iustum matrimonium*) was barred on legal (not moral) grounds. The children were illegitimate in the eyes of Rome, but not of local law.

47. *BGU* 326, 1655, 1696, *P. Coll. Youtie* 64, *P. Oxy.* 2474, *P. Princ.* 38. We also find minute but not necessarily exhaustive listings in what are apparently Greek-influenced *heredis institutiones ex re certa,* which all indicate substantial properties: *P. Oxy.* 907 (vineyards, wheat fields, four silver talents to each daughter as dowry), *PSI* 1325, *P. NYU* inv. 2.15.

48. Figures are simply unavailable, since the size of properties is almost never given (usually just "my wheatfields near..."), and the quality never. *PSI* 1325 and *BGU* 326, both of the second century, list respectively at least 45 arouras distributed and a single legacy of 6¼ arouras; taking Duncan-Jones's median average (*Economy,* 366) for Egyptian land prices, the use of which is dubious on several grounds, these might indicate values of very roughly 9000 drachmas and 1250 drachmas. The smallest estate known to have been left by a Roman will, the 800 drachmas of a freedman in the early third century (*P. Oxy.* 3103) could by that standard easily have included a bit of land.

49. Such evidence as there is deserves a moment's consideration.
Certain funerary societies, *collegia funeratica,* envisage the possibility that some of their members will have left testaments: *ILS* 7212, 1.22–23, 1.29–2.2 (the *cultores Dianae et Antinoi* at Lanuvium) or *AE* 1929.161, 10–14 (the *familia Silvani* at

whether or not people leave a will.[50] This is not simply to say that if you have nothing you leave no will, and if you have something you do; but rather that the chances of your leaving a will increase or decrease substantially with the amount of property you own. In Rome, with a much greater inequity in the distribution of wealth, there is little evidence for testation below a fairly high line, that of relatively prosperous businesspeople, civil servants, professional persons, and landowners.[51]

There is one corroboration of this, an exception which seems strikingly to prove the rule. This great exception is the soldier's

---

Trebula Mutuesca), and possibly *ILS* 7213, 6 (the *collegium Aesculapi et Hygiae* at Rome). Such societies regularly embraced a variety of members, freeborn, freed, and even slaves; and there is no reason why some of their members should not have been well enough situated to contemplate leaving a will, while still maintaining their membership in a group for social reasons which for economic purposes they no longer required. I suspect that they were exceptional.

Again, the famous Bagradas Valley inscriptions from North Africa (*CIL* 8.25902, 4.2–6, cf. 25943; 2) make it quite clear that some of the tenant farmers there left wills. But as a recent study has convincingly demonstrated, these particular *coloni*, far from being downtrodden victims, were men of astonishing economic and political power: D. Kehoe, *The Economics of Agriculture on Roman Imperial Estates in North Africa* (Göttingen, 1988).

In literature, even Trimalchio's *saltuarii* are represented as leaving wills; but this is satire. Either they were slaves, in which case they demonstrated their master's humanity (cf. Pliny *Ep.* 8.16, or *ILS* 7212, 2.2–5, referred to above), or they were free men, in which case they underline their master's phenomenal wealth (with the understanding that normally such people did not leave wills). In any case, hardly reflective of reality.

Take chapter 15 of H. Dessau's *Inscriptiones Latinae Selectae,* "Tituli ministrorum vitae privatae, opificum, artificum," which presents a cross-section of such little people as could afford to erect an inscription: some 451 stones are included. Of these, those that mention or imply a will (under the criteria discussed in chapter 2 above), there are 4 *negotiatores* (one of them a magistrate; 7481, 7524, 7526, 7541); a *solatarius,* a *margaritarius,* and a *cullearius* (7551, 7602, 7660); and a *doctor librarius* and a philosopher (7752, 7784). No cooks, bakers, tenant farmers, brick makers, innkeepers, etc.

There may well be instances of small people—wage earners, craftsmen, and the like—leaving wills, but they will have been the exceptions, the success stories; they do not controvert the main point, that normally such people did not expect and were not expected to leave wills.

50. E.g., A. Dunham, "The Method, Process and Frequency of Wealth Transmission at Death," *University of Chicago Law Review* 30 (1962/63): 241–85, at 245–51; cf. J. W. Deen, "Patterns of Testation: Four Tidewater Counties in Colonial Virginia," *Am. J. Legal Hist.* 16 (1972), 154–76, at 169, remarking that wealthier testators use making a will as an opportunity to review their estates, whereas the poorer tend to leave it until their deathbeds.

51. It must moreover be remembered that "wealth" is an abbreviation embracing a number of related factors, particularly education and experience in its management.

will. It is quite clear from both the inscriptions and the papyri that the rate of testation was much higher among the military (soldiers and veterans) than among the ordinary civilian population at large, of which it was a tiny fraction (less than 1 percent).[52] The key here should lie in the tremendous difference between the military will, with its all but absolute liberty, and the formal testament with bronze and scales, the *testamentum per aes et libram*. The great value of this difference is that it directs attention, not to the commonness of the military will, but to the uncommonness of the civilian.

For a soldier, the simple expression of his intention was sufficient for a valid will; a civilian needed an elaborate ceremony or at least a written document. A soldier could testate in any language; a civilian had to use Latin (before Severus Alexander). A soldier could say anything, name anyone; a civilian must disinherit certain people, must institute an heir at the beginning, must have the correct number of witnesses, must not bequeath things to certain classes of people, and so forth.[53] The excuse for all of this was the simple nature, the ignorance of the soldiers for which the paternal

52. It is here assumed that the samples of praetorian soldiers at Rome and soldiers and veterans in Egypt are representative, and can be confirmed elsewhere. Take for instance Lambaesis in Numidia, first base of *legio III Augusta* and later a *municipium* in the second century, a *colonia* in the third. The inscriptions from that place are divided into military and municipal in *CIL* 8, allowing us to produce some rough figures.

There are about 229 inscriptions (nos. 2781–3010) assigned to centurions and lesser holders of military *munera:* on the criteria discussed in chapter 2, I find 18 that clearly mention or reflect the existence of a will (and several others which suggest it). Of 226 inscriptions (nos. 3011–3287) to private soldiers or veterans of the legion, 19 indicate a will (another six have simply *heres eius*). Not many, perhaps, but then these 226 inscriptions also include several set up *inter vivos*, and many are to the wives of soldiers (who should count as civilians). And their significance lies in their contrast with some 866 (nos. 3319–4185) explicitly sepulchral inscriptions from the civilian community: among these I can find at most 14 which seem to indicate the existence of a will (and these include 4 with children who were heirs of their mothers; after A.D. 178, they could easily have been heirs by intestacy).

Such figures are of course very rough, and any number of factors may affect them, including different epigraphic habits, different social conditions, or the method or care of the observer—among some 1121 common *tituli sepulchrales* from Numidian Cirta, *ILAlg* 2.815–1936, I can find no trace of wills at all. One could, if one wished, argue them away on general principles. But on the face of it, the evidence shows a strikingly higher incidence of testation among the military.

53. In general, Kaser, *Privatrecht*, 680–82; Amelotti, *Testamento*, 81–110. B. Campbell, *The Emperor and the Roman Army 31 B.C. – A.D. 235* (Oxford, 1984), 210–29.

emperor, with an eye to their loyalty, made all possible allowance.[54] But the important point here is that the ignorance of the soldier cannot have been any greater than that of the ordinary populace from which he sprang. Indeed it may have been less, given the aid and information which the army and his comrades could provide him. And yet soldiers made the most appalling mistakes, from the institution of their own unfreed slaves as heirs, to the complete omission of the act of mancipation (the formal sale of his estate by the testator to a straw man) in a would-be formal will.[55] Such basic errors would simply invalidate a normal will. When even men and women of high rank and considerable education forgot to confirm codicils naming an heir, or left legacies to slaves whom they had neglected to free, or made a will without their tutor's approval,[56] how did the average citizen, unprotected by the soldier's legal privileges, stand a chance of leaving a valid will?

It is particularly hard to imagine ourselves in the place of the average citizen in an empire where literacy was rare and education rarer. Even if one wanted to leave a formal *testamentum per aes et libram*, the problems were daunting. The Roman testament was worked out by highly cultivated men at Rome. How forbidding it must have looked, bristling with technicalities and pitfalls, to a tenant farmer or a shopkeeper with little education and shaky Latin. Scribes cannot have been very competent, and there is astonishingly little indication of their employment in the composition of wills.[57]

For some the problems were compounded. In an empire where citizens were for long a minority, men and women in the less Romanized areas might find themselves barred from leaving property under Roman law to their noncitizen children, spouses, and friends (or, from the time of Augustus to that of Hadrian,

54. *Dig.* 29.1.1 pr.; Gaius 2.109, cf. 114.
55. *Dig.* 29.1.40; *BGU* 1695. The *Testamentum Porcelli* is a parody of a soldier's will: Daube, *Roman Law*, 77–81. The will of the veteran M. Antonius Valens verges on unintelligibility: *Suppl. Ital.* 181, improved by O. Cuntz at *JÖAI* 9 (1906): 23–26.
56. Pliny *Ep.* 2.16.1, 4.10.1; Cicero *Fam.* 7.21 (with Watson, *Succession*, 73).
57. That is, strange though it may seem, most testators did it themselves: below, pp. 70–75. There is simply no evidence that the (unattested) uneducated testator— other than the soldier—resorted to professional help, as distinct from mere scribal services.
58. The possibility of leaving property by *fideicommissum* to *peregrini*, unintentionally opened by Augustus, was finally closed under Hadrian: Kaser, *Privatrecht*,

would at least find it difficult).[58] At cosmopolitan Athens under Hadrian, even among professional Epicurean philosophers there were few Roman citizens, and yet the head of the school had to be a citizen (*in angustum redigitur eligendi [facultas]*); therefore special permission had to be sought from the emperor to allow the current head to name a noncitizen as successor, if necessary, in his Roman will.[59] What can the situation have been like in areas with fewer citizens and less knowledge of the law? Even a highly educated Greco-Roman, Plutarch, was struck by the apparent absurdity of a law which made one person heir to the estate and another its purchaser (the *familiae emptor*); what can the act of mancipation have meant to others without his experience of Roman antiquities and Roman formalism?[60]

Ethnic and geographical origin are not especially significant in themselves in determining the likelihood of testation—native Spaniards, Gauls, Egyptians, Syrians, Greeks, all produced Roman wills. The important factors are status, wealth, and the education they bring, the familiarity with the products of Roman culture; a Roman will, however faulty, is a sign of understanding and a mark of self-identification. It excludes not only the noncitizen and the poor, but also those who may well have had "a bit of this and that" to leave yet were daunted by, indifferent to, or simply ignorant of the law governing wills. It includes only by imperial fiat the Roman soldier, not inappropriately for a member of the most visible force of Romanization; and the existence of the ignorant citizen soldier implies the existence of equally ignorant civilians. The making of a Roman will, even by the relatively humble, is a self-conscious mark of identification with Rome and the values propagated by its cultured elite.

---

758. (Inscriptions reveal noncitizens as such fiduciary heirs: e.g., *CIL* 5.2834.) Within that century, Dio of Prusa noted the impossibility of directly naming the heirs desired (*Or.* 73.3). Pausanias, writing afterward, remarked on the problem of citizens whose children were non-Roman being forced to leave their property to strangers or to the state, a problem alleviated by Antoninus Pius' allowing them to leave to their children (8.43.5). Pliny, e.g., requesting citizenship, includes the man's children (*Ep.* 10.11).

59. *ILS* 7784, with, most recently, S. Follet, *Athènes au IIe et IIIe siècles. Études chronologiques et prosopographiques* (1977), 23–24, and J. H. Oliver, *AJP* 99 (1978): 269–70.

60. Plutarch *Mor.* 550 B.

•   •   •

To act thus in a markedly Roman way implies subscription to certain beliefs and expectations.[61] These, in turn, will affect two aspects of testation in a particular way.

First, it must be very dubious that the existence and nature, or the absence, of close family ties had significant general effect on the likelihood of testation. This cautious conclusion should not be misunderstood. We can learn a great deal about choice of heirs or legatees, and about the relative values placed on children, spouses, parents, and close kin; and we can speculate about the reasons for the choices made.[62] But the question here is of a different order: did the existence or nonexistence of children, spouses, or other close relatives affect testation itself? At the simplest, for instance, was a person who had children more likely to leave a will than one who was married but childless, or than one who was simply unmarried? Moreover, ideally, one would like to be able to make fine distinctions: would a person who had both sons and daughters be more likely to make a will than one who had children of one sex only, that is, would he or she feel a greater need to deviate from the equal-handed tables of intestate succession? We do not know. The great gap lies in our ignorance of intestacy among those who had something to leave; but the partial nature of the information which we do have about wills is equally baffling. Thus, we can rarely be sure that the *extraneus* heir named in a legal text or inscription was the sole heir, thus implying the nonexistence of close kin, or (equally possible) the passing over or disinheritance of children and spouse; nor does the mention only of a spouse generally exclude the existence of a child, or vice versa. Data for reconstructing the complete families of testators are simply inadequate.

Nevertheless, several considerations suggest that the simple existence or nonexistence of family, however closely or broadly defined, had little effect on leaving a will. Take the figure with fewer family ties than most, the soldier, legally barred from marriage throughout his career in the two centuries before Septimius Severus. Of the praetorians surveyed (some of them veterans,

61. Outlined in chapter 1.
62. See below, chapters 6 and 7.

some of them serving in the third century and thus able to marry), 59 left heirs of whom we know something: 9 of these were related by blood or marriage (wives, children, siblings, a cousin, a clansman), but some 50 were *extranei,* most often of course comrades, but also fellow townsmen, friends, and freedmen. Clearly, lack of family did not inhibit testation for them. On the other hand, take the 15 cases of intestacy found among the four jurists surveyed in the Digest: 2 of those cases record nothing about family, but of the other 13 individuals, 1 left behind a cousin, 2 left siblings, and no fewer than 10 left children (2 of them a spouse as well).[63] Equally clearly here, natural affection did not guarantee a will. Both of these instances are admittedly fragile; unknown factors may weigh heavily (the unique advantages of soldiers and the substitution of camp for family, for instance;[64] or, among civilians, simple inadvertence, or contentment with the law of intestacy), and the evidence is miserably inadequate—but they are suggestive.

More important are the reasons for making a will in the first place, the idea of a duty of testacy which embraced the married and the single, the childless and those with children alike. The urge to praise and to blame, the need to select a proper heir, the duty to repay obligations and reward friendship, and in the end the passionate desire to preserve one's own memory: all were universal motives for which the existence of a family was strictly irrelevant, and even a man who was ill and dying, childless and without kin, could still feel the need to make an oral will in order (among other things) to leave property to a friend.[65] The paradigm here should be Martial's friend Vestinus, who was spared long enough in his last hours to divide his great wealth among his friends: by so doing, says the poet, he seemed to have died in the old age which was in fact denied him.[66] If we consider testation as deviance from the rules of intestate succession, there is no difference discernible to us between the married man who chooses as heirs his children and the unmarried man who nominates his friend. Family obviously affected the choice of an heir, with preference shown for one child over another, or for a spouse over a

---

63. References at n.16.
64. Cf. R. MacMullen, "The Legion as Society," *Historia* 33 (1984): 440–56.
65. *Dig.* 32.39.1 (Scaevola).
66. Martial 4.73.

brother, for instance; but it does not seem to have affected the decision to choose an heir in the first place. That decision was predetermined by society.

Similarly, on the evidence alone, there is no significant correlation to be drawn between age or health and the incidence of testation. Ideally, we should like to know the age and physical condition of the testator at the time of the first will, age and condition at the time of the final version or final codicil, and age at the time of death. Rarely do we have record of even one of these, never of all three. There is sufficient evidence to show that most last wills were probably written or supplemented in contemplation of death, that is, normally during serious illness, on the deathbed, or in what was regarded as old age. The great problem here lies in the word "last": almost never can we be sure that this final document was also the first, and all too often it is clear that it was a revision or replacement of earlier versions; that is to say, the motivation was not so much impending death as constant review.[67] The evidence for this, the general notion of a duty of testacy, and above all the Augustan invention of the confirmed codicil, certainly suggest that in general testators thought about wills long before they thought about dying. Moreover the low incidence of intestacy among those who had something to leave, and the extreme rarity of people known to have put off making a will until the last moment (as did the poet Horace and an anonymous soldier, who both died in the act of testation) should confirm that caution was the general rule.[68]

The question should not be "how old was the Roman testator?" but "how young?" To put the matter into stark perspective, one study of a group of wills in the United States in the mid-twentieth century found that the average testator was 66 when he or she executed a last will.[69] Most Romans, elite or otherwise, simply didn't live that long, nor did they require anyone to point out to them that life was short and disease and accidents common. To take an arbitrary age, minors under 25 years are certainly on

67. See below, pp. 64–70.
68. *Dig.* 29.1.40 pr.; *Vita Horati; P. Vindob. Gr.* inv. 25819. Kaser, *Privatrecht*, 680 nn. 17, 22, for references. Cf. Epstein, *Wills and Wealth*, 44, on the rarity of oral wills at Genoa.
69. Dunham, "Wealth Transmission," 279.

record as leaving wills, the youngest known being the 18-year-old who left his mistress as heir.[70] Of some ninety-one praetorians in *CIL* 6, ten died testate between the ages of 20 and 24 (and another twenty-six between the ages of 25 and 29); did their profession encourage them to make wills earlier than their civilian counterparts? But such random figures are not necessary. An important recent study has offered strong reason to believe that roughly 50 percent of Roman males would be fatherless at the age of 14, rising to 60 percent by the age of 20 and over 80 percent by 30—that is, the majority of Roman males would be *sui iuris* in their teens and twenties, *patresfamilias* (fathers of families, in legal terms) and possibly owners of property.[71] The effect of demography mixed with the duty of testation should be clear, so clear indeed that an axiom may be propounded: if a Roman male citizen were fourteen or over and *sui iuris,* and if he had property worth leaving, he would be expected to have a will.

Cato's audience was thus restricted. Beyond it may lie those intestate millions whose actions rarely concerned historians, orators, jurists, Egyptian bureaucrats, or anyone who erected an epitaph. But among Roman men and women of property and some education, it can be assumed that intestacy was generally considered abnormal and unfortunate, that there was a shared sense of the duty of testation which transcended family and age, some effects of which will be seen in the next chapter. That sense of duty was shared by both sexes, and they acted on it in similar fashions despite the great disparity in the numbers of men and women who left wills—a disparity which will be returned to later.

70. Quintilian 8.5.17. *Dig.* 12.6.67.4 (minor, probably); 33.7.3.1 (under 20); 34.3.20.1 (minor); *CIL* 6.1637 (a knight aged 24), 3516 (a 19-year-old).
71. R. P. Saller, "Men's Age at Marriage and Its Consequences in the Roman Family," *CP* 82 (1987): 21–34, esp. 33. Cf. Hopkins, *Death and Renewal,* 70 ff., 146ff.

# 4

## The Act

### *Frequency—Composition—Witnesses*

Sharing a sense of duty, individuals and society must have worried how to get it right, how to ensure that the document was a precise reflection of the testator's true last judgment. This concern manifested itself in various forms: in a concern for revision, in a concern for authorship, in a concern for the proper choice of witnesses, and in a fear of illegal or immoral interference by outsiders. In one way or another, this chapter and the next will pursue the proper performance of the duty of the testator.

First, should not the *supremum iudicium* truly contain the last judgment?

To begin at the end: a will from Egypt dated 14 February 169 was opened 3 June that same year; another dated late April or early May 186 was opened within a month. The testament of C. Longinus Castor, dated 17 October 189, was opened 21 February 194, but it had attached to it a codicil dated simply 7 February, that is, perhaps as little as two weeks before the document was opened. The will of L. Ignatius Rufinus, written 3 March 210 while its author was infirm, was opened 3 June 211. Aurelius Chaeremon's will, written 21 July 224, was opened the following 12 September. And the will of Aurelius Hermogenes, dated 1 June 276, was opened in late June or July of the same year.[1] Thus far the slight but consistent evidence of the wills preserved on papyri: they were signed in the shadow of death.

To them can be added chance references in other testamentary papyri to imminent death or serious illness.[2] Improving anecdotes in literature also closely connect the making of wills with the

---

1. *BGU* 1655, 2244, 326; *P. Coll. Youtie* 64; *P. Oxy.* 2348, 907. Add now *P. Oxy.* 3758.134–155: a will opened the day after it was written in March, 325.
2. *BGU* 361; *P. Col.* 188. *P. Vindob. Gr.* inv. 25819 records the nuncupative will of a dying woman.

onset of death: Horace, cut off before he could sign the prepared document; Claudius, murdered perhaps because of the contents of his will; Sulla, warned by a dream at Cumae and writing his will on the very day of his death; the dying governor of Britain, Q. Veranius, who combined adulation of the emperor with boasts of what he would have accomplished had he lived another two years; the man who wrote so quickly in his infirmity that he had no time to make a friend heir to one-twelfth, as he had intended; the *paterfamilias* who made his will two days before his death; the noble matricide who had his will written in prison before his execution; the African landowner mortally wounded by bandits, who fled to his villa and there made his will; Martial's young friend Vestinus, begging time from the Fates to leave a will for his friends' sake; soldiers making their wills before battle; even the piglet, M. Grunnius Corocotta, begging time to make his last wishes known before falling under the butcher's knife.[3] People's thoughts at death turned, not surprisingly, to their testaments. The obvious inference to be drawn is that most people did not think of wills until very late, in contemplation of imminent death.

But another inference, equally valid, is that wills were subjected to frequent revisions, of which we hear only of the last. The argument from silence does not outweigh this inference. That is, simply because there is no mention of previous wills we cannot in any of these cases assume that they did not exist—indeed, many of the anecdotes could easily be taken as referring to codicils—nor is it likely that Sulla or Claudius had reached their seventh decade of life and mastership of the world without making a will. At the same time, for what they are worth, other anecdotes do explicitly depict the deathbed will as a revision: the seriously ill Verania, allegedly pressed by Regulus into adding a codicil with a legacy for him; the rich consular Velleius Blaesus, who "wished to change his will" on his deathbed; C. Oppianicus, allegedly poisoned by his villainous brother, crying out too late that "he wished to change his will."[4]

3. *Vita Horati;* Suetonius *Claud.* 44.1; Appian *BC* 1.105; Tacitus *Ann.* 14.29; *Dig.* 36.1.63; 32.102.1; *Rhet. Her.* 1.23; *Dig.* 29.5.2; Martial 4.73; Caesar *BG* 1.39; *Testamentum Porcelli.*
4. Pliny, *Ep.* 2.20.1–6, 2.20.7–8; Cicero, *Cluent.* 31. Cf. Fronto *Ad Am.* 1.14: canceled codicils claimed to be deathbed revisions.

An illuminating group of cases is offered in the fifteenth and sixteenth books of Tacitus' *Annals*, all of them involving men sound in mind and body who were faced with sudden death in the direct aftermath of the Pisonian conspiracy or in the subsequent period of uncertainty: wills figure prominently in the narrative. First, in the year 65 the senator Flavius Scaevinus was accused among other matters of having sealed his will the day before the projected attack on Nero; in defense against that particular charge he claimed that he had often sealed his will without particularly noting what day it was. Moved by love for his wife, Piso himself included in his will the basest flatteries of the emperor— doubtless trying to save part of his wealth for her. Seneca, faced by Nero's messenger, called for his will and, when his request was refused, told the assembled friends that he could leave them only the image of his life; his intention had clearly been to add a codicil rewarding his last companions, not to make a new will (Tacitus elsewhere records one that already existed with a codicil of funeral instructions). The praetorian prefect Faenius Rufus chose to bemoan his fate in his testament. L. Antistius Vetus refused to make Nero a major heir, even to safeguard the interests of his grandchildren. In 66, P. Anteius Rufus could find no one brave enough to witness his will until the scoundrel prefect Tigellinus intervened. Seneca's brother, Annaeus Mela, added codicils to his will which assigned a large sum to Tigellinus and his son-in-law in order to preserve the remainder, and which complained about the iniquity of his undeserved fate when other real enemies of the prince still lived. And Petronius Arbiter, far from praising Nero and Tigellinus in codicils added to his will "as many others had done," set down a list of the emperor's sexual crimes, complete with the names of partners and novelties, and sent it under seal to the emperor.[5]

It is easily arguable that these eight men had already made wills when they were faced with sudden death. The emphasis is on last-minute change, change effected or thwarted or rejected, on the addition of lamentation or praise and even of legacies; Tacitus

<hr />

5. *Ann.* 15.54.1 and 55.3; 15.59.8; 15.62.1 cf. 64.5–6; 15.68.2; 16.11.2; 16.14.5; 16.17.6; 16.19.5. J. G. Keenan, "Tacitus, Roman Wills and Political Freedom," *BASP* 24 (1987): 1–8, dealing with these items, arrived too late to be taken into account here.

notes explicitly that "many of the dying" added codicils to their wills (16.17.6). Such senior men simply would not have lived without testaments until the last minute; nor did they. The prime exhibit is the stout defense of his actions by Scaevinus, a defense which momentarily confounded his prosecutors with the apparently truthful claim that he had often sealed the tablets of his will without noticing the date—the implication is surely that for him this was an occurrence of no little frequency.

A norm can be postulated, despite the scarcity of direct evidence. To be sure, the papyri include wills written (though in one case revised as well) not long before death, without any indication that they superseded previous documents; legal and epigraphical sources normally deal as a matter of course with the final and operative testament only; and we are told little even of the circumstances surrounding wills made in contemplation of death. But all this need not matter. Take the will of Julius Caesar, dated some six months before his unexpected death: we could safely have presumed the existence of a previous version, even had we not known of at least three.[6] Similarly, the wills of Augustus, dated 3 April A.D. 13, seventeen months before his death, and of Tiberius, written some two years before his death in 37: other wills are casually recorded for them as early as 24 and 6 B.C., respectively, the existence of which could have been surmised regardless.[7] Not to labor the point, Scaevinus ought to be taken as a paradigm for the frequency of revision, to be joined by the poet Archias, whose advocate pointed out in a dispute over his citizenship that he "has often made his will in accordance with our laws."[8] Hence the satirists merely exaggerate reality when they depict frequent revision as a ploy of the would-be victim of captators: Petronius' Eumolpus, masquerading as a great landowner, pretends to revise his will every month; Martial's Charinus bankrupts the poet, who must give him presents each of the thirty times he revises his will in one year.[9]

6. Suetonius 83.1: from 59 to 49 his heir was Pompey. Thus, a third document, effective between 49 and 45 is to be presumed, and at least one before 59 (his father had died in 85).

7. Suetonius *Aug.* 101, *Tib.* 76. The elder Drusus (died 9 B.C.), C. and L. Caesar (died 2 B.C. and 1 A.D.) had all been instituted heirs by Augustus previously: Suetonius *Claud.* 1.5.

8. Cicero, *Pro Archia* 11.

9. Petronius, *Sat.* 117; Martial 5.39.

To such anecdotal indications can be added more general considerations. First, the duty of testation among those who have
anything to leave must imply an absolute necessity to keep the will
up-to-date. The birth or adoption or emancipation or death of a
*suus heres* could invalidate or seriously imperil a will in law; the
acquisition or loss of friends and relatives must have constantly
rearranged a testator's emotions and moral sensibilities. The two
men censured or pitied by the younger Pliny for leaving out-of-
date wills were surely not the norm: one omitted some of those for
whom he cared most and favored some who were no longer
friends, while the other may indeed have become a proverb for
un-Roman indifference.[10] These men were simply derelict in their
duty. The conscientious Roman would imitate the 60-year-old
Cicero who, two years before his death, newly divorced and re-
married, his grandson born and his daughter recently dead, duly
made a new formal will.[11]

Second, that revision was common is suggested by the matter of
intestacy. Just as dying without a will at all is rarely recorded in the
*Digest*, so of the 687 wills noticed in the four jurists, only 8 were
automatically annulled by the law, normally because of the appearance of an unexpected or unsuspected *suus*.[12] Similarly, in the
papyri, from the dozens of examples of intestacy in the Roman
period before the Constitutio Antoniniana, not one instance concerns a Roman law will.[13] In this light, most people seem to have
been prepared (whether well or ill) for the sudden accident that
might take them off without warning, and being prepared meant
having a valid will. Indeed, some were overprepared, leaving the
problem of two wills to be sorted out by the survivors.[14]

10. *Ep.* 5.5.2 (C. Fannius) and 8.18 (Domitius Afer). The antiquity of Afer's
will was the subject of interested concern to a newer friend: Quintilian 6.3.92. *Dig.*
31.89.1 shows problems caused by a five-year-old will.
    11. *Att.* 12.18a.2. Cf. *Dig.* 28.5.93: *Pactumeio [herede instituto] occiso...mutavit
testamentum Noviumque Rufum heredem instituit.*
    12. *Dig.* 40.4.29 unsuspected son, 28.2.19 disinherited son, 29.7.11 posthu-
mous daughter, 29.1.36.2 posthumous daughter, 38.8.9.1 deaf testator, 31.77.23
*nullo iure*, 40.5.38 *non perfectum*, 49.14.9 posthumous son.
    13. See above, pp. 42–46.
    14. Tacitus *Ann.* 2.48.1 (Pantuleius); [Quintilian] *Declam.* 308; Josephus, *Ant.*
17.221 (Herod); Cicero, *Q. Fr.* 3.7.8 (a man who signed the wrong one of two wills
prepared for him). *Dig.* 28.3.11 (Ulpian) has two wills, both signed by the same
witnesses; cf. 29.1.27 and especially 29.2.97.

And third, a widespread urge to revise wills must lie behind the recognition, sometime in the reign of Augustus, of a new legal institution, one designed specifically to fill that need, the confirmed codicil.[15] A great array of evidence shows the codicil being employed to supplement the will in every respect, from leaving legacies and *fideicommissa* of all kinds, to naming tutors, to manumitting slaves, to setting down instructions about the funeral and the tomb. Implicit in all, explicit in some, is the idea of change, simple change of mind or reaction to changed circumstances: adding to largesse in existing legacies, shifting the charge of legacies from one heir to another, changing distributions among heirs, changing the nature of legacies or the person of *fideicommissarii*, adding legacies for a newborn heir, removing an ungrateful freedman or freedwoman as heir, adding a condition, making provision for a second husband.[16] "It occurred to me afterwards," began one testator in his codicil, feeling that he should describe more exactly the contents of the property which he had left to one heir by preception. Another, having arranged in his will for one man to bring his body home if he died abroad, added in a codicil written the same day, that his heirs were to care for his body and place it in the tomb of his sons in Campania.[17] The codicil could do everything but name an heir; hence it provided a needed outlet for the worried or the conscientious testators who wanted their wills to represent their most recent internal and external condition, without going to the extra trouble of drawing up a new document.[18]

15. Kaser, *Privatrecht*, 693f., and now A. Metro, *Studi sui codicilli* 1 (Milan, 1979). The exact date is unknown: see Champlin, "Miscellanea testamentaria I–III," *ZPE* 62 (1986): 249–51.

16. Examples from the Digest: (respectively) 34.1.18, 32.27; 31.33.1, 34.1.13 pr.; 34.4.30.3, 36.1.80.8; 31.88.8; 34.4.30 pr.; 34.1.18.3; 32.37.2; 28.7.27.1; 31.34.7.

17. *Dig.* 33.7.20 pr. (*postea mihi venit in mentem*); 34.4.30.2.

18. Two other aspects of the codicil deserve mention. First, its frequent connection with imminent death, as the ultimate revision. A codicil could particularly be the vehicle of final emotions, consolations to the relatives, prayers or flattery addressed to the emperor with the intent of protecting the survivors, laments at the iniquity of one's fate. Equally, perhaps, it might be the first display of true emotion such as one might not entrust to the will, as in Petronius' final act: hence the title chosen by Fabricius Veiento for a work which scurrilously attacked senators and priests, *Codicilli* (Tacitus, *Ann.* 14.50). Otho left consolation and funeral instructions: Suetonius *Otho* 10.2.

Second, and related, the use of codicils by sons-in-power to express their dying wishes where legally they lacked the right to leave a will. Here the poet Lucan, who before suicide left a codicil with instructions for correcting some verses, is

In short, there is every reason to believe that in both theory and practice a good Roman citizen would not wait until death was imminent before making a will. The necessity for a current will leads to frequent revision, and the frequency with which the Romans made and remade their testaments affected several aspects of their composition.

Next, how to ensure that the testament truly captured the exact intentions of the testator? Modern lawyers toast with gratitude "The man who made his own will." Scaevola, in the third book of his *Responsa*, records the opening words of a real will: "I have written this my testament without any jurist, preferring to follow the promptings of my soul rather than excessive and miserable diligence; and if I shall have done anything less than legal or less learned, the will of a sane man ought to stand as legitimate."[19] With straight face Scaevola briskly recalls that the document was indeed invalid, and how he saved the *fideicommissum.* Conscientious testators wished to express themselves as fully as possible, but they were obliged to do it in words prescribed by others to ensure the validity of their wishes; hence there was room for conflict between personal and legal requirements. How far then were wills the testators' own compositions, how far did they rely on experts?

First, a distinction must be drawn between scribes and jurists, a distinction suggested by the epitaph of a freedman scribe at Venafrum "who wrote wills for twenty-five years without a jurist."[20] A freedman *sevir* at Cadiz recorded his activity as a writer of testaments, *testamentarius.* A schoolmaster of Greek extraction at Naples

---

matched by the anonymous Sicilian whose brief request for a monument and for the manumission of two slaves is preserved on stone at Cefalù: *Vita Lucani; FIRA* 56; cf. *CIL* 8.26482; *Dig.* 35.2.18 pr.

19. *Dig.* 31.88.17.

20. *ILS* 7750, *sine iuris consult.* As Amelotti pointed out, in M. Amelotti and G. Costamagna, *Alle origini del notariato italiano* (Rome, 1975), 7–12, "sine iurisconsulto" may not mean without expert help, but rather without legal controversy and therefore recourse to jurists. This is probably true; there is a similar usage on sepulchral inscriptions, e.g., *ILS* 8365, *huius monumentum dolus malus abesto et iuris consult:* M. Kaser, "Zum römischen Grabrecht," *ZSS* 95 (1978): 15–92, noting a divergence between civil and sacral law. The distinction between scribe and jurist still holds in this case. On scribes in general, see M. Amelotti, "Notariat und Urkundenwesen zur Zeit des Prinzipats," *ANRW* II.13 (1980): 386–99.

mentioned that he also wrote testaments faithfully (*cum fide*).[21] These are humble drawers-up of documents, men whose professional lives included other areas; and five quite colorless references to *testamentarii* in the Digest (all Severan) add nothing to the picture.[22] By contrast, a *test[amentarius]* who was also a jurist and a senator of consular rank apparently turned up in standard versions of the so-called *testamentum Dasumii* of A.D. 108, but he is an anomaly on several counts and in fact a chimera: the man in question is clearly not a *testamentarius* but a witness, and the passage should be restored as a standard mancipatory clause.[23] Scribes were clerks; their clients relied on them for the correct forms, particularly if Latin were not their native tongue (there is no reason even to believe that the clients were necessarily humble or illiterate).[24]

At the same time there is almost no evidence that anybody turned to professional jurisconsults for guidance through more intricate problems; only one source mentions them directly in this connection, Suetonius' account of the cash-hungry Nero (*Nero* 32), who not only drew into his treasury the estates of those who showed themselves "ungrateful" to the prince, but also punished in some way the legal experts who had written or dictated those wills. Yet nowhere does anyone mention a jurist in his or her will or render thanks for advice, and most striking of all is the complete absence of recorded consultations of jurists by testators in all of the hundreds of testamentary cases in the Digest which turn on legal problems to be resolved after the fact. This observation recalls a dictum of F. Schulz, that by the first century B.C. the leading jurists were withdrawing more and more from giving legal advice. However, Schulz further assumed without demonstration that the gap was filled for the public by smaller men, minor jurisconsults and scribes, while the great lawyers reserved themselves for friends, important people, and knotty problems. In the classical period "the jurisconsults continued to some extent

---

21. *ILS* 7749, 7763.
22. 28.5.9.3 and 6; 29.6.1 pr.; 36.1.3.5; 48.10.15.6; 48.10.22.10.
23. *FIRA* 48, on which see Champlin, "Miscellanea," 251–55.
24. On the subject, not here too relevant, see now J. M. Fröschl, *Imperitia litterarum: Zur Frage des Analphabetismus im römischen Recht," ZSS* 104 (1987): 85–155, particularly at 110–22.

to assist parties in private acts such as testaments and contracts; a testament in particular was hardly ever made without professional assistance," he concluded, adducing as sole proof the man in Scaevola who wrote *sine iurisconsulto*.[25] But *sine iurisconsulto* probably did not mean what Schulz thought it meant, and if it did, the exception would hardly prove the rule. There is almost no hint of professional assistance in the composition of wills anywhere, be it from learned jurist or humble scribe.[26] This silence might not be significant, were it not that there is a very strong case—curious perhaps in a world familiar with scribes and jurists—for believing that the citizen was expected to do it himself.

First, there is a quantity of evidence, mainly legal. There is the *paterfamilias* who died two days after dictating his will, or the soldier who died while dictating to a notary.[27] Likewise, there is the woman of standing who was allegedly bullied into adding a legacy to her will, the recipient watching her as she wrote it out; the advocates of the condemned senator who brought him tablets in prison, wrote out his will in his presence, and arranged for proper witnessing; the senator who proved how intimate he had been with the man he was now accusing by producing his own will written out in his friend's hand.[28] And, more generally, there are the numerous occasions, particularly last moments, when people revised or added to their wills, with no mention of scribes or lawyers being hurriedly summoned.

This very personal aspect of the will appears most strikingly in connection with charges of forgery. A decree of the senate (the *senatusconsultum Libonianum*) of early imperial date, an edict of Claudius, imperial constitutions as late as Diocletian, and jurists from Celsus onwards: all were concerned with the specific crime

---

25. F. Schulz, *History of Roman Legal Science* (Oxford, 1953), 49, 90, 109–10, 155.

26. See note 20. The closest we get to a consultation—one not by a testator—comes in the well-known and startling exchange of letters from the fifteenth book of Celsus's *Digesta* (28.1.27). Domitius Labeo inquires whether the writer of a will can be asked also to witness the document, to which Celsus replies, after a greeting, "I don't understand what you are consulting me about, or yours is a quite silly question, for it is more than ridiculous to doubt that a person can be legally called as witness although he also wrote the tablets of the will." Were there certain areas of the law, notably that of succession, with which everyone was, rightly or wrongly, expected to be familiar?

27. *Dig.* 32.102.1; 29.1.40 pr.

28. Pliny *Ep.* 2.20.9–11; *Rhet. Her.* 1.23; Pliny *Ep.* 6.22.3.

of writing oneself into another's will, and even the physical requirements of documents were changed under Nero to prevent the writer of a will from slipping in a legacy for himself.[29] What does this signify? In most cases, discussions in the Digest are not interested in telling us about the writer of the document; but some are revealing. Thus, the person who wrote his own disinheritance into a will is obviously a *suus heres;* sons and slaves are distinguished elsewhere from *extranei* who write wills; an instituted heir might break the law by writing in a disinheritance, a patron a legacy, a wife her dowry, a creditor his debt; a man with a soldier son might write in a legacy for that son in a comrade's will. Again, an emancipated son writing his father's will is ordered to put in a legacy for himself; another patron gives himself a legacy in a freedman's will; a slave writing a will might be ordered to include liberty for himself; a man dictating to his mother's slave leaves her a legacy; a daughter writing at her mother's dictation gives herself a legacy through ignorance of the law.[30] The evidence thus tends in a single direction, offering frequent tableaux of private writing within the testator's circle of family or servants or friends, and sometimes explicitly at the testator's dictation.[31]

Even where such personal ties are not recorded, family, servants, or friends are surely more likely than hired scribes to have been the subjects of concern over whether a writer inserted legacies to himself, his slave, his son, or his wife, let alone made himself heir—what hireling scribe would presume to do so? Nor would a hired scribe be likely to forge the bequest of a slave to

29. For Digest references, see *Vocabularium Iurisprudentiae Romanae* s.v. "scribo" II. D. 1. b.: *scribit quis testamentum alterius;* and *CJ* 9.23, *de his qui sibi adscribunt in testamento.* The date of the *senatusconsultum Libonianum* (on which see *Dig.* 48.10): R. Talbert, *The Senate of Imperial Rome* (Princeton, 1984), 439, opts for A.D. 16 (or 15 B.C.), but it looks as though Claudius did not know it (*Dig.* 48.10.15 pr.) and there are several later consular Libones. Nero's *senatusconsultum:* Suetonius *Nero* 17; Paul *Sententiae* 5.25.6; Justinian *Inst.* 2.10.3.

30. *Dig.* 37.4.8.6; 48.10.1.8; 48.10.6.1; 48.10.11; 48.15.2, 4, 5; 29.1.15.3; 34.8.1; 48.10.15 pr. 48.10.1.7, 6 pr.; 48.10.18 pr.

31. The Codex fully supports the picture in the Digest, in the section referred to above (9.23): there we see an emancipated son who wrote himself heir at his father's behest; a writer of a codicil who received a legacy or *fideicommissum* in it; a husband who wrote legacies for himself in his wife's will; a soldier, summoned to write his comrade's testament, who received a slave from that will; and a slave who gave himself freedom at his master's order.

himself with a *fideicommissum* from the testator to manumit, or to insert himself as tutor in a will.[32]

Professional scribes and lawyers are thus conspicuously absent in the composition of wills in the Digest and in literature: what of the actual documents themselves, as preserved on papyrus? Should we necessarily assume the widespread employment of scribes among Roman testators in Egypt? Among the Roman citizens in Egypt who left wills, illiteracy is all but unheard of; there is only one certain case, the late (295) will of a woman.[33] Some testators signed and acknowledged in Greek their Latin wills; some confirmed subsequent additions in their own hand, or signed and sealed by them (apparently not an empty formula); two stated "I have read my will."[34] Two testators, each of considerable rank and property, explicitly announce that they have dictated their wills, but there is no sign whether to a scribe, a family member, or a slave.[35] The man who wrote the will for the illiterate woman certainly looks like a friend rather than a hireling.

Egypt of course adds the problem, before Severus Alexander, of producing legal Latin versions from Greek originals.[36] At the end of the surviving copy of the will of Longinus Castor we find a Roman lawyer who vouches for the authenticity of the preceding Greek version, which agrees with the real (Latin) will.[37] Who wrote the original Greek version is a mystery. It is not at all clear that a Roman citizen in Egypt, as distinguished from a Greco-Egyptian, would go to his local scribe for assistance. He was probably wealthier and surely more literate and, in the case of the soldier, he might move in Latin-speaking circles; could he not have concocted his own will, with the help of friends or family, with the aid even of a formula which was by no means necessarily the property of scribes? Particularly interesting here is the record of the opening of a will on 3 June 169 which includes an imperfect

32. *Dig.* 48.10.17, 18.1.
33. *P. Lips.* 29.
34. *CPL* 221, *P. Coll. Youtie* 64, *P. Berol.* inv. 7124; *BGU* 326; *P. Hamb.* 73.9–11; *P. Mich.* 439 and *P. Yale* inv. 1547; *P. Oxy.* 2857, 2348.
35. *P. Oxy.* 907, 2348.
36. Formularies which had existed in Rome for some time were certainly available for guidance (cf. *P. Hamb.* 72), and we now possess a Greek version of a will on papyrus which is accompanied by a Latin draft (*P. Oxy.* 2857).
37. *BGU* 326.

and highly lacunose Greek version of the will itself.[38] The *mancipatio familiae* at the end is astonishing: the property is purchased not for 1, but for 1000 sesterces, the *libripens* (the holder of the scales at the formal sale) has become a second buyer of the estate, *familiae emptor*, and the formula for the first witness is garbled. Surely this is more likely to be the work, not of a professional scribe, but of a private citizen who was proudly doing his best.

Aside from the evidence or lack of evidence, legal and papyrological, three brief observations can be added. First, testamentary problems occupy a large amount of the jurists' time, if the Digest is any witness.[39] Several factors will account for this, not least a volume of litigation reflecting the economic importance of inheritance; but it might also be wondered whether more legal problems arose over wills than over any other legal documents precisely because the will was the most personal of documents: Romans expected or were expected to make their own wills, as far as possible, whether writing them personally or dictating them to family, friends, or scribes. Second, wills are the only legal instruments in which the assertion of character or personality was not only allowed but expected, and the idiosyncrasies paraded even in that most dry and intellectual of works, the Digest, are fascinating. And third, the highly formulaic nature of the will and the frequency with which it was revised would each, in a different way, encourage a do-it-yourself approach.

As far as we can tell, then, the jurists were not consulted and the scribes did no more than take dictation, which family members or slaves might just as easily have done, and are indeed much more often attested as doing. Both scribes and jurists could well have offered minimal guidance in matters of form, but there is little sign that they did. The duty of testacy should include knowing, or thinking that one knew, what one was doing; and the composition of the document was essentially the testator's own.

After drawing up the document to one's own satisfaction, one needed witnesses, men (and only men) who could attest to their understanding that the document they had signed was indeed the

38. *BGU* 1655.
39. Above, p. 7.

testament of the deceased. The formal requirements for witnessing a will—the *mancipatio familiae*, where and how it could or could
not be done, who could or could not participate—are known in
considerable detail.[40] Yet the social context, and particularly what
degree of ceremony was expected, remain obscure. Whether or
not one went through the *mancipatio* described by Gaius, or pre-
tended to have done so, one at least had to have the seven witnesses (or five plus *familiae emptor* and *libripens*) gathered together.
The occasion itself might be public and solemn, in a temple perhaps, or with leading men of the community in attendance.[41] The
norm was probably simply to invite witnesses to the house—formal
invitations survive—and to dress appropriately for the occasion;
but the whole process seems to have been remarkably casual.[42]
Thus, the will of the emperor Tiberius was witnessed (we are told)
by the most humble of men; M'. Curius, a Roman businessman at
Patrae, took advantage of Cicero's passing through Greece on his
way back to Rome from his province to get his signature, those of
his son and nephew, and those of his companions (the *cohors
praetorii*); Cicero's own will in 45 was witnessed not only by friends
but by members of his own and Atticus' households (*domestici*) as
well, the latter brought over for the purpose; at least one man's
testament was allegedly signed by total strangers.[43] The explanation for this casualness lies in what has gone before: frequency of
revision must have discouraged repeated solemnity, and Pliny and
Seneca both speak of witnessing wills as one of the occurrences of
daily life at Rome.

Preservation of the document itself was equally casual; that is,
it was left up to the testator whether copies were made and where
they were kept. The safest place was probably a temple—once
upon a time, said Fronto in a solemn oration, wills used to be
brought forth from the best-protected temples of the gods—but
there are numerous examples of wills being left with friends,

40. E.g., Gaius 2.104–108, cf. Justinian *Inst.* 2.10.5–14, and especially Ulpian
*Ad Edictum* 39 = *Dig.* 28.1.22.1–7. Imperial constitutions at *CJ* 6.23.1–14. Cf. *Dig.*
28.1.27 (could a witness write the will?); 34.5.14 (could a witness receive a legacy?).
41. Juvenal 8.142; Suetonius, *Claud.* 44.1.
42. Invitations: *P. Mich.* 446 = *CPL* 226; *Dig.* 28.1.30. Best clothes: Pliny, *Ep.*
2.20.10.
43. Suetonius *Tib.* 76; Cicero *Att.* 7.2.3; 12.18a.2; *Cluent.* 37.

slaves, or *tabularii,* and one jurist was moved to note that it was sometimes necessary to have two signed copies, as in the case of the man sailing off somewhere who wanted to take his will yet leave some record of his last wishes.[44] Where the law did take a real interest was in the ascertainment of the document's authenticity when the testator was no longer able to confirm it, after his death —this at least from the time of the establishment under Augustus of the 5 percent inheritance tax. Elaborate procedures for the opening of the tablets (*apertura tabularum*) called for the recognition of their seals by the available witnesses, the inspection of the contents, and the making of copies and inventories; above all, the opening must be done before a magistrate and before the witnesses or a majority of them.[45] The magistrate was there to care for the state's interests, the witnesses to care for the testator's. They ensured the authenticity of the document—though not its contents, which they may or may not have known, as the testator wished—by recognizing their seals. Forgery was, if not widespread, at least much feared, and some of the most prominent men at Rome are accused of having signed testaments they knew to be false. Testators had to choose their witnesses carefully, since the carrying out of their last wishes depended initially on the witnesses.

"My masters and relations, you who are attending this making of my will, let it be signed"—so M. Grunnius Corocotta the piglet, in his last moments. "Who is there," asked Symmachus with rhetorical flourish, "who does not summon his most intimate friends to sign, when last wishes are being established?"[46] So little is known about the identity of witnesses, let alone their relations with testators, that little of broader significance can be said about their role

44. Fronto *M. Caes.* 1.6.5; *Dig.* 28.1.24 (Florentinus), cf. Justinian, *Inst.* 2.10.13. For references: H. Vidal, "Le dépôt *in aede,*" *RHDFE*[4] 43 (1965): 545–87, at 550–53. Other examples of informality: a dying testator allegedly gave his will to a close relative (the relationship was disputed), with a mandate to produce it after his death (*BGU* 361); a will is carried from Greece to Rome (Cicero, *Att.* 7.2.3). Egyptian practice was far more formal: A. H. S. el-Mosallamy, "Revocation of Wills in Roman Egypt," *Aegyptus* 50 (1970): 59–73. (I have not yet seen S. Serangeli, *Studi sulla revoca del testamento in diritto romano,* Milan, 1982.)

45. E. Nisoli, *Die Testamentseröffnung im römischen Recht* (Diss., Bern, 1949), 45ff.; R. Martini, "Sulla presenza dei 'signatores' all'apertura del testamento," *Studi in onore di Giuseppe Grosso* (Turin, 1968) 1: 483–95.

46. *Rel.* 41.4.

in the procedure. Clearly intimacy with the testator was by no means universal: Atticus' servants, Cicero's entourage, Tiberius' humble witnesses, are not friends, nor are the signers of the will of "Avillius" of Larinum, who had no idea of his real identity. Again, there was a certain cachet to be gained, or perhaps a greater feeling of security, from inducing prominent men to witness one's will: the architect Cyrus can have been no intimate of both Cicero and Clodius Pulcher, nor was the knight M. Anneius Carseolanus on close terms with Pompey (who *was* a friend of the heir), nor probably was the emperor Claudius an intimate of "all the magistrates" who witnessed his will.[47] How did one choose one's witnesses?

Only the papyri give some hint as to who the witnesses were, eighteen of them yielding information which ranges from virtually complete lists to barest mention. They allow two observations, neither of them startling. First, soldiers and veterans witnessed the wills of soldiers and veterans, and the witnesses tended to be of the same rank as the testator. Thus, the famous will of Antonius Silvanus, the *stator praefecti* of ala I Thracum Mauretaniae, was witnessed by comrades, two *duplicarii*, a *sesquiplicarius,* and two *signiferi.*[48] And second, there is a strong tendency to choose certain relatives as witnesses. Here the best example is the only intact list, that appended to the will of the veteran C. Longinus Castor in 189, along with that of his codicil in 194. Seven men witness the actual will, and apparently five witness the codicil, three of them having been signers of the will as well: that is, probably nine

47. Cicero *Mil.* 48; Valerius Maximus 7.7.2; Suetonius *Claud.* 44.1. Why Regulus was a witness to the will of Verania is a mystery if he had indeed, some decades before, sunk his teeth into the severed head of her husband: Tacitus *Hist.* 4.42, cf. Pliny *Ep.* 2.20.

48. *CPL* 221. Other examples: Safinnius Herminius, soldier of the Alexandrian fleet, left a will in 157, witnessed apparently by another soldier of the same fleet and by a fellow crewman (*BGU* 1695); in the later second century a soldier of the first cohort of Apameans requested the attendance to witness his will of a soldier in the *legio II Traiana Fortis* (*P. Mich.* 446); the will of the centurion Valerius Aion of 320 is witnessed by seven men who are all Valerii and centurions (*P. Col.* 188). Moreover the second-century wills of Longinus Castor and Iulius Diogenes (*BGU* 326; *P. Select.* 14), both veterans, both have veteran witnesses. It is worth pointing out that in the two cases where we have the necessary information, those of Antonius Silvanus and Valerius Aion, far from being soldiers alone and away from home, both died leaving among heirs or legatees a child, a wife or concubine, and siblings.

different men.[49] Of these, one, C. Longinus Aquila, is clearly a relative.[50] No fewer than four are Iulii; a fifth, Iulius Serenus, who receives a legacy in the codicil, is named *cognatus,* a relative in the female line. One of the Iulii is a Petronianus; another witness is an M. Antistius Petronianus. That is, six of the nine signers bid fair to be relatives, while a seventh, M. Sempronius Heraclianus, turns up in the codicil as procurator, being named his worthy friend, *philos kai axiologos.*[51] From this and five other papyri there is thus some reason to assume that family members (or brothers-in-arms) are to be looked for among the witnesses to wills, for the ordinary citizen in Roman Egypt. Similarly, in more exalted circles, for the emperor Augustus, whose *familiae emptor* was the husband of his niece, the noble consular L. Domitius Ahenobarbus; for Cicero, among whose witnesses was a Publilius, certainly a relative by marriage; or for the rich old ex-praetor Domitius Balbus, whose near relative (*propinquus*) both forged and signed his will in the reign of Nero. Similarly, to be sure, for the cousins (*consobrini*) of M. Grunnius Corocotta.[52]

---

49. *BGU* 326. The interesting problem of the manner in which the codicil was signed is ignored here: *FIRA* p. 152 n. 2.

50. Possibly two men in fact, a Longinus Aquila and a C. Longinus Aquila, father and son. Also, it is by no means clear that the second-last signature on the codicil, C. Longinus Castor, is that of the testator himself. In short, up to three other Longini may be involved.

51. The will of M. Sempronius Priscus (*P. Berol.* inv. 7124: A.D. 131) may likewise preserve the names of all seven witnesses: the *libripens* M. Longinus Longus and the first witness C. Longinus Priscus must be cognates or relatives by marriage, for one of the testator's daughters and heirs is a Longinia. Of the *reliqui signatores,* three at least were veterans; two are Iulii, recalling perhaps a Iulianus mentioned in a section concerning *tutela* of the daughters; and one is a Domitius Clemens, again perhaps recalling the *familiae emptor* M. Lucretius Clemens.

The fragmentary will of Sabinia Apollinarion (*PSI* 1325: A.D. 138/161) preserves the names only of the first witness, the veteran M. Sabinius Rufus, and the witnesses M. Sabinius Rufus and M. Sab....

The will of L. Ignatius Rufinus (*P. Coll. Youtie* 64: A.D. 211) has as witness L. Valerius Lucretianus, presumably a relative of the testator's wife, Lucretia Octavia; another was an M. L...nus.

In the anonymous Latin will of 91 (*P. Yale* inv. 1547) the *libripens* probably and two witnesses certainly were Ti. Claudii.

And in the testament of Aurelius Chaeremon of 224 (*P. Oxy.* 2348) six of the seven witnesses are Aurelii: hardly surprising after the Constitutio Antoniniana, but three of them are Sarapion, Saras, and Sarapiodorus.

52. Suetonius *Nero* 4; Cicero *Att.* 12.18a.2; Tacitus *Ann.* 14.40. The *familiae emptor* for Julius Caesar may have been his father-in-law Piso: W. Schmitthenner, *Oktavian und das Testament Cäsars*[2] (Munich, 1973), 29 n. 2. Note also the ?third century *testamentum Alexandri* ([Callisthenes] 123), whose seven divine witnesses

This unsurprising conclusion leads to a slight paradox: in none of the observable cases—we know all or most of the provisions of some six wills preserved on papyri[53]—in none of these is there any sign of a witness receiving anything under the will. Yet it was not illegal for a witness to profit by the will, as jurists over the centuries agreed.[54] And Symmachus, acting as prefect of the city in 379 and thus a legal authority, found it quite acceptable if witnesses accepted some legacy from the will, a modest honor; what he could not abide was the witness who took a large part of the estate.[55] Cicero mentions not once but twice being named heir in a will which he witnessed. In one, both he and Clodius were heirs and witnesses—how intimate can the testator have been with such bitter enemies, that is, how large were their shares? In the other, an old acquaintance and new friend named him heir to one-fortieth. In neither can we even be sure that he was an heir in the first degree.[56] Otherwise, we have only the story of the outrageous Regulus forcing the testatrix to leave him the clothes off her back at the very signing of the will: was Pliny's reaction prompted as much by Regulus exceeding his role as witness as by his action?

If we set aside these three occurrences, or reduce them to minor amounts, and accept with Symmachus that a witness should receive little or nothing, some pattern may be discernible. Among those few cases in literature and the papyri where we can divine something of the relationship between testator and witnesses, the relatives are normally cognates or affines—that is, relatives through the female line or by marriage—not husbands, sons, or (but for two instances) close agnates (relatives through the male line). It could be concluded from this and from the general absence of mention of witnesses in the surviving documents, that the Roman testator tended to choose as witnesses men who could be

---

are in the Latin version all relatives: Iuppiter Olympius, Hercules *patrius noster,* Minerva, Mars, Hammon (the testator's father), Sol, and the Fortuna of Alexander the king.

53. Antonius Silvanus, Longinus Castor, Ignatius Rufinus, Valerius Aion, Sempronius Priscus, Sabinia Apollinarion.

54. *Dig.* 34.5.14: Marcianus quotes Trebatius and Pomponius on a dubious legacy.

55. *Rel.* 41.3, 5.

56. *Mil.* 48; Att. 7.2.3.

trusted but who would not normally expect to receive much under the will: the cousin, the brother-in-law, the comrade-at-arms, rather than the brother or the intimate friend. In short, the testator would try to guard the will by entrusting its future to people friendly enough to ensure its survival, but not so closely involved as to be swayed subsequently by hopes or fears. Not surprisingly, since the will was felt to be in considerable peril.

Thus far can we trace the actions of the individual testator to ensure that the testament was a true representation of his or her last judgment, by keeping it up-to-date, by creating it personally, and by selecting trustworthy witnesses. Care had to be taken, for there was a constant apprehension of the will coming under attack.

# 5

## Interference
### *Forgery and Captation*

We turn from the hopes of the testators to the fears of the society in which they lived. An inheritance was proverbial for a windfall: in Cicero's words, when a Syrian prince arrived in Sicily, the wicked governor Verres thought that an inheritance had come to him.[1] For Martial, the first element in a happier life was a property not earned but bequeathed. The deaths of a few relatives or friends might raise an impoverished farmer ploughing alone with his single ass into a man of wealth, or degrade a man of moderate means into a terrible miser.[2] To the astrologer inheritance signified power and happiness.[3] But was it just a windfall for everyone? How many potential beneficiaries actively interfered with testators industriously doing their duty? In a word, was the testator's last judgment really his or her own? Unfriendly external intervention with the contents of a will might take two forms, forgery and captation.

So broad was the conception of *falsum* as applied to testaments that no typical case can be constructed. In practice, forgery could range from the substitution of a completely fraudulent document, to insertions or deletions in a legitimate document, to the addition of a forged codicil to a perfectly valid will, to witnessing (even unwittingly) a forgery, even to writing in a legacy to oneself at the behest of the testator.[4] The plaintiffs in such lawsuits were either heirs or persons who would normally expect to be heirs,

1. *Verr.* 2.4.61–62.
2. Martial 10.47; Apuleius *Apol.* 99; Martial 1.99.
3. Firmicus Maternus 3.3.4, 3.7.17, 3.9.7, 3.9.10, 3.10.2, 3.12.4, 3.12.14, 4.9.2, 4.24.6, 5.3.12, 6.3.4.
4. Unwitting witnesses: Cicero *Cluent.* 37; Suetonius *Aug.* 33.2 and probably *Claud.* 9.2. For the very uncertain wording of the prime statute, see J. Crook, "*Lex*

that is, almost always a near relative by blood or a patron, whether or not they had received anything under the suspected document.[5] The defendant, on the other hand, could be anyone who might pass himself or herself off as close to the testator, including family, freedmen, freedwomen, friends; and while there might be a whole range of possible motives, the only one offered is simple greed.[6] So much is obvious, but what did the act of forging a testament signify to the Romans?

The problem of forgery, that is, the counterfeit of coins and interference with wills, occupied legislators continually, and concern was certainly justified in the case of wills not only by their social and economic significance but by the absence of the one person who could guarantee the authenticity of the document. Hence the series of laws following the original Lex Cornelia of 81 B.C.;[7] hence too, exceptional public interest in an action which harmed an individual and disrupted society. This raises a peculiar problem: since forgery was such a bad thing, it furnished a very convenient metaphor.

First, the forgery of wills indicates general disorder. Thus, among other social disruptions the dreaded Bacchanalian conspiracy of 186 allegedly unleashed much forgery of wills (*subiectio testamentorum*), the troubles under Sulla likewise touched off a round of forgeries, the subversive Catiline trained up a cadre of youthful forgers, and centuries later a Christian apologist could fling similar charges against the pagans.[8] Likewise, forgery indicates bad emperors: Pliny praises Trajan for not supporting forged or unfair documents.[9] However plausible such observa-

---

*Cornelia de falsis*," *Athenaeum* 65 (1987): 163–71, and the thorough discussion of F. Marino, "Il falso testamentario nel diritto romano," *ZSS* 105 (1988): 634–63.

5. E.g., Pliny, *Ep.* 6.31.7 (*heredes* challenge codicil); Apuleius *Apol.* 2.10–11 (nephew); Pliny *Ep.* 7.6.8 (mother); *CJ* 9.22.4 (son), 5 (son); *Dig.* 22.1.48 (*heredes*), 48.10.24 (daughter), 45.1.135.4 (daughter), 34.9.15 (heir challenges codicil), 38.2.19 pr. (patron), 48.2.18 (sister).

6. Notably in Juvenal's characterization of the *signator falsi* as a supine Maecenas (1.63–68); cf. Cicero *Off.* 3.73; Tacitus *Ann.* 2.48.1, 14.40; Fronto *Ad Am.* 1.14; etc.

7. See chapter 4, n. 27.

8. Livy 39.8.7, 18.4; Cicero *Par.* 46, cf. *Leg.* 1.43; Sallust *Cat.* 16.2; Arnobius *Ad Nat.* 2.42, cf. Lactantius *DI* 5.9.16.

9. *Pan.* 43.1. When Petronius ostentatiously broke his seal (Tacitus *Ann.* 16.19.5) he was suggesting that Nero would try to tamper with his will.

tions might seem, it is doubtful that they were based on much knowledge, any more than Juvenal's paradigm of the corrupt nobleman signifies an actual, living forger of wills.[10]

At the same time, forgery is an all-too-convenient charge to hurl at one's enemies. The prime example is Cicero. If we can trust his report, the atrocities of his nemesis Clodius in Gaul included the writing of dead men's wills.[11] Or again, the blackening of Oppianicus in the *Pro Cluentio*. It was Oppianicus who allegedly induced a crony to masquerade as someone else, had his suppositious will signed by witnesses, and then murdered the man whose will had been forged. Equally criminal were his supposed machinations over the will of his mother-in-law, which instituted her grandson, his son, as heir: he rubbed out legacies with his finger in so many places, presumably to save money for his son, that after the old lady's death his worry over the resulting mess drove him to write the whole thing out again and to forge all the seals.[12] The point here is not the guilt or innocence of Clodius or Oppianicus, or of the Bacchanals, but that *falsum* was a standard charge to blacken reputations. The problem is substantiation.

Cicero, writing this time without apparent malice, and Valerius Maximus both record similar versions of a curious scandal in the 70s B.C.[13] A rich man, L. Minucius Basilus died, apparently in Greece. Certain others, unnamed, brought a forged testament to Rome and, in order to secure his fortune, wrote down as their coheirs M. Crassus and Q. Hortensius, "the most powerful men of the time." These two, although they suspected the document to be false, were not accomplices—but they did not hesitate to accept the fruits of other people's crimes. The great men thus received the fortune while the true heir, Basilus' sister's son, inherited nothing more than his name. All of this is related in a matter-of-fact manner, as something everyone knew. Yet apparently the heirs named in the allegedly forged will kept their loot, and if there was a trial the nephew will certainly have lost. The reason is clear. The law might thunder against interference with wills, all the world

10. 8.142.
11. *Har. Resp.* 42.
12. *Cluent.* 37, 41: Oppianicus was conveniently dead at the time of the speech.
13. Cicero *Off.* 3.73–74; Valerius Maximus 9.4.1.

might suspect and disapprove of the forgers who lurked every-where, but the fact is that forgery must have been extremely difficult to prove. The document involved was formulaic and therefore easy to concoct; the alleged author of it was usually dead; and there were no techniques of scientific analysis. If the testator were dead, if any genuine will had been destroyed, and if accomplices remained silent, how great a risk can a forger have run?

Charges of *falsum* were by no means uncommon; the question is, how many were proven? Papinian records two successful suits, one involving a codicil which gave a slave liberty; a pair of Severan rescripts deal with a forged will and forged codicils; Suetonius mentions in passing that Claudius had witnessed a will later deemed by the senate to have been forged; and a letter of Marcus Aurelius has revealed a case of forged codicils in Athenian high society.[14] Most notorious is the case of A.D. 61, recorded by Tacitus, which will be considered below.

On the other hand, for what the figures are worth, we know of slightly more cases where the lawsuit failed. Thus, after a great contest before the prefect of the city, Apuleius' enemy Sicinius Aemilianus continued to impugn as false the will of his uncle which the prefect had judged to be genuine. In another case Pliny successfully defended the freedmen and heirs of a young man whose mother had accused them of murdering him and forging his will—this in appeal by the mother from an earlier adverse decision; and again, Pliny's incomplete record of a case against a Roman knight heard by the emperor himself has been rounded out by an inscription showing the defendant to have served later as a procurator in the imperial service, strong indication that he was acquitted.[15] Scaevola considers cases of heirs failing against a widow, of a daughter failing against her coheir, and of another daughter failing against the heirs; Papinian and Ulpian have a case against a patron's daughter failing; Ulpian alone has a patron

14. *Dig.* 37.1.14, 40.4.47; *CJ* 6.11.1, 7.4.2; Suetonius *Claud.* 9.2; *SEG* 29.127. L. Audasius, the aged and infirm rebel against Augustus, was only *falsarum tabularum reus* (Suetonius *Aug.* 19), that is, he was not necessarily convicted. The third and fourth century rescripts in *CJ* 9.22, "Ad Legem Corneliam de Falsis," are remarkably unhelpful, being generally concerned with points of law and procedure.

15. *Apol.* 2.10–11, 3.1; *Ep.* 7.6.8, 6.31.7 with *AE* 1975.849, on the correct dating of which see W. Eck, "Zum konsularen Status von Iudaea im frühen 2. Jh.," *BASP* 21 (1984): 55–67, at 65–66.

failing to prove forgery; and Modestinus has a man failing against a *propinquus.*[16]

The most notorious of forgery cases was one that involved Roman senators and knights in the middle years of Nero's reign. His childlessness and his wealth exposed the aged ex-praetor Domitius Balbus to the snares of the unscrupulous. A young relative destined for a senatorial career concocted a will and was caught: six accomplices were named, one a collusive lawyer, one a Spanish ex-quaestor, one an ex-consul of distinguished family, one a senator of unknown rank, and two knights.[17] This for Tacitus was one of the two extraordinary crimes of 61, the other being nothing less than the murder of the prefect of the city of Rome. Why extraordinary? Doubtless the high rank of the conspirators contributed to the scandal, but others of equal standing were involved in other cases. Much more likely an explanation is that clear and proven cases of forgery were rather rare; indeed this one may have come to light only because the testator was still alive.

In short, the evidence suggests that it was much more convenient to accuse someone of forgery than to prosecute. Chances of proving your case in court were not good, and if you failed you might lose your rights in the inheritance.[18] Moreover, in addition to the allegations of a Cicero, there are several instances of charges hurled against individuals without any sign of prosecution.[19] Forgery obviously existed and concerned society, but there is a great gap between perception and reality. The allegation was easy to raise and fraught with moral overtones, but so difficult to prove (and therefore to document). It should be taken as indicative more of social anxiety than of social reality, the recurrence of charges and allegations, both general and particular, as reflecting the sacrosanctity of the will rather than the frequency of the

16. *Dig* 22.1.48, 48.10.24; 45.135.4; 38.2.42.3 and 38.2.6.1; 38.2.19 pr; 5.3.47.
17. Tacitus *Ann.* 14.40–41, cf. *Hist.* 2.86.
18. *Dig.* 34.9.15, cf. *CJ* 9.22.6, *Dig.* 48.10.24.
19. Fronto *Ad Am.* 1.14, urging Marcus to take up an inheritance despite the existence of a forged codicil; Tacitus *Ann.* 2.48.1, Tiberius awarding an estate of which he was part heir to a consular who had been instituted in an "earlier and unsuspected will"; Suetonius *Dom.* 2.3, Domitian accusing Titus of tampering with their father's will. *Dig.* 48.2.18 concerns a woman caught up in procedural problems who continued to assert the falseness of her brother's will. Most interesting is Lucian's attack on his pseudonymous enemy in the *Adversus Indoctum*, which includes (19) the charge that he had written himself into an old man's will.

crime. The significance of this is perhaps best brought out by turning to the other form of interference in the last will and testament of an individual, *captatio.*

Where *falsum* was a legal crime, easy to charge and difficult to prove, *captatio* was a moral crime, easy to charge and all but impossible to prove. *Captatio* is a subject made so familiar by the satirical and philosophical literature of the late republic and early empire —the classic handbook being Teiresias' advice to Ulysses in the underworld, in Horace's *Sermo* 2.5—that there is a real danger of confusing literature, or cultural values, with life. It is usually assumed, by historians as well as literary critics, that *captatio* was a common phenomenon and captators a significant social problem in the period of the late republic and early empire.[20] Before that is accepted, before we can talk of its historical significance, there are three questions to be answered. First, how precisely is *captatio* to be defined? Second, what do our ancient literary sources actually tell us about the practice? And third, how is it to be described as an historical phenomenon?

To call *captatio* "legacy hunting," as it is commonly translated, is seriously to mislead. To be precise, it is "testament hunting," but the better translation of the word is "inheritance hunting." The distinction implied is crucial.

All of the elements of captation turn up in earlier republican literature, indeed most are present in the *Miles Gloriosus* (around 200 B.C.), but the terminology was first coined by Horace in the 30s B.C. with the phrase *captare testamenta* and the noun *captator.*[21] The metaphor is, obviously, drawn from fishing, specifically from angling with bait to attract the fish; alternatively it can be used of hunting, specifically of snaring with nets. Both ideas are picked

20. For sources, see appendix IV. Captation has, as a common satirical theme, attracted far more bibliography than any other aspect of ancient testation. Most important recently are the collection of evidence by V. A. Tracy, *"Aut captantur aut captant," Latomus* 39 (1980): 399–402 ("Captation was a common phenomenon in ancient Roman times from the days of the Republic"), and the broader discussion by Hopkins, *Death and Renewal,* 238–42. Much of what follows here is based on the conclusions reached in the unpublished work of A.R. Mansbach, *Captatio: Myth and Reality* (Diss., Princeton University, 1982). Mansbach provides an anthology of modern conceptions of captators as a "class of schemers" (G. Highet), "a social category" (T. Reekmans), "a special breed of legacy hunters" (K. Hopkins).

21. *Sermo* 2.5.23–24, 57.

up and developed by subsequent writers, particularly Seneca and
Martial, with much play on fish swimming into nets and so forth.
This metaphorical convention is clear enough, and subsequent
readers could be expected to catch on immediately; but what
exactly did they understand was being hunted and fished for?

For Horace, it is *testamenta* that are being captated, not *legata*:
that is the whole drift of Teiresias' advice and examples to Ulysses.
The cases in Latin literature where legacies pure and simple are
being hunted are very rare indeed.[22] Obviously that was possible,
and Seneca and Pliny can both speak simultaneously of hunting
legacies and inheritances,[23] but in the overwhelming majority of
instances, fictional and otherwise, the whole inheritance, the *hereditas,* is the object of captation. Thus Cicero, in the *Paradoxa Stoi-
corum,* speaks of the hope of inheritance (*spes hereditatis*) which
prompts a friend to pay court to a sick and childless old man; in
the *De Officiis,* of *hereditates* wrongly gained through simulated
*officia.* Similarly Petronius (*captare hereditatem*), Martial, Pliny, and
others.[24] Indeed the point is immediately obvious in the synonym
sometimes used for *captator: heredipeta* (inheritance seeker).[25] And
that inheritance is at stake is supported by the emphasis found, in
every writer, on captation of the childless, that is of those for
whom there were no *sui heredes.*

The simple difference between *legatum* and *hereditas* is central.
The two words have precise and very different legal meanings,
and no Roman would confuse them: a legacy is merely a gift of
some value taken out of the inheritance; an inheritance is everything. The difference is significant both socially and economically. Unworthy heirs seriously upset the stability and morality of
society, far more so than unworthy legatees, not merely because of
their own dubious moral and often social position, but because in
choosing them testators have left an unambiguous last judgment
on the deserving friends and relations who were cut out. There is
certainly considerable censure of unworthy heirs (and testators),
but there are few disparaging remarks by a Cicero or a Pliny
against unworthy legatees; similarly, legislation barred unworthy

22. Martial 9.9; Pliny *Ep.* 2.20.2.
23. *Ben.* 4.20.3; *Ep.* 2.20.11.
24. *Par.* 39, *Off.* 3.74; *Sat.* 117, Martial 6.63, 9.48; Pliny *Ep.* 8.18.
25. Petronius *Sat.* 124.2; *Schol. ad Juv.* 3.129; cf. Jerome *Ep.* 117.8.

heirs in certain situations, but not unworthy legatees. Moreover, we do read of large individual legacies, and legislation did exist to bar excessive legacies, but the very strong impression given by all of the legal and documentary evidence is that, proportionally to the properties involved, most legacies constituted only a minor part of most inheritances. In short, the social and economic stakes were incomparably higher than the words "legacy hunting" suggest: legacy hunting may be scandalous, inheritance hunting is an outrage.

A clear and consistent picture of the elements in captation can be drawn from the sources.

First, captators in literature come in all shapes and sizes—wives, fathers-in-law, cognates, mistresses, lovers, gigolos, freedmen, freedwomen, friends, priests, magistrates, even the emperor. But they have one feature in common: they are invariably *extranei*, that is, they are people who would not stand to inherit automatically from their prey if he or she died intestate.[26] Possible intestate heirs do not appear. Children, usually *sui heredes*, are never portrayed as captators, nor is the *proximus agnatus*, be it brother or sister, uncle or aunt, or cousin. Moralists, jurists, the law, and society at large expected people to leave their property to their children, and Plutarch summed up succinctly: sons did not act like captators, since they knew that the inheritance was theirs of right.[27] One can easily imagine situations where a brother or sister schemes to supplant siblings in their parent's affection, or cousin courts cousin to keep the money in the family, and surely such campaigns took place in reality. Yet *captatio* as presented by historians, satirists and moralists does not allow for that possibility. In short, captation connotes to them the denial of family claims, the rupture of family ties, the triumph of the outsider—the possibility of a member of the family captating as well is out of the question.

Bait falls into three simple categories. First, gifts: anything from admission to the games, to free lodging, to the loan of a slave—and above all money and food, choice tidbits of fruit, honey

---

26. I exclude only two fathers alleged to have captated their emancipated sons: Pliny, *Ep.* 4.2.2 (Regulus); Juvenal 16.51 (father of a soldier).

27. *Mor.* 497 A–C. Cf. Pliny *Pan.* 37.2; *Dig.* 5.2.4, 28.2.19; and the *querela inofficiosi testamenti*. On disinheritance, see above, p. 5, and below, pp. 107–11.

cakes, mullet, boar, pigeon, or fine wine.[28] Second, words: praise, flattery, anything to demonstrate interest and respect, from the humble "Did you sleep well?" to praise for the victim's bad verses.[29] And third, deeds, *officia:* mainly physical attendance on the prey, morning salutation, presence at recitations, accompaniment in the street, support in court, presence at dinner. Here three actions stand out as particularly captatorial. One is, again and again, attendance at the sickbed, a common career hazard: Epictetus offers a too vivid picture of captators wiping the noses of their victims and washing their faces, while Juvenal remarks (in effect) that you need a strong stomach for the job.[30] A second is ostentatiously to pray for the health of the victim, a sort of variant being to name your prey in your own will (with the implication that he will outlive you).[31] And a third *officium*, in a class by itself, is the provision of sexual services to the lonely rich, you the captator either acting as pander (Ulysses in Horace), or giving yourself (especially to old men or old women), or giving yourself or your child in marriage.

With the exception of sexual services, all of this falls within the normal range of what friends—whether equal in status or not—did for their friends in real life. And in fact there is a notorious historical example of one man giving his wife to another, which some saw as a high act of disinterested friendship.[32] The point here, something remarked on by ancient writers, is that captation and friendship were indistinguishable in their attributes—motive alone separated them.

The quarry of the captator is easily summed up in three words: *orbus, locuples,* and *senex.* All three, or synonyms, are found in Horace and earlier. Above all, as you would expect, he or she is childless, sometimes a bachelor, sometimes bereaved of an only child, sometimes widowed without children. But they are also rich; and they are old and often ill. "You are childless and rich and were born

28. References for the various kinds of bait are drawn from the sources listed in appendix IV; examples are also given by Tracy, *"Aut captantur."* On the expense involved: Juvenal 3.161; Pliny *Ep.* 9.30.1.

29. A checklist at Martial 12.40.

30. Epictetus 4.1.148; Juvenal 10.198–202. Cf. Cicero *Par.* 39; Seneca *Ben.* 4.20.3; Pliny *Ep.* 2.20; Ovid *Ars* 2.332; Martial 12.56; Lucian *Dial. Mort.* 15(5).

31. Martial 12.90; Lucian *Dial. Mort.* 18(8).

32. Below, pp. 98–99.

in the consulship of Brutus: do you imagine that you have true friendships?" asks Martial, rather savagely.[33] The concatenation of these three attributes is so constant, their presence so overwhelming, that we should assume that when Romans heard the word *captatio*, regardless of context, they automatically thought of people who were childless, old, and rich. In short, a clear profile for the would-be captators to tack up on their garret walls: someone without a close intestate heir; someone worth pursuing; someone whose capture was imminent. But they should beware.

Strange to say, there is no Latin word for this person, the captator's victim. With *captatio* there is a real danger of optical illusion. The powerful images of corpses and carrion birds, the strong disapprobation expressed by ancient authors for the captator, the sad tableaux of sick and helpless old men and women besieged even on their deathbeds: these are rather misleading. *Captatio* is commonly reprehended as immoral, its spread through society is decried; but there is little indication, fictional or otherwise, that it was particularly successful. What disgusts moralists and satirists is more the process than the result, the siege of the testator by the unworthy, rather than their capture of him. Much more often than not, the captator is portrayed as unsuccessful, more victim of his or her own traps than predator. The cheated captator is a repeated theme in Martial, for instance, while all of the relevant Dialogues of the Dead by Lucian deal with captators whose tricks have failed.[34] The captator lived on hope.

The most striking recurrent theme in the literature is not the unworthiness of the captators, nor the helplessness of their prey, but the power of the captated. Thus Seneca speaks of childlessness, *orbitas*, giving rather than taking favor, *gratia*, and of lonely old people acquiring power, *potentia;* the elder Pliny mentions the supreme *auctoritas* and *potentia* won by *orbitas;* his nephew muses on the rewards, *praemia*, of *orbitas;* and Tacitus writes variously of the rewards of *orbitas*, of powerful *orbitas*, of the old and the rich and the powerful, of one powerful through wealth and *orbitas*, of another powerful in his wealthy *orbitas* and old age; and so forth.[35]

---

33. 11.44.1.
34. E.g., Martial 5.39, 9.9, 12.56.
35. Seneca, *Consolatio ad Marciam* 19.2; Pliny *HN* 14.5; Pliny *Ep.* 4.15.3; Tacitus *Germ.* 20.5, *Dial.* 6.2, *Hist.* 1.73, *Ann.* 3.25.2, 13.52.2.

Hence we read repeatedly of the conscious encouragement of captation, led off by the cunning Miles Gloriosus; and a recurrent character is the *simulatus aeger,* the testator who pretends to be ill—there is even a supposedly historical example, that of Julius Vindex, the future rebel against Nero.[36]

There is an important corollary to this: if you want to get richer, don't have children, because captators don't like them. (And as a variant in some cases, if you have children hate them or pretend to hate them.)[37] Again the Miles Gloriosus provides the paradigm: courted by everyone, he asks, "What need have I of children?" If you have children you don't get presents.[38] One warning out of many is that given to Petronius' company of travelers on their way to Croton: "You will find no fathers there, for those with *sui heredes* are regarded as pariahs. A father is someone who is never invited to dinner, never entertained, who, in short, is compelled to spend his life, outcast and excluded, among the poor and obscure. Those, however, who remain bachelors in perpetuity and have no close relatives are held in high honor and esteem: they and they alone are men of honor and courage, brave as lions, paragons without spot or flaw."[39] Exaggerated perhaps, but Plutarch has exactly the same message: it is the childless "whom rich men feast, whom great men court, for these alone do advocates plead gratis.... Many who had many friends and much honor, the birth of one child has made friendless and powerless."[40]

Here again a curious refusal by the ancient writers appears. It is after all the capricious testator, not the captator, who wields the real power to disrupt the family by alienating its wealth, not merely by not having children, but by passing over near relatives in favor of extraneous parasites: the captator may urge the testator on, but the responsibility is that of the testator who ignores duty or natural affection. But, that said, there is very little adverse comment by anyone against such people, and what there is dwells

---

36. Plautus *Miles* 705–715; good examples at Martial 6.63 (*scis captari*); Pliny *Ep.* 8.18; Petronius *Sat.* 117. *Simulatus aeger:* e.g., Seneca *Brev. Vit.* 7.7 (the phrase is his); Petronius 117; Martial 2.26, 40; Pliny *HN* 20.160 (Vindex).

37. E.g., Juvenal 10.236; Pliny *Ep.* 8.18.3; Seneca *Consolatio ad Marciam* 19.2 (*odia filiorum simulent*). Mansbach *Captatio,* 26–28.

38. E.g., Juvenal 6.37; Lucian *Dial. Mort.* 16(6).3; Musonius 15b Hense.

39. *Sat.* 116, translated by W. Arrowsmith.

40. *Mor.* 497 A–C (Loeb translation, W. C. Helmbold).

on their various individual failings of character, not on their failing to act as proper Roman citizens should in testamentary matters. True opprobrium is reserved for the poor captator, working ever hopefully toward an easy retirement.[41] One explanation of this may lie in the perceived sanctity of the testament, the very early recognition that within limits the testator's last wishes were to be upheld. But the unwillingness to recognize the true cause of the problem of *captatio,* the selfish testator for whom there is no term in Latin, suggests that we should look closely at the phenomenon before we accept the ancient picture of it.

Easily the fullest and finest illustration of what the ancients thought was going on, is to be found in a text never apparently cited in connection with *captatio,* the *Timon* of Lucian. The god of wealth, Ploutos, explains to Hermes why some men get rich quickly:

> When I am to go from one man to another, they put me in wax tablets [i.e., the will], seal me up carefully, take me up and carry me away. The dead man is laid out in a dark corner to be fought over by weasels, while those who have expectations regarding me wait for me in the public square with their mouths open, just as the swallow's chirping brood waits for her to fly home. When the seal is removed, the thread is cut, and the tablets opened, they announce the name of my new master, either a relative or a toady or a lewd slave held in high esteem since the days of his wanton youth, with his chin still shaven clean, who in this way gets a tremendous recompense, deserving fellow that he is, for many and various favours which he did his master long after he had earned a discharge. Whoever he may be, he snatches me up, tablets and all, and runs off with me, changing his name from Pyrrhias or Dromo or Tibias, to Megacles or Megabyzus or Protarchus, while those others who opened their mouths in vain are left looking at one another and mourning in earnest because such a fine fish has made his escape from the inmost pocket of their net after swallowing quantities of bait. As for the man who has been flung head over ears into riches, an uncultivated, coarse-grained fellow who still shudders at the irons, pricks up his ears if anyone casually flicks a whip in passing, and worships the mill as if it were the seat of the mysteries, he is no longer endurable to those who encounter him, but insults gentlemen and whips his fellow-slaves, just to see if he himself can do that sort of thing, until he falls in with a prostitute or takes a fancy to

41. The same is true for the caduciary aspects of the Augustan marriage laws: attention is focused on the heir or legatee, not on the testator.

breed horses or goes himself into the keeping of toadies who swear
that he is better looking than Nereus, better born than Cecrops or
Codrus, sharper witted than Odysseus and richer than sixteen
Croesuses in one; and then, in a moment, poor devil, he pours out
all that was accumulated little by little through many perjuries,
robberies and villainies.[42]

What is the historical reality corresponding to this Hogarthian
realism? One modern account tells us: "The very existence of a
special word for [captators] in Latin is evidence enough that their
activities became a well-established element in Roman life. In
surviving literature there are frequent suggestions that legacy-
hunting had reached pathological levels."[43]

Some preliminary observations may help to clear the ground.
First, that "the Romans had a word for it" has been taken as proof
of its historical existence. But did they? The term was invented by
Horace and developed in subsequent Latin literature. But neither
the word nor the concept of *captatio* appears on inscriptions,
though all sorts of other complaints about life do. Neither word
nor concept appears in the Digest, and it is worth remembering
that captation was neither crime nor delict: certain actions associated with interfering with another person's will, specifically
force and fraud, were later considered as *institutiones captatoriae*
(captatorial practices), but under the principate simple intent to
gain someone else's property by posing as their friend was not
actionable.[44] And neither word nor concept appears on the papyri
dealing with Roman law, though again there were considerable
opportunities for their expression. Indeed, while the Romans may
have had a word for it, the Greeks did not, not even satirists like
Lucian, who wrote about it—somehow "hunting," *thera*, does not
quite capture it. We might well not expect to find the word else-

---

42. Lucian, *Timon* 21–23 (Loeb translation, A. M. Harmon).
43. Hopkins, *Death and Renewal*, 239.
44. With *captatoriae institutiones* the jurists apply the metaphor to their own
concerns: J. Tellegen, "*Captatio* and *Crimen*," *RIDA*[3] 26 (1979): 387–397. The only
hint of *captatio* in the Digest appears at 31.77.24 (Papinian, *Responsa*) on a *fideicommissum: Mando filiae meae pro salute sollicitus ipsius, ut, quoad liberos tollat, testamentum
non faciat: ita enim poterit sine periculo vivere.* The fear may be of captation, but
without the context we cannot be sure; nor, if *captatio* is at issue, can we be sure
whether the fear was justified. Cf. 36.1.76 pr: a testator likewise commands his
daughter to make no will until she has borne children; but this was clearly due to a
wish to see her property revert to her brother.

where; but the point is that with *captatio* we are breathing a rather rarefied literary air, specifically that of Roman satire: it is not a word in daily currency.

Within the restricted circle of Greek and (mostly) Latin letters, one can easily trace the progress and development of central ideas from author to author, from Horace through to Lucian—for instance, the same image of the corpse and the bird of prey recurs in Petronius and Seneca and Martial. This repetition of a figure of speech from author to author, or variations on a theme such as we find in Martial, should emphatically not be taken as a measure of historical frequency.[45] Moreover, one suspects that satirists and moralists have weighted the concept with unavoidable baggage; that is, that close study of sober historians such as Tacitus and Pliny would show them moving into code or cliché when they come to describe such scenes or personalities.

The historical value of two common elements in the literature is particularly dubious. One is the notion of anonymous "crowds" of captators hovering around, not only in the fictions of Plautus and Horace, of Petronius and Lucian—a crowd of 50,000 in one case—but in more overtly historical, or at least anecdotal, writers like Plutarch and Aelian. Without specifics they must be discounted. The other is a very recognizable figure, the upstart, especially the freedmen, freedwomen, and lovers (of either sex) familiar from Petronius, Martial, and Lucian. One or two dubious cases aside, there is no actual instance on record of a parvenu taking the place as heir of a solid Roman citizen; and moralizing aristocratic writers would surely have savaged such targets if they saw them.[46] Moreover, in the numerous historical cases in literature and the Digest where blameless favorite freedmen and freedwomen were left as heirs, they were invariably coheir with someone else, normally a respectable friend of the testator.[47] That is, the exaggerated scene of the unworthy favorite taking everything, as in Lucian

45. Mansbach, *Captatio*, 68. Cicero *Par.* 43 is very similar to *Off.* 3.74; Seneca. *Ep.* 95.43 to *Ben* 4.20.3. *Captatio* is particularly useful in Stoic treatments of servitude and liberty.

46. Possible cases: the father who disinherited Scopelian in favor of his cook, at Philostratus *VS* 517–18 (but no sign that they were Roman citizens); and the deformed freedmen Geganius Clesippus of Pliny *HN* 34.11 and *ILS* 1924 (but no sign that he was the heir).

47. Chapter 7, below.

and elsewhere, has no known historical counterpart. There would
certainly have been lawsuits if it had actually occurred.

Satire and its concerns apart, the historical record for captation
is meagre: one is soon struck that *captatio,* like *falsum,* was a charge
far more convenient to bring than to prove. It comes in two forms.

First, there is *captatio* as general denunciation, part of a standard list of sin (forgery of wills is another) which is trotted out in
times of perceived decline or disruption. It is a sign of universal
moral decay. The prime witness for this, and the one most quoted,
is the elder Pliny:

> Later generations have been handicapped by the laxity of the world
> and by our multiplicity of resources. After senators began to be
> selected, and judges appointed, on the score of wealth; and wealth
> became the sole adornment of magistrate and military commander;
> after lack of children to succeed one began to occupy the place of
> highest influence and power; and *captatio* ranked as the most profit-
> able profession; and the only delights consisted in ownership: the
> true prizes of life went to ruin, and all the arts that derived their
> name "liberal" from liberty, the supreme good, fell into the opposite
> class, and servility began to be the sole means of advancement.[48]

Here Pliny is echoing in general terms the commonplaces of (say)
the preface to Columella, or the remarks of Sallust's Catiline.
Precisely the same strictures appear near the end of the surviving
portion of Longinus *On the Sublime,* with its talk of the universal
slavery of today and how this slavery of all is death to oratory in
the service of the state, how love of money and pleasure enslave
us, judges are bribed for their verdicts, everyone is governed by
bribery and hunting after wills—and so on.[49]

There is a distinction to be made here between opinion and
observation. To take another Plinian example, in a much-quoted
aphorism he asserted that "*latifundia,* great estates, have destroyed Italy." Whatever he may have meant, this is simply and
òbservably not true; even if we could not test it, it is unsound to
take such an assertion literally.[50] Similarly, both Pliny and Lon-

48. *HN* 14.5 (Loeb translation, H. Rackham).
49. Longinus 44.9. Late antiquity follows the same track, e.g., Lactantius *DI*
5.19.16 (*qui hereditates captant, testamenta supponent*).
50. *HN* 14.5. M. I. Finley observed of this passage, "Moralizing statements
are...not helpful,...not even when they imply factual statement, no matter how

ginus link inheritance hunting with (in effect) the decline of
polite letters. However, Petronius makes the same connection in
speaking of Croton, where *captatio* is the sole way of life and
"literature and the arts go utterly unhonored; eloquence there
has no prestige; and those who live the good and simple life find
no admirers."[51] No one would claim that the Satyricon should be
taken as a historical record—indeed, in this passage Petronius
may be satirizing not contemporary life at Rome but a contemporary attitude to it, that of the Plinies and the Longinuses of his
day. The point is this: there can be no doubt that Pliny and other
commentators saw *captatio* as a rampant evil, and that is important; but they do not provide evidence for its historical nature or
extent.

When we move from general observations to particular instances, a handicap at once appears. Seneca remarked in one of
his letters: "Someone sits at the bedside of a sick friend: we approve. But another does it for the sake of an inheritance: he is a
vulture waiting for a corpse. The same deed is base or honorable:
it matters how and why it is done." Similarly, in *De Beneficiis:* "Let
him do everything a good friend and one mindful of *officium*
ought to do. If the hope of gain is in his mind, he is a captator and
casts his hook...he hovers over a cadaver."[52] All very true, but not
helpful, since we never know what is going on in the friend's
mind. *Captatio* lies in the eye of the beholder.

This can be illustrated first by its suspicious absence. Our
knowledge of Pomponius Atticus derives from his friends Cicero
and Cornelius Nepos; in the unlikely event that he had any enemies, their feelings have not survived. Nepos notes in his biography that Atticus acquired inheritances "for no other reason than
his goodness." That may be, but his greatest such acquisition was
the inheritance of his uncle Caecilius, a man who up until the end
had sworn that he would leave his benefactor Lucullus as his
heir—his was the corpse dragged through the streets by an out-

---

often they are quoted in modern accounts": *Studies in Roman Property* (Cambridge,
1974), 2. Pliny's gloomy picture of decay was prompted by a discussion of trees.
    51. Petronius *Sat.* 116 (trans. W. Arrowsmith).
    52. *Ep.* 95.43 (trans. R. Gummere); *Ben.* 4.20.3 (trans. J. Basore).

raged mob, as Valerius Maximus tells us, without mentioning the actual heir. Everything went to Atticus, but Atticus gets a good press; what would an enemy call him? Similarly, of the emperor Antoninus Pius, while still a private citizen, we are told that he cared for his relatives scrupulously, so that he was enriched by inheritance from cousins, his stepfather, and many relatives by marriage. Again, what would a hostile observer make of that? It was rather rare to leave an affine as heir.[53]

In some cases we do have differing and hard-to-reconcile points of view on the same situation. One is that of the notorious Domitius Tullus, a loathsome old man who, Pliny assures us, had encouraged captators (unnamed), but confounded them by leaving everything to his niece and adopted daughter and her descendants, thereby disproving the popular belief that wills were the mirrors of people's characters. Pliny particularly praises Tullus' excellent, but anonymous, second wife for bearing with and caring dutifully for an old and infirm man, crippled and deformed in every limb, one who needed someone even to clean his teeth for him. She received an enormous legacy, all the more deserved since she had been greatly censured for marrying him. Pliny clearly approves of her, but others had reprehended her for marrying a man who was fabulously wealthy, without natural offspring, old, ill: surely captation was suspected. It is now clear that Juvenal transformed the virtuous wife of the anecdote into a scheming prostitute-captatrix, in his tenth satire.[54]

Even more sharply divergent are the two ancient versions of a notorious affair in the life of the younger Cato, retold by Plutarch. "This part of Cato's life," he says, "like a drama, has given rise to dispute and is hard to explain." In the mid-50s B.C., Cato divorced his wife Marcia so that his good friend Hortensius could marry her and produce children and heirs; a few years later, in 50, Hortensius died and his wife returned to Cato with a good part of his fortune. Cato's hagiographer attributed to him the most altruistic of motives: the act was one of true friendship, and any children born would be a benefit to the state. But Caesar, in his

---

53. Nepos *Att.* 21.1; *HA Pius* 9.1.
54. *Ep.* 8.18; Juvenal 10.232–39, with R. Syme, "Juvenal, Pliny, Tacitus," *AJP* 100 (1979): 250–78 = *RP* 3 (1984): 1135–57, at 258/1141.

*Anti-Cato,* charged that Cato had enticed his friend into wanting Marcia, with the specific intent of inheriting from him: "the woman was at the first set as bait for Hortensius, and lent by Cato when she was young, that he might take her back when she was rich." Where the truth lay is perhaps beside the point.[55]

Another most dubious historical example is the simple assertion by Seneca that two senior senators of the reign of Tiberius, Arruntius and Haterius, made a profession of the art of captation. This is fragile on several grounds, not least because Seneca gives no further information, and we have no clue as to his motives here. Moreover there is no hint elsewhere of this depravity; indeed one of these men is portrayed in a speech in Tacitus as incorrupt and magnanimous. But worse, why should we believe Seneca's charge, when he himself was accused by an enemy of exactly the same misconduct, captation?[56] If captation lies in the eye of the beholder, it is hard to imagine captators ever recognizing themselves in the mirror.

If asked to identify just one captator, most students would immediately name the great Regulus of Pliny's correspondence. In letter 2.20 he stands in his glory, villain in three outrageous affairs, the man who dupes a testator with mumbo jumbo, one who upbraids doctors for prolonging a testator's miserable existence (only after he has wormed his way into the will), one who extorts as a legacy at the signing of the will the very clothes off a testator's back. But Regulus, most conveniently, is not just a captator, he is a monster of all possible depravity, a rags-to-riches decayed aristocrat, an arch-intriguer, a protector of the wicked, an informer, a bad orator and an offender against good taste. It need hardly be said that Pliny is not a reliable witness on Regulus, and that for most accusations against him we can find contrary evidence (some of it provided by Pliny himself). A recent paper has carefully investigated Pliny's profound detestation of all that Regulus stood for, his fundamental lack of moderation, moral, so-

---

55. *Cato Minor* 25.3–5, 52.3–5 (Loeb translation, B. Perrin). An excellent account of these and other motivations attributed to the actors can be found in M. Griffin, "Philosophy, Politics, and Politicians at Rome," in *Philosophia Togata: Essays on Philosophy and Roman Society,* ed. M. Griffin and J. Barnes (Oxford, 1989), 1–37, at 24–25.

56. *Ben.* 6.38.4; *Ann.* 11.6, 13.42.4.

cial, and rhetorical.[57] One feature that emerges, and something which would not have been lost on contemporaries, is in what literary terms the immoderate Regulus is painted a villain. Here, Pliny certainly introduces the *captatio* letter with the word *fabula*— "have your penny ready," says the story-teller—and it contains the traditional three tales; one's suspicion is heightened when one observes that Regulus' actions at the sick testator's bedside are uncomfortably similar to those of a doctor in a poem in the Greek Anthology.[58] In this, the most upsetting of the three tales, Regulus turns up at the bedside of the gravely ill Verania, a woman who hates him, and dupes her into adding a codicil in his favor to her will. If she loathed him so much, if he was so notorious a captator, why was he even allowed into the house? Perhaps he was not quite so black as he was painted.

There are two striking elements in these historical examples of captation. One is that, to put it mildly, there was always room for dispute between friendly and hostile observers of the same incident. The other is that, even then, there are precious few examples of the charge actually being leveled: the ones just considered are all there is. If one subtracts generalizing moral condemnations and the repetitions and embellishments of the satirists, there is almost no factual evidence for the existence of *captatio* as a historical phenomenon.

Thus, there is no evidence that *captatio* existed as a widespread social practice. There is certainly no evidence that it happened to increase in the very period of the late republic and the early empire when our literature is the fullest. And there is absolutely no evidence that there was an identifiable "class of schemers" called *captatores*.

On the other hand, Roman writers are deeply concerned by it, and there can be no doubt that it existed. Certainly several ele-

---

57. R. Scarcia, " '*Ad tantas opes processit*': Note a Plinio il Giovane," *Index* 13 (1985): 289–312 = *Labeo* 30 (1984): 291–316. See also my "Pliny the Younger," in *Ancient Writers: Greece and Rome*, ed. T. J. Luce (New York, 1982), 1040–41.

58. 11.382, Agathias, first noticed by M. Schuster, "De Agathiae scholastici epigrammate quodam (*AP* xi.382)," *WS* 45 (1926): 120–22. True, Agathias is writing centuries after Pliny, but as Scarcia points out (294–95), the version of Agathias looks primary (the actions are appropriate to a doctor), while Pliny's is a secondary application; that is, the two authors are probably drawing on a common source.

ments in the social climate of the late republic and the early empire would foster captation. One is the wide freedom of testators to dispose of their property as they saw fit, a freedom early recognized at Rome and even at that late date relatively little hampered by restrictive legislation. At the same time, there were exceptionally strong social pressures on testators to recognize and reward friendship posthumously. Combined with this might be the vertical distribution of wealth, with its concentration in the hands of the few—the stakes would be higher—and the severely restricted ways of striking it rich in Roman society. Again, rates of fertility and mortality might provide the incentive. Demographers have estimated that roughly one-fifth of Roman marriages produced no surviving children (and another one-fifth only females, which might be equally undesirable for some testators).[59] And generations certainly turned over far more rapidly than today—producing more chances at the jackpot per annum, as it were. So there were more than enough pressure points in society.

First, it should be underlined that captation was nevertheless not the epidemic suggested by overheated ancient writers and their modern followers. If the surviving evidence, literary, legal, epigraphical, and papyrological, is any guide, we can say with confidence that the overwhelming majority of Roman law testators left as heirs their relatives within the third degree, that is, children, grandchildren, parents, siblings, and nephews and nieces, where they existed.[60] That is to say, despite all the social and demographic pressures to the contrary, over 90 percent (probably well over), of testators followed the dictates of duty or natural affection. However strong the social pressures in favor of friends may have been, obligations to the family were much stronger. Of course, even 10 percent or 5 percent of all testamentary inheritance would provide prizes worth having; but the proportion is more significant than the sheer numbers.

It is enough that the social pressure points existed; they need not have been heavily abused. Ancient writers treated *captatio* as a moral and not a social problem, and in this they were basically correct. When one finds charges like captation flung about con-

---

59. Hopkins, *Death and Renewal*, 99–103.
60. See the following two chapters.

stantly, when figures like the captator become stock characters, there are two possible reactions, not mutually exclusive. One, perhaps the natural one, is to conclude that there was a lot of it about. The other, less obvious perhaps, is to look to quality, not to quantity: not that it was necessarily common, but that it was felt to be very, very bad. Undoubtedly schemers flattered and lonely, foolish, rich old men and women succumbed: as a phenomenon of social history they are negligible, certainly unquantifiable, almost nonexistent. But there is no mistaking the fervor or the sincerity of a Pliny the Elder on captation. What is central here is captation's symbolic role in the standard perception of the evil effect of wealth on Roman society, of avarice and selfishness both tearing the family apart and perverting friendship absolutely. Given their great concern with wills, it is not surprising that Roman writers should express such evil in terms of inheritance hunting. Captation ignites the tensions at a major social frontier, between family and friendship, at a time of great danger, the succession of generations.

Forgers and inheritance hunters assuredly did exist, though in unknown numbers; but the significance of *falsum* and *captatio* lies elsewhere. Concern about them, their erection into metaphors for social disruption and decline, only reinforce a sense of the solemn importance accorded the will in Roman moral life. And their relatively minor historical role should suggest that, however influenced by outside pressures, the dispositions made by a Roman testator truly represented his or her own last judgment. It is to those dispositions that we now turn.

# 6

## Family

*Disinheritance—Sons and Daughters—*
*Husbands and Wives—Kin*

At the heart of the testator's universe lay, normally, his or her close family, and by far the majority of the testator's final thoughts as reflected in the will are centered on it.

In the last generation our understanding of the Roman family and of its historical role has undergone profound revision. Particularly relevant to testation is an outstanding recent group of papers by R. P. Saller and B. D. Shaw on what might be called the physical aspect of the family, raising questions on such topics as fertility and mortality, the age of men and women at marriage, and the structure of the family itself. So important is some of this work as a key to the mental universe of the Roman testator that, at the risk of oversimplification, a brief review is essential.

First, in a fundamental paper published in 1984, Saller and Shaw offered a model of the Roman family based on tombstone inscriptions and differing significantly from earlier views.[1] Where ancient literary and legal sources might lead us to think that the Romans conceived of the *familia* or *domus* as (in our terms) the extended family or as the household-with-slaves, dedicatory epitaphs show the nuclear family (mother-father-children) as overwhelmingly predominant, at least in the urbanized civilian popu-

---

1. "Tombstones and Roman Family Relations in the Principate: Civilians, Soldiers and Slaves," *JRS* 74 (1984): 124–156. Extended by Shaw in "Latin Funerary Epigraphy and Family Life in the Later Roman Empire," *Historia* 33 (1984): 457–97. J. C. Mann offered a criticism of their methods in "Epigraphic Consciousness," *JRS* 75 (1985): 204–06, concluding: "Stone inscriptions do not give us information about the total population of an area. They merely tell us something about the people in that area who used stone inscriptions." But for our purposes, testators are almost invariably the kind of people who use stone inscriptions. Note also R. P. Saller, "*Familia, Domus,* and the Roman Conception of the Family," *Phoenix* 38 (1984): 336–55.

lations of the West. This conclusion is based on statistical analysis of varied and extensive samples of inscriptions which record the relationship between the dedicator and the deceased: members of the nuclear family—parent, child, sibling—provide between 75 and 90 percent of Roman epitaphs. The importance of this lies in the fact that these were funerary inscriptions, that is, dedications erected by survivors; and Saller and Shaw note, in a review of Ulpian's discussion of funerary requirements in his *Ad Edictum*, that "the statements in the Digest suggest that where the deceased is associated with a named commemorator...the latter is very likely to be the heir or, failing that, the family member thought to be tied by the strongest bond of duty."[2] From this we should be justified in concluding that the large majority of Roman testators left as heirs their children or their spouse, or both. Such a conclusion is indeed fully consonant with all of the ancient evidence and will be taken for granted.

Second, the same scholars have turned to the age of Roman men and women at marriage, with startling results. In a pioneering paper published in 1965, K. Hopkins argued that the modal age of marriage for Roman women lay between 12 and 15, a conclusion that has become embedded in the literature. But now Shaw has modified it substantially. Using a different method and a much larger sample, he has concluded that while the early to middle teens might be appropriate for the upper classes, most girls tended to marry later, in their late teens. In this he followed the path broken by Saller, who has argued that Roman men, apart perhaps from some senators, tended to marry in their late twenties.[3] The resultant ten-year gap between men and women at first marriage is profoundly important for the structure of Roman society itself, and it directly affects inheritance practice. Thus, there is now a significant explanation for the observably common

2. Saller and Shaw, "Tombstones," 126, based on *Dig.* 11.7. Add perhaps Pliny *Ep.* 6.10.5, implying that commemoration of the dead is a duty of the heirs: *tam rara in amicitia fides, tam parata oblivio mortuorum, ut ipsi nobis debeamus conditoria exstruere omniaque heredum officia praesumere.*

3. K. Hopkins, "The Age of Roman Girls at Marriage," *Population Studies* 18 (1964–65): 309–27; B.D. Shaw "The Age of Roman Girls at Marriage: Some Reconsiderations," *JRS* 77 (1987): 30–46; Saller, "Men's Age." Men and women of senatorial rank presumably married younger, as Saller notes, and cf. R. Syme, "Marriage Ages for Roman Senators," *Historia* 36 (1987): 318–32.

phenomenon of the second marriage, or the threat of a second marriage, most often of course by the wife.[4] The attention of testators and lawyers is naturally drawn to the tensions both between stepparents and stepchildren, and between the widow and her own children, and testators demonstrate great concern for their children's well-being.

Third, not surprisingly, is the high mortality expected of a preindustrial society. It is generally agreed by historical demographers that the life expectancy at birth for Romans would be in the neighborhood of 20 to 30 years.[5] Saller, following on work by Hopkins, has suggested the demographic likelihood that at age five about 84 percent of Roman children would have their fathers still living, at ten 68 percent, at fifteen 54 percent, at twenty 41 percent, at twenty-five 30 percent, at thirty 19 percent, at thirty-five 12 percent, and at forty only 6 percent.[6] Saller's purpose was to demonstrate how misleading is the stereotype of the Roman family, and how severely limited *patriapotestas* must have been in real life. If his propositions are accepted, roughly 50 percent of Roman males who reached 14 (and legal maturity) were already *sui iuris* and thus capable of making a will. Moreover, a parallel set of figures provided by Hopkins suggests that of any group of contemporary males (such as the fathers of Saller's boys), over 50 percent did not survive beyond 20.[7] This immediately lends support to the proposition that Roman males (at least) could be expected to make their wills much earlier than a modern American or British male: most of them were legally capable at the earliest possible age (and there might be considerable familial or social pressure), and the possibility of their own imminent death must have been much more a part of everyday life. Be that as it may, we should at the least look for an intense concern for the

4. Admirably discussed by M. Humbert, *Le remariage à Rome* (Milan, 1972), 76–112. Likewise, questions will arise about the dowry of a daughter married more than once, such questions touching the law of succession as well.

5. Discussion and full bibliography in B. W. Frier, "Roman Life Expectancy: Ulpian's Evidence," *HSCP* 86 (1982): 213–51, and "Roman Life Expectancy: The Pannonian Evidence," *Phoenix* 37 (1983): 328–44.

6. Saller, "Men's Age," cf. "*Patria Potestas*," and "*Pietas*, Obligation and Authority in the Roman Family," in *Alte Geschichte und Wissenschaftsgeschichte: Festschrift für Karl Christ zum 65. Geburtstag* (Darmstadt, 1988), 393–410.

7. Hopkins, *Death and Renewal*, 70–73.

well-being of offspring who were children in both senses of the word; that is, who were not only the testator's offspring, but physically children as well. We, with a life expectancy in the seventies, tend to think of the testator as an elderly person with mature offspring. Nothing could be further from the Roman reality, and foremost in the mind of the testator would be both the protection of the child and, if disaster occurred, the appointment of a substitute heir.

Fourth, demographers have likewise considered questions of fertility in historical societies, and particularly of the probability of fathers leaving surviving children. Again, roughly speaking, one could expect that about 20 percent of Roman fathers would have no child living at the time of their death, another 20 percent would have a daughter or daughters but no son, 30 to 35 percent would leave one son, and 25 to 30 percent two or more sons.[8] That is, one-fifth of Roman males would have to look either to their wives or to siblings or other kin, and another one-fifth might be tempted to look for a male heir not of their descent. How did they react?

Some of these demographical observations will directly affect the conclusions about the strategies of testators to be offered below. At the least, they sharply remind us, despite the familiarity of the testament, how very foreign to us was the physical, and hence mental, world of the Roman testator.

On intestacy in classical Roman law, the praetor, the magistrate in charge of the legal system, would modify statute law to allow possession of the estate (*bonorum possessio*) to relatives in four classes of heir, in order: children; agnates; cognates to the sixth degree; and spouse. But the mental map of the Roman testator is far more complex and will prove to have quite different aims. Seldom would a testator assign to joint heirs the simple, equal shares of the estate envisioned by the praetor. Unequal division might arise from sheer favoritism, but it was much more likely to be part of a calculated strategy in which the testator employed legacies and trusts (*fideicommissa*) to alter drastically or even to reverse the overt intention of the *institutio*, the part of the will naming the heirs. And there are two figures who are difficult to fit

8. Hopkins, *Death and Renewal*, 97–100, citing J. Goody and E. A. Wrigley.

into the schematic legal conception of the family. One, to be considered later, is the servant (slave or freed), who might fall between family and friend, and part of whose estate (in the case of freedmen) could revert to the patron's family at death.[9] More important, indeed crucial to the testator's conception of the family, is the other; the close female relative. For testators of both sexes, how do daughters fare relative to sons, sisters to brothers? And where do wives fit in, relative to the male testator's children and kin?

Normally testators preferred any children they might have to all other heirs, and society generally held that children should inherit—that disinheritance was to be avoided.[10] Legal opinions and literary anecdotes to that effect have been cited earlier, to which more could be added: a testatrix who in a rage upset the "natural order" of the will, disinheriting her children (Augustus set the will aside), or Apuleius begging his wife not to disinherit her son.[11] Best is Pliny's solemn defence of his acceptance of part of an inheritance from a woman who had disinherited her son: he held a formal investigation with *consilium* into the reasons for the disinheritance, before deciding that it was justified and that he could take up his share.[12]

That strong emotion could lead to disinheritance goes without saying. The jurist Ulpian even provides a selection of acceptable circumlocutions for ill-disposed testators who could not bear to write the offending child's name: "the person not to be named," or "the person who is not my son," "the brigand," "the gladiator," "the one born of an adulterer."[13] Children could always find ways of upsetting parents, from getting divorced to taking bribes, and even the innocent could fall to the wiles of a wicked stepmother.[14]

Yet disinheritance as disavowal is extraordinarily rare in the literature, and here a clear line must be drawn between life and

9. See below, pp. 131–42.
10. Cf. above, pp. 15 and 89.
11. Valerius Maximus 7.7.4 (cf. 7.7.3, a man who forfeited the name of father by disinheriting his son); Apuleius *Apol.* 99.
12. *Ep.* 5.1.
13. *Dig.* 28.2.3 pr.; cf. 28.2.14.2, a child disinherited because not the testator's son.
14. *Dig.* 24.3.44.1; Cicero *Cluent.* 135; Pliny *Ep.* 6.33; *Dig.* 5.2.4.

death. During the testator's lifetime relations with his or her offspring might be stormy indeed; and declamatory works overflow
with scenes of fathers repudiating their sons for every conceivable
offense.[15] But this repudiation in lifetime is something quite different from disinheritance after death, although the Latin word
*abdicatio,* used of it, is often translated as "disinheritance".[16] Not a
legal act in itself, it is in fact rarely mentioned outside of the
classroom. Moreover, a suggestive study of the social and moral
ties of the late antique family has argued that, for all the abuse
and punishment meted out by fathers to sons, "the usual bonds of
power held": sons obeyed their fathers, on whom their future
welfare depended, and fathers dominated their sons.[17] And, at the
end, parents were as much bound by *pietas* as were their children.[18]
In brief, society and lawyers both frowned on disinheritance effected without good reason; parents and children were both
caught up in a web of obligations; and despite all the tension the
ultimate repudiation of disinheritance was not common.

But disinheritance need not be an act of anger. When it happened in real life it was far more likely to be an act, if not of love,
at least of cool calculation; that is, there was a good and acceptable, as well as a bad, disinheritance. In many cases, where the
documents themselves survive or legal opinions are recorded, no
reason for the action is given or can be deduced, but where a
reason is offered, it rarely involves rejection of the child. Two
general and related tactical patterns can be discerned.

The clearer of the two is the use of the fiduciary heir. Ulpian
explicitly noted that "many testators disinherit their offspring not
to disgrace or to harm them, but so that they may look out for
their best interests, just as for young children, and give an inher-

15. E.g., Seneca *Controv.* 1.1, 4, 6, 8; 2.1, 2 (a daughter), 4; 3.2, 3, 4; 5.2; 6.1; 7.1,
3; 8.3, 5; 10.2; [Quintilian] *Declam.* 256, 257, 258, 259, 279, 281, 283, 285, 286, 287,
290, 291, 295, 296, 300, 330, 357, 373, 375, 376, 378, 387.
16. Brief discussion in S. F. Bonner, *Roman Declamation in the Late Republic and
Early Empire* (Liverpool, 1949), 101–3.
17. B. D. Shaw, "The Family in Late Antiquity: The Experience of Augustine,"
*Past and Present* 115 (1987): 3–51, at 21–28.
18. Saller, *"Pietas,"* 399–403. P. Veyne has exaggerated the tension between
fathers and sons to the point that he must assume that parricide was astonishingly
frequent at Rome, something neither likely nor much attested: "La famille et
l'amour sous le haut-empire romain," *Annales ESC* 33 (1978): 35–63.

itance via a trust."[19] The *heres fiduciarius* is, generally, an heir named with a *fideicommissum* to pass all or part of the estate on to another person. Here again, there seem to be two distinct forms in practice.

One thinks first of the testator who named a fiduciary heir in order to circumvent the law, to have that heir pass on the estate or a part of it to someone barred from regular inheritance, such as certain women under the Lex Voconia, certain bachelors (under the Lex Julia de maritandis ordinibus), Junian Latins or (at one time) peregrines.[20] In many of these cases a child of the testator may have been involved, as when the parent was a citizen and the child not, or as (most notoriously) in the late republican case of the wealthy Fadius Gallus, who entrusted an untrustworthy friend with passing on the estate to his daughter, to avoid the Lex Voconia.[21] But disinheritance is largely irrelevant here, and the estate was presumably to be handed over immediately: this is less a strategy than a tactical response to unfavorable circumstances.

A more creative strategy closely connected disinheritance and the fiduciary heir, and it occured often enough for us to perceive it as a regular practice. Here, clearly intending to hold the family together and to protect the interests of young children,[22] the testator institutes as heir the surviving spouse (or, on occasion, a friend or relative), with a trust to pass the estate on to the child at death or when the child reaches a certain age (16, 20, and 25 are mentioned).[23] (Similar *fideicommissa* may also be found directed to helping children who were not the testator's own, but instances

19. *Dig.* 28.2.18: *Multi non notae causa exheredant filios nec ut eis obsint, sed ut eis consulant, ut puta impuberibus, eisque fideicommissam hereditatem dant.* On this, see most recently M. Kuryłowicz, "*Heres Fiduciarius:* Bemerkungen zum römischen Erbrecht in den lateinischen Grabinschriften," *ZPE* 60 (1985): 189–98.

20. Gaius 2.274, 275, 110, 285. Possible examples in the Digest: *Dig.* 32.41.14; 35.2.86; 36.1.26 pr.; 36.1.80.1. At *Ep.* 10.75, Pliny finds himself as heir, with the bulk of the estate to be passed on to two cities. D. Johnston, *The Roman Law of Trusts* (Oxford, 1988), 29–41, doubts for various reasons that such evasive trusts worked well.

21. Cicero *Fin.* 2.55.

22. In the light of p. 63 above, it goes without saying that, even where it is not recorded or implied, both testator and children are likely to have been young.

23. *Dig.* 22.1.3.3, a *propinquus* heir, passing the estate to a daughter at a certain age; 33.1.21.2, wife to son at twenty-five; 35.1.77.3, wife to daughter at death; 36.1.23 pr., stepfather to stepsons at their father's death; 36.1.48, friend to son at sixteen; 36.1.59.2, wife to sons at death; 36.1.76.1, wife to son at twenty; 36.1.80.1,

are few.[24]) Here the temporal element is central, aligning the practice with usufruct.[25] In both the surviving spouse is provided for, with eventual reversion to the children; but the fiduciary heir is in a much stronger position than the usufructuary, being in full enjoyment of all or part of the estate, rather than in limited enjoyment of part only. Appointing the surviving spouse as a fiduciary heir and hence at law the owner (rather than assigning a usufruct) is thus the strongest possible vote of confidence in a trustee who will essentially administer the estate until the time comes to pass it on, and a strong incentive to maintaining family unity after the death of the testator, since inevitably there must have been some provision out of the estate for the physical well-being of the children in the interim. Disinheritance of the children, a necessary first step, is thus here a sign of careful planning for their future.

Less clear are the other cases of disinheritance, where such a *fideicommissum* is not involved. Between inheritance via a trust and the paradigm—beloved of rhetors but rare in life—of the enraged parent cutting off the disobedient child, there lies a large middle ground wherein children are disinherited with no overt signs of dislike. An emancipated son or one who has been adopted out of the family might be ignored,[26] a daughter who has received or will receive her dowry might be disinherited.[27] Some disinherited children are given legacies of land, goods, money, or mainte-nance, *alimenta*.[28] And in some cases where there is no hint of

---

sons to grandsons at twenty-five; 36.1.80.9, husband to son at death; 36.1.80.10, husband to son and grandson at death; 36.1.80.14, wife to son at death; 36.1.80.15, son at twenty; 36.3.18, father to son at death. Also Phaedrus 4.5: wife to three daughters (after assigning portions).

24. E.g., *Dig* 36.1.11.2, (extraneous) heir to *liberta, cum nubilem aetatem comples-set;* 36.1.80.12, heir (unknown) to *alumnus* at fifteen: quasi-filial relationships?

25. *Dig.* 33.2.37: usufruct of the estate to the widow until the daughter reaches 18. Cf., independently, D. Johnston, "Successive Rights and Successful Remedies: Life Interests in Roman Law," in *New Perspectives in the Roman Law of Property: Essays for Barry Nicholas* ed. P. Birks (Oxford, 1989), 153–67.

26. E.g., *Dig.* 37.5.6, 22, Valerius Maximus 7.7.2.

27. *Dig.* 27.2.4; 28.5.62; 31.34.5; 31.77.9. Cf. 33.5.21, a daughter to receive a legacy of 100 in cash plus ten slaves at the time of her marriage.

28. *Dig.* 28.2.19; 28.5.38 pr.; 30.108.13; 31.77.9; 33.4.7 pr.; 34.1.10.2. In the one case of disinheritance recorded by the papyri, *P. Princ.* 38, a woman institutes her mother and disinherits her sons, but also bequeaths substantial lands to their father, her husband.

property passing there are sure signs of the testator's affections in the naming of disinherited children as substitute heirs (which includes the assignment of a legacy)[29] or in the appointment of a tutor for them.[30] The common element in these is not merely an absence of malice but a sense that the child has in some way been taken care of—the most extreme examples being those of men who handed over most of their property to their emancipated sons before death.[31]

Without the details in any single case one cannot yet say whether this is a part of any larger strategy in the distribution of a partible inheritance, particularly as in any individual case the testator might so engineer his dispositions that a legatee's portion could approach in value that of a burdened heir. Certainly there are hints of the latter: one testator carefully requested that his dearest daughter keep what he had given to her in his lifetime, and not be angry that her brother received a larger portion of the estate, since his was the greater burden and he would be paying out the legacies.[32] Again, whatever the motive and the context, the testator took some thought for the future of the disinherited child: the purpose of that thought, the limit of the care, is seldom clear in the sources.

Disinheritance as a rejection of the child is rarely attested, then; and when we see the fact shorn of context, particularly in the Digest, there is no need to assume an emotional repudiation. Rather the reverse is true: disinheritance is more often associated with a testator looking out for a child's interests while protecting the family fortune.

As one would expect from the law of intestate succession, there is no hint of customary primogeniture in Roman testaments.[33]

---

29. *P. Oxy.* 2857 and probably *BGU* 326 (with A. Watson, "The Identity of Sarapio, Socrates, Longus and Nilus in the Will of C. Longinus Castor," *Irish Jurist* 1 (1966): 313–15 (*P. Select.* 14 has a very similar situation); *Dig.* 35.2.87.7; 28.6.47. I shall assume throughout that substitute heirs were always given compensatory legacies; this is sometimes explicitly recorded (*BGU* 1696; *P. Mich.* 437; *CPL* 221; Suetonius *Aug.* 101 + *Claud.* 4.7; probably *CIL* 6.10229; *Dig.* 31.89.2).

30. *Dig.* 26.2.26.2; 35.1.77.3.

31. *Dig.* 32.37.3; 32.78.1.

32. *Dig.* 31.34.6.

33. *Dig.* 31.76.5 shows a testator leaving a *fideicommissum* to his daughter that even if she bore other children a larger share of her inheritance should go to

O. Montevecchi, in her study of Egyptian wills, found two kinds of division among children, one allowing equal shares to all, another tending to favor the eldest son, for instance through the assignment of a double portion.[34] But there is nothing approaching prescription here, and the practice is Greco-Egyptian, indeed is absent from all Roman law wills from Egypt. Instead, three patterns are discernible in Roman testators' treatment of their children.

First, it was quite possible simply to name all surviving children without assigning shares, or explicitly to divide the estate equally among them, without any initial regard to sex or maturity.[35] But record of this is rare, and beyond the *institutio* the testator was quite free to upset the balance of inheritance by assigning the burdens of legacies and *fideicommissa* to one or another of the heirs.

Second, it was equally possible to name an *extraneus* as coheir along with one's children. Here testators turned to siblings, nephews, patrons, even brothers-in-law or *liberti*.[36] The emperor also appears as a coheir, but that was under exceptional circumstances, and even the conventional bad emperor would hesitate to accept where children survived.[37] Most of all, testators turned to their spouses (in the large majority of cases, their wives), who may or may not have been parents of the surviving children.[38]

The naming of the *extraneus* as a coheir with children is a puzzle which may not have a single solution. One aim it does not seem to

---

Sempronius; but this is clearly favoritism toward a beloved grandchild, and requested specifically *in honorem nominis mei*. A royal will like Herod's is not relevant. At *Dig.* 31.77.21, a father gives keys and ring to his elder daughter, but not with any presumption of priority.

34. Montevecchi, "Ricerche," 101–3.

35. *P. Ber.* inv. 13857, sons and daughter; *P. Oxy.* 907, three sons and two daughters, with specific legacies to certain individuals; *Dig.* 5.4.6 pr., daughter and four sons; 31.34.6, daughter and son; 33.2.32.1, two sons and one daughter; 33.4.14, two daughters and one son.

36. Siblings: *P. Cair. Goodsp.* 29, *P. Col.* 188; Plutarch *Cato Min.* 11 (half-brother); *Dig.* 23.4.30. Nephews: *Dig.* 28.5.79.2, 32.32 pr., 34.9.16. Patrons: *Dig.* 31.83, 48.10.14. Brother-in-law: Macrobius *Sat.* 3.15.6. Libertus: *Dig.* 37.14.12. Unknown: *Dig.* 5.2.19, 28.6.34.1, 31.77.7.

37. See below, pp. 150–54. Individual instances at Dio 53.20.4, 58.4.5; Tacitus *Agricola* 43.4; Suetonius *Nero* 6.3. The policy of a good emperor is stated at Suetonius *Aug.* 66.4.

38. E.g., Suetonius *Aug.* 101, Tacitus *Agric.* 43.4; *P. Col.* 188, *P. Oxy.* 3692, *BGU* 388; probably *CIL* 6.10229; *Dig.* 31.89 pr., 32.41 pr., 32.41.7, 33.1.21.2, 33.5.21 pr., 34.1.16.3, 35.2.25, 36.1.80.14, 40.5.14, cf. *CJ* 3.28.12.

have had is protection of the child's interests (excepting always the rare placation of the emperor): in one case only is the coheir also identified as a tutor,[39] and there is no hint of special care to be taken by the *extraneus* coheir for the child heir, no *fideicommissum* (such as is found in other circumstances) to look out for the child's interests, to keep the household together, or to return part of the estate to the child. One common element is (the emperor again excepted) that almost all of these *extranei* are potential heirs by intestacy or, to reverse the observation, *amici* do not appear as heirs where there are surviving children who have not been repudiated (a striking confirmation of the primacy of family).[40] Wealthy freedmen and freedwomen of course had little choice but to recognize their patron's right.[41] And there may have been a tendancy to prefer a male heir, even an outsider, where only daughters existed.[42] But the simplest (and probably correct) general explanation is that instituting as coheir with one's children one who was not *suus heres*—typically, a spouse—was a mark of special esteem. A promotion, as it were, from legatee to heir, this would not be a devaluation of the children, but a recognition that a special outsider, normally a near relative, was as important to the testator as his or her children.

A third pattern in the treatment of children involves not the recognition of equality among them, nor promotion of the special *extraneus* into their number, but discrimination among them. Clearly matters of individual emotion come into play here, particularly in the question of disinheritance. Unlike the Digest, literary sources occasionally give some details of senatorial scandals: the testatrix who, in a furious will, left one daughter heir, cutting the other off with a modest legacy; the man who left one son heir while disinheriting the other for a criminal act; the man who, as a mark of displeasure with his son, left him his mother's property (*bona materna*) only.[43] The *querela inofficiosi testamenti* was not infre-

---

39. *Dig.* 26.9.8.
40. See below, pp. 142–46. The *libertus* coheir of *Dig.* 37.14.12 was *quasi et ipsum filium*. The cases of Pomponia Galla and Valerius Paulinus in Pliny recall offended (not loving) parents.
41. Gaius 3.40–42.
42. See below, pp. 142–43, and on testamentary adoption, pp. 144–46. *Dig.* 32.32 has a daughter heir to 1/4, two nephews receiving the other 3/4; 5.2.19 has an *extraneus* heir to 3/4, a daughter to 1/4.
43. Valerius Maximus 7.8.2; Cicero *Cluent.* 135; Philostratus *VS* 558.

quent. Again, legacies to one heir before the division of the estate (*praelegata*), or the charging of more legacies, might increase or decrease the face value of that heir's share. Yet these dramatic interventions involve questions of individual emotions in which, without more detail than now exists, it is difficult to discern patterns. Behind these, however, is clearly visible a pattern of systematic, customary discrimination against daughters in the period of the late republic and early empire, a discrimination which must be carefully defined. Two different manifestations can be adduced, with support culled mostly from the Digest.

First, in those cases where both sons and daughters are heirs and the portions are known, sons are clearly preferred. Not untypical are those instances where a son received one-half, his sisters one-fourth each; or a son three-fourths and his sister one-fourth; or one son five-twelfths, another one-third, and a daughter one-fourth; or a son one-half; his sister one-third, and his mother one-sixth; or the grandson who received two-thirds, his sister one-third from the *honestissimum testamentum* of their grandmother; or a daughter who received far less than her brother; or a daughter who must take one-sixth of her inheritance and transfer the rest to her brother and coheir; or a daughter who was to take certain property and hand everything else over to her brother.[44] Very similar to these last instances is that of the testator who, leaving son and daughter as heirs, added a *fideicommissum* to the daughter to make no will until she had children; as the emperor concluded, this was tantamount to a trust to transfer the inheritance to her brother.[45] It may be that males were customarily selected to discharge debts or pay out legacies[46]—but even then there is no suggestion anywhere that their portions were intended thereby to be reduced to equality with those of their sisters. The

44. *Dig.* 31.77.30, 32.27.1, 36.1.80.5, *CJ* 3.28.12; Pliny *Ep.* 7.24.2; *Dig.* 35.2.94, 35.2.14 pr.; 36.1.58. *P. Stras.* 41 + *P. Lips.* 32 is a unique case in that the daughter received 11/12, the son 1/12. But the bypassed son here was adopted, not natural; and the daughter was bidden by *fideicommissum* to turn over 5/12 of the estate to the son's daughter when she married: not typical, but hardly a weighty exception.

45. *Dig.* 36.1.76 pr. (Paul *Decreta* 2). Cf. 31.89.5: a daughter is to return her dowry to her brother if she dies childless.

46. Explicitly at *Dig.* 31.34.6 (son's portion larger since he must pay the legacies and the daughter had already received some property in the testator's lifetime), 32.34.3 (son to pay legacies and debts).

likelihood is that sons were, in general, intended to obtain the bulk of the inheritance; and three items in the Digest concerning posthumous children give direct insight into the intention of testators as the jurists perceived or recorded them. In his *Digesta*, Julian postulated a testator who directed that if a son were born he should be heir to two-thirds, his wife to the remaining one-third, but if the child were a daughter she should receive one-third, the mother two-thirds.[47] This is not merely hypothetical, for Africanus records in his *Quaestiones* a testator who instituted his daughter as heir: if a son were subsequently or posthumously born, he would be heir to three-fourths, the daughter to one-fourth; if a daughter, she would receive one-fourth and the elder sister three-fourths. And Paul, also in *Quaestiones*, names a testator who had carefully disposed of posthumous children thus: if a son appeared, he would be heir; if two sons or two daughters, they would share equally; but if a son and a daughter, the male was to receive two-thirds, the female one-third.[48] In short, all things being truly equal, one expected a daughter to receive less than a son when both were heirs.

Alternatively, one could simply disinherit the daughter in favor of the son. Occasionally just this is baldly recorded, but so often are daughters noted elsewhere as being disinherited but otherwise provided for that, where details are lacking, the presumption must be that they were normally looked after, rather than that they were cut off in anger.[49] Very rarely we do read of daughters being instituted while sons are disinherited and given a legacy.[50] The great majority of cases record the reverse; that is, daughters are apparently excluded from the inheritance and their welfare is taken up either directly through legacies or indirectly through *fideicommissa* to the heir. Sometimes the simple fact that the disin-

---

47. *Dig.* 28.2.13 pr. If both son and daughter were born, how to distribute the *as*? The answer: son 4/7, wife 2/7, daughter 1/7. A similar situation is postulated by Tryphoninus at *Dig.* 28.2.28.4.

48. *Dig.* 28.5.48.1; 28.5.82 pr. In the latter case, two sons and one daughter appeared, and portions were assigned 2:2:1.

49. *Dig.* 5.2.16 pr. (a son disinherited as well: he brings *querela*, she does not), 28.6.47, 30.108.13, 33.5.21, 37.7.6 (a successful *querela* by a daughter), *CJ* 6.28.1. At *Dig.* 31.77.7, a daughter is heir, a son disinherited. On legacies to children in the Digest, see above all the pioneering paper of L. Boyer, "Fonction sociale," 355–60; it should be noted here and later that Boyer's references are far from exhaustive.

50. Daughters heirs, sons legatees: *Dig.* 5.2.13, 28.2.19.

herited daughter received a legacy survives.[51] At the other extreme, in one rare papyrus considerable detail emerges: a daughter (she a peregrine, her brothers citizens) is to receive 4000 silver drachmae, one-third of a particular house, a slave, and money for the funeral.[52] Best of all, a daughter may occasionally win a *legatum portionis*, a legacy of her intestate share of the estate, free of the burdens of an heir.[53] But mostly a brief description of the legacy to the disinherited daughter suffices, including all of the normal types: land, be it farms or a house, or something more particular like a shop or a suburban estate; cash; slaves; and occasionally *alimenta*, that is, support in one form or another.[54] In short, there is considerable evidence that the disinherited daughter was to some extent cared for through normal legacies. This leads to the matter of dowry.

On the evidence, of all possible bequests to the disinherited daughter, ownership of her *dos* was probably one of the most common.[55] In an excellent discussion of the size and function of dowry at Rome, R. P. Saller has attempted to fix the position of Roman dowry on a spectrum of possible uses which stretches from a token amount, for little more than a trousseau, through to what is "in most societies" essentially a settlement of the wife's claim to

51. *CPR* 6.2.76; *Dig.* 33.2.39; Dio 56.32.4.
52. *BGU* 1662.
53. *Dig.* 31.77 pr.; *CIL* 6.10230 (*laudatio Murdiae*).
54. Land: *BGU* 1655; *P. Select.* 14 (possibly illegitimate); *Dig.* 33.3.6 (probably not an heir). (Also, unknown if heir: 32.91 pr., 35.1.101 pr.; heir 32.92 pr.)
   Cash: 31.45.2 (conditional on marriage), 33.5.21, 35.1.28 pr., 36.1.76.1; *BGU* 1662; Valerius Maximus 7.8.2.
   *Peculium:* 33.8.6.4 (unknown if heir), 34.4.31.3.
   Slaves: 31.77.17 (probably), 33.5.21, *BGU* 1662. (*P. Oxy.* 907 to an heir.)
   *Alimenta: Dig.* 34.1.10.2. 33.1.22 has a conditional annuity for a daughter who was probably not an heir.
   Jewelry and other items considered particularly feminine do occur, but surprisingly rarely, and they happen not to be attested specifically as transferred to a disinherited daughter: *margarita* (*Dig.* 30.108.13); *vestum mundum muliebrem lanam linum et alias res* (33.2.39); *argentum muliebre* (33.7.12.47); *ornamentum omne meum muliebre cum auro et si qua alia muliebria apparuerint* (34.2.32.4); cf. Phaedrus 4.5.21, *mundum muliebrem.*
   55. *Dig.* 27.2.4; 28.5.62; 31.34.5 (by *fideicommissum*), 31.45.2; 31.77.9; 31.89.5 (probably); 34.1.10.2; 35.1.28. (35.1.101 pr., unknown if heir, but unlikely; daughter heir gets dowry at *P. Oxy.* 907, *Dig.* 23.3.85, 23.4.30(?), 33.4.13.) *Dig.* 33.5.21 is a legacy to a daughter of 100 in cash plus ten slaves when she marries within the family. (32.41.7 appears to recall the same will: both extracts, with elaborate instructions from the testator, derive from the twenty-second book of Scaevola's *Digesta*.) And above all, note *Dig.* 35.2.14 pr, discussed below.

her father's estate.[56] He argues that Roman dowries, compared to those in other societies, were "relatively small but not negligible," and hence concludes that they must fall in the middle of the possible spectrum, serving "to support her [the wife], her children and her entourage in her husband's house—a function that makes good sense in the context of the high divorce rate." In the absence of an explicit ancient statement on the purpose of dowry, the argument depends on inference from the modest size of dowries relative to the size of family fortunes, a relationship itself based on very slim evidence yet highly probable. In essence, the argument is that dowries could not represent the daughter's portion because they were too small to be an equal share. But in light of Roman testamentary practice, the opposite may be true: they were relatively small because they did represent the daughter's share.

We have seen two converging trends in the practice of Roman testators, that is, the institution of daughters as heirs with sons, but to a smaller portion of the estate, or their disherison and the allotment to them of some form of legacy. Either path ensured that daughters received a smaller share than sons. One of the commoner forms of legacy is that of dowry, to which we might add various kinds of marriage gifts, and some texts in the Digest are particularly revealing as to the testator's purpose. In one, other details aside, Papinian in consideration of an actual case seriously entertains the possibility that a father may have disinherited his daughter in consideration of the dowry and allowance which she had already received.[57] This is particularly valuable because it concerns not just one father's action but what an experienced jurist thought worth pondering. In another, a testator wrote bluntly, "I have disinherited you, daughter, because I wanted you to be content with your dowry."[58] In yet another, a father instituted his son and divorced daughter coheirs with a *fideicommissum* that, after deducting one-sixth as compensation for her dowry, the daughter hand over her share to her brother—the figure was

56. R. P. Saller, "Roman Dowry and the Evolution of Property in the Principate," *CQ* 34 (1984): 195–205.

57. *Dig.* 6.1.65.1, from *Responsa* 2.

58. *Dig.* 28.5.62. Was he unusual in the wish, or only in the explicit expression of it? (The legal question was whether this constituted a sufficient disherison.)

arrived at *in Falcidiae ratione*, that is to say, the one-sixth, equivalent
to one-twelfth of the entire estate, would satisfy the requirement
of the Lex Falcidia that the heir receive at least one-quarter of
what she would have received on intestacy.[59] There is, in brief,
evidence to support the notion that some Roman fathers did
consider the dowry to represent a daughter's share, a lesser share,
of the estate.

Great progress has been made toward a better understanding
of the lives of women in antiquity, particularly through study of
the ancient family.[60] With this progress has come a more positive
view of women's role both public and private, and particularly a
tendency to see a progressive amelioration of their lot through the
Roman era.[61] At the same time, doubts may be entertained as to its
nature and extent.[62] Certainly as far as literate, propertied classes
are concerned, many women not only held considerable wealth
but (more importantly) exercised virtually unlimited control of it.
Their independence, and the independence of the relatively
humble women known from inscriptions and papyri, are striking.
Yet in what remains a valuable contribution to the study of the
Roman family, F. von Woess concluded after careful consideration
of all the legal evidence that the law was much more favorable to
daughters than was custom, insofar as their rights of inheritance
were concerned.[63] Thus the simple restrictions of the second-century Lex Voconia were steadily circumscribed or circumvented by

59. *Dig.* 35.2.14 pr.
60. The bibliography grows constantly. Very useful recent introductions to it
may be found in papers by M. Corbier, "Les Comportements familiaux de l'aristo-
cratie romaine (IIe s. av. J-C – IIIe s. ap. J-C)," *Annales ESC* (1987): 1267–85, and
M. Golden, review of B. Rawson, *The Family in Ancient Rome, Classical Views* 22
(1988): 78–83. A succinct legal account of "Women in Roman Succession" is
offered by J. Crook, in *The Family in Ancient Rome: New Perspectives*, ed. B. Rawson
(Ithaca, N.Y., 1986), 58–82, and see most recently J. Gardner, *Women in Roman Law
and Society* (London, 1986), and S. Dixon, *The Roman Mother* (London and Sydney,
1988). In addition to her pioneering work on women in the ancient world in
general and on the women of Hellenistic Egypt, S. Pomeroy offers a useful "preliminary study" of "Women in Roman Egypt," in *Reflections of Women in Antiquity*,
ed. H. Foley (New York, 1981), 303–22.
61. E.g., Pomeroy, "Women in Roman Egypt," or Hopkins, *Death and Renewal*,
84–95.
62. Gardner, *Women in Roman Law*, 257–66, criticized by R. P. Saller in review,
*CP* 83 (1988): 263–65. Shaw, "Family," 28 ff., characterizes the relationship of
wives to husbands in late antique North Africa as one of servile dependence.
63. Von Woess, *Erbrecht*, 65–121. Cf. above, pp. 46–49.

subsequent laws (such as the Lex Falcidia, the Lex Papia Poppaea, and the sanctioning of *fideicommissa*), and the basic rules of intestate succession were always more favorable to daughters than were the wishes of testators. But (as has been suggested above) testators usually preferred sons to daughters in the final distribution of their estates. This provides the missing element in an equation. It has already been observed that the great majority, perhaps 80 percent or more, of known Roman testators were men, and it was suggested (again following von Woess) that this was a result of their owning proportionally more property than Roman women. The primary reason why men owned more is that they inherited more.[64]

Wealth tended into the hands of men, but von Woess must be modified, or supplemented, in one important respect, and here the matter of discrimination against daughters should be seen in context. Individual women could and did inherit on a large scale, and there is considerable evidence for their consequent economic activity. That they did inherit so much must be explained.

In a study of women as property owners in Roman Egypt, D. Hobson observed that two general principles governing the distribution of property in wills emerged from the papyri: "that every member of the immediate family should be provided for as his or her circumstances require," and "that the property should remain within the immediate family if possible."[65] It is here suggested that these eminently sensible observations hold true for all Roman testators in the period under consideration. The idea of rigid equality between sons and daughters would have struck a thinking Roman of the fifth century B.C. as yet another horrible consequence of intestacy; in the standard conception, women were the

64. This seems to be the crucial factor. Obviously men had a far greater range of possibilities for economic activity than women, and women had greater social and legal restrictions on them, but wealth started with inheritance. (For the proportion of 4:1 between men and women in the ownership of property, compare L. Huchthausen, "Herkunft und ökonomische Stellung weibliche Adressaten von Reskripten des *Codex Iustinianus* [2 und 3 Jh. u.Z.]," *Klio* 56 [1974]: 199–228: about 19 percent of the recipients of these imperial rescripts were women.) Further to this, and significant for the extent to which society subscribed to the process, there is virtually no evidence to suggest that female testators deviated from the general practice, by favoring daughters over sons. Indeed, no significant difference is visible between the actions of males and females over the whole range of testamentary practice.

65. Hobson, "Women as Property Owners," 320–21.

end of the family. But we can say that, at least by the time of the
late republic (when our evidence begins), this attitude would have
been considerably altered: when a testator without a son was
forced to choose between a daughter and an extraneous male,
however close, the daughter succeeded; where sons did exist,
some testators treated daughters as their equals; and most testators allowed them some portion of their estate. Daughters were
not equal to sons, but the demands of natural affection were
strong. The family as perceived by the testator was not the larger
agnatic family of archaic times, but his own descendants, with
male taking precedence over female. In brief: sons before daughters, but daughters before everyone else.

The large question then remains, if children were to be preferred to all others, how did Roman testators treat their spouses?
In particular, how did men treat those intruders into the heart of
the family, their wives? The latter is the central, perhaps the only
real question: if women tended to be a decade younger then their
husbands at first marriage, more wives outlived husbands than
the reverse; and if men accounted for four-fifths of the wills
produced, wives had four times the chance of being mentioned in
their spouse's will than had husbands. Much good work has been
done on the testamentary treatment of wives by their husbands—
and what follows is deeply indebted to it.[66]

Again, von Woess demonstrated the essential: that the testamentary position of wives was the reverse of that of daughters.
The law was unfavorable to wives, particularly in the rules of
intestate succession, which moved only from not recognizing any
intestate claims at all, to recognizing those of spouses in the very
last place. But society treated them well. That is to say, testators
gave vent to their natural affection, and jurists tended to favor the
claims of wives. It can be taken for granted that most widows
received something from their husbands' wills.

One reason for this discrepancy between law and practice lies
in the commonly perceived decline of the *manus* marriage by the
time of the late republic. The original intestate rules reflected a
much earlier time when *manus* marriage was the rule rather than

66. Von Woess, *Erbrecht*, 45–65; Boyer, "Fonction sociale," 374–95; Humbert,
*Remariage*, 189–263.

the exception; and since in such a marriage the wife would be in the position of a daughter-in-power to her husband, she would have an intestate claim equal to that of her children. When, by the time of the later republic, the marriage would normally be *sine manu*, she lost that natural right. Compensation must be made. Praetorian law clearly relegated surviving spouses to a position of taking on intestacy after children, agnates, and near cognates. Husbands, however, tended to place their wives close after children but before all other near kin.

For husbands, there was not only a need to demonstrate marital affection; several other considerations might enter their calculations, particularly the problems raised by remarriage. Would the wife's fortune be subjected to plunder by a second husband, perhaps even the dreaded captation by adventurers in the guise of suitors? Could a surviving stepmother be entrusted with the care of stepchildren where property was at stake? Could even a mother be trusted to subordinate her own interests to those of her children? Could one possibly ensure that the family unit survived in some form, until the children reached maturity? The main task, then, thoroughly analyzed by M. Humbert from the point of view of remarriage, was to reconcile the profit of the widow with the protection of the children, to reward and yet in some way to restrict the powers of the surviving parent, and to ensure that the property remained in the original family. Two distinct strategies appear, with notable resemblances to the treatment of daughters.

First, the wife could be left as an heir. Wives were only rarely left sole heirs or even heirs to the greater share of the estate. Occasionally we read of them succeeding where there were no surviving children, or being named heir with their children as substitutes (the presumption by the testator must have been that the children should succeed the wife eventually), or inheriting with a *fideicommissum* to transfer the estate at some specified time to a child.[67] But easily the commonest treatment of the surviving

67. No children: *Schol. ad Juvenalem* 4.81; Petronius *Sat* 71.3 . This would appear to be contrary to the Lex Papia Poppaea (Kaser, *Privatrecht*, 724): exemptions, particularly through the *ius liberorum*, were presumably not uncommon. Children as substitutes: *P. Oxy.* 2857; *Dig.* 28.6.43.2. Fiduciary heir: *Dig.* 31.77.12; 32.41.14; 36.1.59.2; 36.1.76.1; cf. 33.1.21.2; Phaedrus 4.5 (and 100,000 legacy). Cf. Humbert, *Remariage*, 214–22. Named as heir, but no sign whether children existed: *Dig.* 31.89.7 (*ex asse*); 33.1.13.1; 34.9.13.

wife as heir was to appoint her to one-half or (more often) less of
the estate—shares of one-twelfth, one-tenth, one-sixth, one-
fourth, and one-third are attested, but never more than one-half
—along with, most often, sons or daughters, but sometimes near
relatives instead.[68] As an alternative to this, she might receive a
legacy equal to a share of the inheritance, but unburdened.[69]
Hence the relative position of wives as heirs can be neatly plotted:
a wife may very well not be an heir at all, where children survive;
she may be coheir to a lesser share than children or even near
relatives; but she will not be dismissed with a legacy only, where
the heir is an *extraneus*.[70]

However, it would be far more common for a wife to receive a
legacy.[71] Often these are not specified in our sources; often they
run in the normal range of land and chattels.[72] Beyond these there
are four distinctive groups of legacies which are particularly identified with settlements in favor of wives.[73]

One outstanding mode is the assignment of her dowry, or part
of it, or its equivalent (*legatum pro dote*) to the widow.[74] Close to this,

68. Sons: Suetonius *Aug.* 101 (1/3 to wife); Plutarch *Cato Min.* 52.5–7; *BGU* 388; *P. Oxy.* 3692 (1/4?); *Dig.* 31.89 pr.; 32.41 pr.; 33.1.21.2 (1/4); 33.5.21; 34.1.16.3 (1/2); 36.1.80.14? (1/3). Cf. Conclusion. Daughters: Tacitus *Agric.* 43.4; *P. Col.* 188; *Dig.* 31.77 pr. (*fideicommissum*); 31.89.3 (codicil); 40.5.14 (1/2); 40.5.41.14. Children: *Dig.* 31.87.4. *Extranei: P. Col.* 188 (siblings); Pliny *Ep.* 6.33 (nephew); Tacitus *Agric.* 43.4 (emperor); Quintilian 8.5.19 (*meretrix;* 1/10 to wife); *Dig.* 31.88.16 (mother); 49.14.9 (sister; 1/4 to wife and her father). Near relatives should be the norm; the cases of both emperor and *meretrix* were generally shocking. Unknown: *Dig.* 31.34.3; 32.42 (1/12).
69. *Dig.* 22.1.48 (usufruct of 1/3), 34.2.18 (1/10); *BGU* 600?
70. There is only one instance of the latter: *P. Coll. Youtie* 64, where a brother is named heir and the wife receives a legacy.
71. This should not need arguing, given the absolute supremacy of the cogna-tic family (and the preference of testators for male heirs). However, the sheer number of references to legacies in the Digest should not mislead: legacies and related subjects absorb by far the greatest share of the lawyers' interest.
72. Land: Pliny *Ep.* 8.18.8; *P. Coll. Youtie* 64 (5½ iugera, one-half of house); *P. Mich.* 439 (including house's contents); *P. Oxy.* 907; *P. Oxy.* 2474 (one-half of house and contents, one-fourth of land); *Dig.* 32.33 pr. (part of house); 32.37 pr. (*fundus*); 33.4.9 (*fundus*); 33.5.22 (*praedia*); probably 33.10.13 (*pace* Modestinus). Slaves: *P. Oxy.* 2474; *Dig.* 31.88.7; 34.2.18 pr.; 34.4.31 pr.; 34.5.28. Wine, oil, grain, vinegar, honey, and pickled fish: *Dig.* 33.6.7 pr. Unknown: heirs with *fideicommissum* to alienate estate (n. 23 above): at *Dig.* 32.41.14, legacies for the fiduciary heir are explicitly mentioned. Substitutes: *Dig.* 28.6.47; 29.4.27 pr.; 36.1.26 pr.; 40.5.41.10.
73. Basic here is Boyer, "Fonction sociale," 374–95: I have considerably recast his typology.
74. *Dos: Dig.* 24.1.54; 31.88.7 (*praelegatum*); 33.4.9; 33.4.12; 33.4.16; 33.4.17 pr.; 33.4.17.1; 36.2.31 (if not heir); 40.5.19.1. Dotal land: *Dig.* 31.77.5. *Pro dote: Dig.* 33.4.8. The subject merited a chapter in the Digest, 33. 4, "De dote praelegata."

in a sense, is the legacy of what the husband had already given to
the wife while alive: gifts between husband and wife being illegal,
the legacy transferred ownership of something already in the
wife's possession.[75] And here we should add the *legatum debiti*, the
repayment of what was owed by the husband to his wife.[76] What
binds these three together is that each gives or returns to the wife
something that is in a sense already hers or, to put it another way,
none involves a posthumous diminution of the patrimony.

A second and equally important mode is headed by the assignment of usufruct to the widow, including under that term the
varieties of temporary enjoyment of property (*usufructus, usus,*
and *habitatio*). Normally a life interest for the widow is intended,
though a time limit is perfectly possible. And, again normally, the
interest is either in all or part of the testator's estate, or in specified farms or houses.[77] Alongside usufruct should be set various
forms of annuity to be paid by the heir in cash, income, or provisions.[78] Usufruct and annuity share the important characteristic
that each provides for the welfare of the widow without perma-
nently reducing the patrimony, both being temporary and usually
closely restricted in nature.

Third, the personal possessions of the wife, generally described as *uxoris causa parata,* and embracing clothing (*vestis* or
*vestimenta*), jewelry (*ornamenta*), and aids to beauty (*mundus muliebris*).[79] These three appear together often enough for us to suspect
that they were regarded as a unity. Here, again, the wife receives
something which is already in her possession, and there is no

75. *Dig.* 32.33.1; 34.2.13.
76. *Dig.* 32.93.1; 34.3.28.13.
77. Usufruct: Cicero, *Caec.* 11 (all goods); *Dig.* 22.1.48 (1/3); 33.2.32.2–4
(house and all contents); 33.2.35 (villa for 5 years); 33.2.37 (goods until daughter
reaches 18). *Usus: Dig.* 7.9.11 (house). *Fructus: Dig.* 33.2.24 pr. (goods); 33.2.25
(*praedia*).
78. Cash: *Dig.* 33.1.5 (10 *aurei*); 33.1.10.2 (100 *aurei*, but determined by Papinian to be a single payment). Income: *Dig.* 33.2.22 (*patrimonii reditus*); 33.2.38 (*fundi
reditus*). Provisions: *Dig.* 33.9.1 pr. (*penus*).
79. Combinations: *Dig.* 32.100.2 (*vestem mundum muliebrem ornamenta omnia
aurum argentum*); 33.2.39 (*vestem mundum muliebrem lanam linum et alias res*); 34.2.13
(*mundum muliebrem omnem ornamenta et quidquid vivus dedi donavi eius causa compara-
vi confeci*); 34.2.30 (*mundum ornamenta seu quae eius causa paravi*); 34.2.32.6 (*vestem
mundum muliebrem omnem ornamentaque muliebria omnia lanam linum purpuram versi-
coloria facta infectaque omnia*); cf. 33.4.17 pr. (*quidquid ei paravi*). Jewelry: *Dig.*
31.88.7 (*ornamenta*); and the combinations just listed. Beauty aids: *Dig.* 34.2.39 pr.
(*mundus muliebris*). *Quae usus eius parata sunt: Dig.* 31.35.

reason to believe that they were anything but a minor part of the estate, of practical or sentimental value.

Fourth, and in a class by itself, comes the legacy of money, bullion, and plate.[80] This is worth noting because it was not the sort of legacy children received, being normally assigned to friends or relatives. Some of it will have been of sentimental significance, and although it did diminish the patrimony it was not income producing; its value relative to the whole estate was presumably modest.

Thus, the testamentary treatment of wives shows clear if not universal tendencies. Wives could of course be heirs to all or a major part of the estate, or they could receive the same legacies as anyone else: individual factors could sway every case, above all the absence of children. But the norm was different. Particularly favored wives were left one-half or less of the property, an equal or greater share going to the testator's blood relations, his children before all—in these cases the husband surely assumed that his widow would in her turn bequeath her property to their children (a result sometimes explicitly arranged through a *fideicommissum*). Otherwise legacies to the wife who was not an heir fall into recognizable categories, embracing significant but otherwise minor goods, lifetime support, or the grant of what was already hers. In brief, and generally speaking, wives were fondly remembered and their welfare carefully considered, but they were firmly separated from the bulk of the patrimony. The gap between law and practice is not so wide as it initially appears.

This treatment of the wife was replicated in the treatment of a surviving parent, who for legal and demographic reasons was almost always the widowed mother, where the testator was childless and normally unmarried. That is to say, she was left a coheir or received a *legatum partitionis,* or she was given temporary enjoyment of all or part of the estate through a fiduciary inheritance or

---

80. Money: Pliny *Ep.* 8.18.8; Cicero *Cluent.* 33 (conditional); Phaedrus 4.5 (100,000); *CPL* 221 (50 silver drachmae); *CPR* 6.2.76 (one silver talent); *Dig.* 31.88.7 (10); 32.30.5 (200); 33.4.12 (10 denarii plus *dos*). Bullion: Cicero *Caec.* 12 (*grande pondus argenti*). Plate: *Dig.* 32.100.2 (*aurum argentum quod eius causa factum paratumque esset*); 33.5.22; 34.2.40.1 (*argentum balneare*); 34.2.32.3 (*argentum escarium*). Statues or busts: *Dig.* 34.2.18 pr. (*species argenti*).

a legacy of usufruct or annuity—in a word, for inheritance purposes, she was the wife of the testator's father.[81]

Naturally, most of our evidence concerns the treatment of widows, but female testators subscribed to the same principle as male, that is, that surviving spouses were to be treated well but kept separate from the property which was passed on to the children. They faced, however, a problem not faced by men: if their husband survived them there was a good chance that any children would be in his *patriapotestas*, hence that any property left to them would automatically pass into their father's possession. Society assigned to the *bona materna* a special significance, recognizing the child's prior claim to it, and the custom arose that fathers should either turn such property over to the children as *peculium* or bequeath it to them at death.[82] But no law bound anyone to following that custom. Therefore, a wife could institute her child heir in her will with the attachment of a condition of emancipation or a *fideicommissum* to the father to emancipate.[83] (And, by the same

81. Only heir named: *P. Oxy.* 2857; *P. Princ.* 38; *CIL* 3.656; *Dig.* 31.77.23. Coheir: *Vita Persi* (with testator's sister); Apuleius *Apol.* 97.4 (brother); *Dig.* 31.88.16 (with wife et al.); 33.1.20 pr.; 34.1.18.3 (with father and *postumi*); 36.1.82 (with uncle and creditors). *Legatum partitionis:* Cicero *Caec.* 12 (*partem maiorem bonorum*); Cicero *Cluent.* 21. Fiduciary heir: *Dig.* 34.4.31.1 (to father-in-law); 49.14.48.1 (to X at death). Usufruct: *Dig.* 33.2.32.1; *test. Alexandri* 116 (*habitatio*). Annuity: *Dig.* 33.9.7 (*penus*); *test. Alexandri* 116. *Dig.* 32.37 pr. records a testator who bequeathed to his mother a property owned by her, with *fideicommissum* to transfer it to his wife.

82. Humbert, *Remariage*, 246–52; Y. Thomas, "Droit domestique et droit politique à Rome: Remarques sur le pécule et les *honores* des fils de famille," *MEFRA* 94 (1982): 527–80, at 555–61. A prime case is offered by Tacitus at *Ann.* 13.43.8. Cf. Philostratus *VS* 558, Herodes Atticus assigns his wife's goods to their unpleasing son; *HA Marcus* 7.4, Marcus assigns their mother's goods to his dead sister's son; probably Tacitus *Ann.* 3.18.1; *Dig.* 31.77.20, mother's goods to brothers; 31.77.19 (*praelegatum* of wife's goods to daughter); 33.7.2 (*praelegatum* to son of mother's property).

83. Humbert, *Remariage*, 226–32. E.g., Suetonius *Vit.* 6; Pliny *Ep.* 4.2.2 (Regulus' wife); *Dig.* 5.3.58; 29.7.6 pr., 35.1.70; *CJ* 3.28.25; 6.25.3; 8.54.5. *Dig.* 37.1.23 pr. concerns a *fideicommissum* left by a divorced wife to go to her sons after their father's death, so imposed in the belief that he would not emancipate them while alive. The families of the father, an ex-praetor in rank named Brasidas, and of his wives have been elucidated in great detail from inscriptions by A. J. S. Spawforth, in "Families at Roman Sparta and Epidaurus: Some Prosopographical Notes," *PBSA* 80 (1985): 191–258, esp. 224 ff.; and the legal issues are discussed by J. F. Gardner, "Another Family and an Inheritance: Claudius Brasidas and His Ex-wife's Will," *LCM* 12 (1987): 52–54. Ironically, the property fell into the hands of the descendants of the husband and his second wife through a subsequent cousin-marriage.

token, a near relative of the wife could leave property to her children imposing the same condition on her husband.[84]) The cause of this may have been discord between the wife (or her relatives) and the husband, possibly a divorce compounded by the danger of the husband's remarrying and producing more heirs; but that problem is seldom explicitly recorded, even when the observer had good reason to do so.[85] That is to say, as with disinheritance, the act was probably less one of anger than one of cool calculation, an effort to make likelihood certain.

Consideration of kin outside of the nuclear family shows how neatly bound was the universe of the Roman testator: whether as heirs or as legatees they are strikingly unimportant beyond siblings and their descendants. This is not so banal an observation as it might appear: in a preindustrial, largely agricultural empire geographical mobility would be relatively low, and at Rome vestiges of the claims of gentile ties remained in the law well into the classical period. Even the rules of intestate succession as modified by praetorian law recognized not only the claims of any agnate but those of cognatic second cousins and their children; that is, a far greater range was permitted on intestacy than was ever considered by testators.[86] To put the matter in another perspective: beyond the nuclear family testators were far more likely to look to friends and freedmen for heirs and legatees, than to first cousins as such.

Kin are occasionally discovered as coheirs of a testator with surviving children, wife, or parent, but only scandalously did they exclude the testator's survivors altogether.[87] More normally, close kin shared the inheritance with them, and the circumstances are so clearly delimited that a pattern can be claimed: the Roman testator with children would normally institute a close male rela-

84. Pliny *Ep.* 8.18.4. Possibly *Dig.* 28.5.47; 35.1.77 pr. (grandmother and grandson); 36.1.52; 36.2.27. At 35.1.93, a grandmother has her son emancipate his children.

85. E.g., Pliny *Ep.* 4.2.2. Only at *CJ* 3.28.25 is there explicit indication of suspicion of the husband's character.

86. To be precise, intestate succession recognized cognate heirs up to the sixth and in some cases seventh degree of relationship; in practice, testators very very seldom looked beyond the third (nephews and nieces).

87. Pliny *Ep.* 6.33, 8.18.

tive (sometimes a female) as heir only if he was to share the inheritance with a closer female (daughter, mother, wife), or with a prepubescent son.[88] The concern here will have been less with the continuance of the patrimony in the family than with the proper execution of the terms of the will.

The relatives most frequently named as heirs or legatees are brothers.[89] After them, in roughly the same numbers, come sisters and nephews (both brothers' and sisters' sons).[90] Nieces, however, are never mentioned.[91] The preference for the male—for brothers over sisters, for nephews over nieces—and for the nearer over the more remote, is clear, and unsurprising. Equally to be expected, in parallel with the treatment of daughters, is the lack of distinction between agnatic and cognatic nephews. What is striking is the absence of nieces, for here the rules of intestacy and the wishes of testators come very close together: except for the blurring of the distinction between brothers' and sisters' sons, practice exactly parallels the rule in effect from the late republic onwards, that the intestate category of *proximus agnatus* included no female beyond sisters.[92]

---

88. Daughter: Plutarch *Cato Min.* 11 (half-brother); *P. Col.* 188 (siblings and wife); (*Dig.* 22.1.3.3 [*propinquus* fiduciary heir]); 32.32 (nephews).

Wife: Cicero *Att.* 13.26.2, 28 (brother); *P. Col.* 188 (siblings and daughter); (*P. Coll. Youtie* 64 [brother *ex asse*]); *Dig.* 49.14.9 (sister and father-in-law).

Mother: Cicero *Caec.* 10–12 (cognate); Cicero *Cluent.* 21, 33 (nephew); *Vita Persi* (sister); Apuleius *Apol.* 97.4 (brother); *Dig.* 36.1.82 (uncle and creditor).

*Pupillus:* Suetonius *Claud.* 1.5 (stepson); Macrobius *Sat.* 3.15.6 (brother-in-law).

89. Heir: Pliny *HN* 7.176–77; Cicero *Fam.* 13.30; *Fam.* 13.26 and 28; Valerius Maximus 7.8.4; Cicero *Quinct.* 14, 15, 38–39; *Att.* 6.1.10; *Verr.* 2.1.123–24; Pliny *HN* 7.177; *P. Col.* 188; *P. Coll. Youtie* 64; *Stud. Pap.* 20.35; *Dig.* 19.1.13.5; 28.5.86 pr.; 28.7.23; 31.69.3; 31.77.14; 34.3.28.10; 36.1.80.2 and 3.

Legatee: *CPL* 221; *Dig.* 28.6.46; 31.77.20; 33.7.27.5; 34.4.30.4; 36.2.26 pr.

Tutor (and presumably legatee): Cyprian *Ep.* 1.1.1; Cicero *Verr.* 2.1.130–53; *Dig.* 26.7.47 pr.; 36.1.38.1. *Fideicommissarius* (and presumably heir or legatee): *Dig.* 31.77.31; 34.3.20 pr.

90. Sisters: Suetonius *Gaius* 24.1 (heir); *Vita Persi* (coheir); *P. Col.* 188 (coheirs); *P. Oxy.* 2474 (legatee); *PSI* 696 (coheirs); *PSI* 738 (heir); *Dig.* 25.4.4 (legatee); 29.5.22 (heir); 33.1.18.1 (coheir); 33.7.20.7 (legatee); 33.7.27.4 (legatee); 35.2.15.1 (heir); 49.14.9 (coheir).

Nephews; Pliny *Ep.* 6.33? (coheir); Valerius Maximus 7.8.5 (coheir); Suetonius *Nero* 34.5 (heir); Cicero *Cluent.* 21, 33 (heir); Cicero *Off.* 3.73–74 (heir); Suetonius *Claud.* 6; *Dig.* 29.4.27.1 (substitute); 28.5.79.2 (substitute); 31.86.1 (legatee); 32.32 (coheir); 32.41.12 (legatee); 34.9.16 pr. (substitute); 35.1.36 pr. (legatee); 36.1.80.8 and 9 (legatee); 38.8.9.1 (coheir). Great-nephews: Suetonius *Caes.* 83 (coheirs); *Claud.* 4.7 (legatee).

91. The one exception being the legacy of Matidia Augusta to her great-nieces: Fronto *Am.* 1.14.

92. Gaius 3.14; Ulpian *Reg.* 26.6; Justinian *Inst.* 3.2.3a.

Beyond siblings and their offspring, testators showed very little interest in their relatives as such. Uncles and aunts are almost never mentioned (age is obviously of some relevance), and cousins of any degree were very rarely heirs, that is, they appear mostly as legatees, fiduciary heirs, tutors, and the like.[93] Here then is the boundary of the testator's familial universe: it included kin to the third degree in the descending but not ascending generation. Regardless of the historical origins of the family, and of the rules of intestate succession, beyond this point testators turned to their friends and their servants before their more distant kin, as both heirs and legatees. One of the more striking illustrations of this is the aristocratic practice of instituting heirs with a condition that they take on the testator's name ("testamentary adoption"): with the exception of the occasional nephew, testators looked to their friends rather than to blood kin to carry on the name.[94]

The location of the border between kinship and friendship is further defined by the testator's treatment of half-blood and affinity. Stepsons and half-brothers might join or even exclude other relatives,[95] but far more commonly remembered were certain close relatives by marriage, sons-in-law (Pompey was Caesar's heir when married to Julia), daughters-in-law, and fathers-in-law.[96] By benefiting these near affines the testator

---

93. Heir: cf. *Dig.* 31.77.29 (*consobrina*); Valerius Maximus 7.7.2 (*sanguine coniuncti*); Cicero *Fam.* 13.29.3–4; Tacitus *Ann.* 14.40 (*propinquus*, but forged); Seneca *Tranq. Anim.* 11.10 (but forced by Caligula); Plin. *Ep.* 4.10 (cognate ?, with *extranei*). Heir with *fideicommissum: Dig.* 19.1.13.3; 36.1.28.16. Legatee: *Dig.* 29.5.26 (*frater patruelis*); 33.7.3.1; 35.1.101; Tacitus *Ann.* 1.8 (*propinqui* substituted with *amici*); Cicero *Caec.* 10–12 (probably *cognatus*); Plutarch *Cato Min.* 6.7; *BGU* 326. Tutor: *HA Hadr.* 1.4 (*consobrinus*); *BGU* 388; *P. Hamb.* 70.

94. Below, pp. 144–46.

95. Stepson (*privignus*): Suetonius *Aug.* 101.2 (coheir with sons); Plutarch *Sulla* 2.8 (heir); *HA Pius* 1.6 (coheir); *Dig.* 34.4.31.2 (legatee).

Half-brother: Cicero *Cluent.* 21, 33 (heir); Plutarch *Cato Min.* 6.7 (coheir with daughter); *Vita Vergili* (coheir with friends).

96. Son-in-law (*gener*): Suetonius *Caes.* 83; Valerius Maximus 7.8.1 (heir); *Dig.* 23.3.48.1 (legatee); 35.1.71.3 (legatee); 36.1.80.8 and 9 (legatee; also nephew).

Daughter-in-law (*nurus*): *Dig.* 35.1.101.3 (legatee conditional on remaining married); 36.1.77.1 (heir by *fideicommissum*, to pass to son).

Father-in-law (*socer*): *Dig.* 34.4.31.1 (legatee); 49.14.9 (coheir with daughter and testator's sister).

Brother-in-law: Macrobius 3.15.6.

*Adfines:* Pliny *Ep.* 8.18 (legatees: all remembered *pro officio*); *Dig.* 33.7.27.1 and 2 (legatee); 34.3.28.5 (legatee); *CIL* 6.10229 (legatee with *fideicommissum*).

presumably hoped to protect the interests of their mutual descendants.[97]

The boundaries of familial affection are thus clear. Beyond the nuclear family, and clearly behind them in terms of interest and affection, only siblings and their children were normally important to the Roman testator as having a call upon their common blood. In practice then, testators had little interest in kin as kin, beyond (in Roman terms) the third degree.[98]

This practice may be compared with two kinship boundaries (*Verwandtschaftsgrenzen*) in law. First, civil and praetorian law were considerably more liberal or cautious in their estimate of the furthest possible extent of family affection, when it came to determining the disposition of property. The Lex Cincia de donis et muneribus (204 B.C.), for instance, allowed gifts over a certain value (no longer known) to be given only to persons within the fifth (in one exception the sixth) degree of kinship to the donor.[99] The subsequent Lex Furia testamentaria (before 169) extended this boundary by allowing legacies valued at over 1000 asses to go only to relatives within the sixth (in one exception the seventh) degree, that is, to second cousins (or the child of a second cousin); and that degree of kinship became fixed as the notional limit of family affection. Accordingly, unmarried or childless kin within that boundary were probably exempted from the penalties of the Augustan marriage laws, normally applied to people in their position, and thus all relatives within that boundary were allowed *bonorum possessio* on intestacy in the class of cognates (any relative beyond the boundary having to cede to a surviving spouse).[100]

97. On the importance of common descendants as a bond between affines, see Pliny *Ep.* 8.10.3.

98. It is of course possible that more distant kin did often appear as heirs and legatees, but were not identified as kin. If so, the lack of specificity is itself the significant element. A very similar testamentary ranking can be observed in early modern times: K. Wrightson, "Kinship in an English Village: Terling, Essex, 1500–1700," in *Land, Kinship and Life-cycle*, ed. R. M. Smith (Cambridge, 1984), 313–32, at 324–25.

99. *Frag. Vat.* 298–299 (Paul).

100. Lex Furia: *Frag. Vat.* 301 (Paul). Lex Iulia et Papia Poppaea: *Frag. Vat.* 216–19; for discussion of the exact degree exempted see A. Wallace-Hadrill, "Family and Inheritance in the Augustan Marriage Laws," *PCPS* 207 (1981): 58–80, at 73–78, and R. Astolfi, *Lex Iulia et Papia*² (Padua, 1986), 72–78. *Bonorum*

The sixth or seventh degree was the limit of what was allowed, to satisfy the testator or to ensure the transmission of property within a family. The inner boundary, the limit of what was compelled, was recognized by the law in the *querela inofficiosi testamenti* at, essentially, the third degree: ascendants, descendants, and (in certain circumstances) siblings of the testator.[101] In practice then, testators adhered much more closely to this inner boundary, with little inclination to move beyond the nuclear family: here lay the *officium pietatis*.

Thus duty and affection clearly predominate over weaker obligations to the extended family or kindred, an observation confirmed by the preference for close half-blood and affinity, people physically closer to the testator, over more distant cognates. Hence it is not surprising that, beyond the family and very near kin as defined and as treated in the modes discussed, Roman testators turned to their servants and their friends.

---

*possessio:* e.g., *Dig.* 38.8.1 (Ulpian). Probably to be mentioned in this context as well is the exemption of the "closest relatives" from Augustus' new 5 percent inheritance tax: Dio 55.25.5.

101. Third degree: it is virtually unthinkable that such a suit might ever be brought in real life by a great-grandparent or a *sui iuris* great-grandchild (both in the fourth degree).

# 7

## Servants and Friends

### Freedmen and Freedwomen—
### Slaves—Friends—Emperor

Natural affection extended little beyond the nuclear family, there to be replaced by a social affection for those who had helped and supported the testator through life. Outside the family lie two sharply delineated categories of individuals with personal ties to the testator, ties recognized by particular modes and patterns of bequest: friends and servants.[1] The latter, historically in close relationship with the family, and normally living with or near it, are essentially slaves and former slaves. From a testator's point of view these fall into three distinct groups: freedmen and freedwomen manumitted by the testator while alive, *inter vivos*; slaves freed by the will or following its instructions; and slaves who remained unfree, property. All appear frequently in wills and each is treated very differently.

Ties between *liberti* or *libertae* and their former masters could be extraordinarily strong, not simply legal and economic, but emotional as well, and they continued after death: Pliny mentions with approval the extreme example of *pietas* offered by P. Catienus Philotimus, whose patron had instituted him heir to all of his property, yet who so loved his master that he threw himself onto the funeral pyre.[2] More illuminating are the shafts of light cast by the Digest: one testator knows what affection his *liberti* feel for his

---

1. There is also a category of people lying between family and friends/servants: *alumni*. A careful recent study concludes that the alumnal relationship is one of quasi-adoption, marked by affection on both sides and by the "adopter's" concern for the economic future of the *alumnus*: H.S. Nielsen, "*Alumnus*: A Term of Relation Denoting Quasi-adoption," *C&M* 38 (1987): 141–88. Since the relationship is one of superior and dependent, since the majority of *alumni* appear to be of slave origin, and since they are often mentioned as legatees as a group rather than individually, they are perhaps best treated with *liberti*.
2. *HN* 7.122.

children; another appoints them tutors for his children; a third takes care that three of them, old and infirm, will be allowed to grow old in peace in their current residence; and yet another affirms that his heir will know which of them were dear to him.[3] And beyond these explicit marks of affection are those implicit in the bequests themselves. Conversely, there is little in wills about ingratitude: not that all was amity between masters and their former slaves, but that the law provided ample recourse against ungrateful freedmen or freedwomen, who had no claim upon the estate under any circumstances. The ungrateful intrude occasionally where testators have changed their minds after (or even while) making their wills, but more often where they are excepted by name from the benefit of burial assigned to the testator's *liberti libertaeque* as a group.[4]

The most favored *liberti* or *libertae* might be instituted as heirs, in certain circumstances. First, they were not normally sole heirs. So regularly are they named as coheirs, if only with their fellows, that in the rare cases where no other heirs happen to be mentioned we may assume that there too they shared the estate with other *extranei*.[5] But second, they were probably never admitted to heirship when the testator had surviving children. In only one case do we hear of a freedman coheir with children, and that case is rather unusual: "Gaius Seius, dying, named as heir among his

3. Cf. Boyer, "Fonction sociale," 355; *Dig.* 32.39 pr.; 33.2.33.2; 34.1.5; 26.7.58 pr. On patronal/libertine affection: G. Fabre, *Libertus: Recherches sur les rapports patron-affranchi à la fin de la république romaine* (Rome, 1981), 242–52.

4. *Dig.* 32.37.2: a *libertus* instituted and then subsequently removed, *de me nihil merito.* 34.4.29: a legatee later termed *ingratus* in the same will. *CIL* 6.12649 is an extract from the will of a man devastated by his daughter's death. Their bones were to be mixed in an altar: *Circa aram libertis libertabusque posterisq. eorum et quibus permiserint [? sollemnia facere liceat] hac lege, ut quotiens quis eorum suis coronas ponent, et aram nostram coronent. Atimeto lib. cuius dolo filiam amisi, restem et clavom, unde sibi alliget. CIL* 6.10229.92: "Dasumius" excepts from his tomb Hymnus *pess[ime de me merito].* For other such exceptions, see chapter 9.

5. Coheirs: Cicero *Att.* 13.12, 13, 50 (+ 3 *amici*); *Caec.* 10–12 (+ husband and *amicus*); *Fam.* 13.46 (+ at least 1 *amicus*); *Verr.* 2.1.123–24 (+ several *amici*); Petronius *Sat.* 76.1 (+ emperor); Suetonius *Vit.* 14.2 (+ emperor); *Dig.* 28.5.79 pr. (*bona materna*); 33.7.27.3 (*in parte*); 33.8.23 pr. (1/2); 34.4.30.1 (1/12); 37.14.12 (+ sons); 39.5.35 pr. (2/3); 40.7.40.2 (*ex parte*).
*Ex asse*: Pliny *HN* 7.122; *Dig.* 32.37.2 (2 *liberti*).
Simple mention as heir(s): *Dig.* 32.38.1; 38.2.35; *CIL* 2.1359. *Dig.* 33.2.34.1 has two *nutrices* to 1/10 each and an *alumnus* to the other 4/5, the former probably, the latter possibly freed. Fabre, *Libertus*, 278–81.

children his freedman Julius, to a share, as if he were himself a son."[6] Normally, the coheirs will have been friends of the testator, and the estate split up: there is, interestingly, in Cicero's matter-of-fact accounts of such affairs, no hint of any stigma arising for a friend when he was named to share the estate with former slaves of the deceased. Close relatives of the testator are conspicuously absent in these cases, suggesting again that affection overcame mere kinship as the basis for institution.

Clearly the most favored *liberti* and *libertae* were on a level with friends and in some cases preferred to them, in a quasi-filial or amorous or fraternal relationship: one is like a son, another the *deliciae* of his former master, a third the foster sister of her mistress.[7] But unlike most *amici*, they had taken their masters' names; now they were actually their heirs and in a very important sense they carried on the family.[8]

There is a tremendous gap between the favored few left as heirs and the far more common legatees. Legacies to freedmen and freedwomen tended to be more circumscribed in their natures than legacies to others, being commonly in a broad way either terminal or conditional, or both: seldom did a testator bequeath ownership of a thing to them directly and without strings. Two modes of legacy dominate in the Digest.[9]

The first is, in effect, a pension payable by the heir. This can, and does, come in a few common forms, all discussed at length by the jurists, who are almost the only source for it. The simplest is the recurrent grant of food, *cibaria*.[10] This might be expanded to embrace clothing, *cibaria et vestiaria*.[11] And these in turn, when added to housing, *habitatio*, are subsumed under *alimenta*, which should be everything necessary to sustain life—the best-known example of this is the huge sum of 1,866,666 2/3 sesterces left by

6. *Dig.* 37.14.12 (Modestinus). Phaedrus tells of a case (3.10), purportedly resolved by Augustus, wherein a freedman, hoping to be named substitute heir by his master, plotted the destruction of the master's wife and son.

7. *Dig.* 37.14.12; Petronius *Sat.* 76.1 (C. Pompeius Trimalchio Maecenatianus); *Dig.* 34.4.30.1. At *Dig.* 28.8.11, the freedman is a son: perhaps common?

8. See below, pp. 175–80.

9. Cf. Boyer, "Fonction sociale," 342–55, to which the following is heavily indebted, but which is here modified in several ways.

10   *Dig.* 34.1.5; 34.1.18.1; 34.1.19; 34.1.15.1.

11. *Dig.* 34.1.12; 34.1 pr.; 34.1.15.2; 34.1.16.2; 34.1.18.5; 34.1.9.1.

the younger Pliny in the early second century for the support of one hundred of his freedmen.[12] The modalities of these pensions could vary: they could be granted in kind or in cash;[13] the quantity could be specified (where applicable) or not, or "what I gave while alive," or left to the heir's discretion;[14] and while lifetime support would be tacitly understood, the testator could easily set a terminus or a condition.[15] Beyond these, but for the same alimentary purposes, the testator could simply allot an annuity (sometimes the income generated by a particular property, *ex reditu fundi*), or direct that the freedman continue to receive the same pension which the testator had granted while alive (*quae vivus/a praestabam*).[16] In short, the pension offered a form of liberality to old servants which was valuable but restricted in scope and duration.

Closely aligned with the pension in purpose and effect were usufruct and the related servitudes. These tended to be limited only by the lifetime of the beneficiary and, where shared by more than one, shares accrued to survivors.[17] They are in fact very rare for freedmen and freedwomen. Here testators were presumably less generous than they were in the bequest of usufruct to their spouses, and tended more to the granting of simple *habitatio*, even of particular rooms or apartments (*diaetae*).[18]

The other major mode of legacy attested by the Digest was, at first sight surprisingly, the ownership of land.[19] Normally only one piece of property is involved, but it is given to all of the testator's ex-slaves or to a specified group: this generosity may have a par-

---

12. *Dig.* 34.1.6; 34.1.8; 34.1.13.1; 34.1.14.3; 34.1.16. pr.; 34.1.16.1; 34.1.16.2; 34.1.18 pr.; 34.1.20.1; 34.1.23; 35.1.84.1. Pliny: *CIL* 5.5262. The North African senator Q. Servaeus Fuscus Cornelianus later arranged *cur. universae libert. liberte* [sic] *et fili eorum alimentis annuis foti*: *CIL* 8.22721 = *ILS* 8978 (Gigthis).

13. *Dig.* 33.1.13.1; 31.88.11.

14. *Dig.* 34.1.15.1; 34.1.16.1; 34.1.15.2.

15. *Dig.* 34.1.13.1.

16. Annuity: *Dig.* 33.1.13.1; 33.1.19 pr.; 34.1.20.2; 35.3.3.4. *Quae vivus/a praestabam*: *Dig.* 33.1.10.3, 33.2.33.1; 34.1.16.1.

17. *Dig.* 7.2.1; *AE* 1940.94. Possibly *Dig.* 34.1.4 pr.; 33.2.34 pr. The norm is outright gift of the land (see below).

18. *Habitatio*: *Dig.* 32.41.1; 33.2.18; 33.2.33.2; 33.2.34.

19. Ownership of other kinds of property is recorded by the jurists, but was presumably of less interest to them: money (*Dig.* 31.29 pr.; 32.39 pr.); clothing (39.5.16); *tessera frumentaria* (5.1.52.1); *militia* (32.102.2, presumably cash); own *contubernalis* and children (32.41.2); no rendering of accounts (34.3.31.1).

ticular purpose. Very often, the ownership is bound by a *fideicom-missum* that the property not pass from the *nomen* (the family name) of the testator and his *liberti*, or that they not alienate it, or that shares accrue to survivors. Such legacies have long reminded observers of the scores of tomb inscriptions which show the build-ing of monuments for oneself, possibly for one's near relatives, and, time and again, for one's freedmen and freedwomen and their descendants, *libertis libertabusque suis posterisque eorum*, often with prohibitions of the property leaving the name of the testator. Further consideration of the coincidence and of the testator's motives is perhaps best left to the discussion of tombs and memo-ry, in Chapter 9.

Conditions and trusts imposed on freedmen and freedwomen, other than those mentioned, are not uncommon. Three stand out in particular.[20] First, an effort may be directed to the support of the testator's surviving family, by making legacies to freedmen and freedwomen conditional on their remaining with the testa-tor's children, wife, or parent.[21] Second, in line with this, *liberti* may be directed not only to care for the burial but to remain by the tomb.[22] And third, they may be directed to transfer all or part of their bequest to another person.[23]

In brief, legacies to *liberti* and *libertae* were closely hedged. Some were temporary inroads on the estate, either pensionary—and therefore paid by the heir and terminated at death or a predetermined date—or (more seriously restricting the heir, and therefore less common) personal servitudes such as usufruct. Others were bound by conditions or requests, most notably the demand that the freedman or freedwoman continue to perform services (*operae*) for the survivors. And where the actual ownership of property was transferred, such property was either insignifi-cant or, when it was land, closely tied with the preservation of the

20. Others include acting as tutors (*Dig.* 26.7.58 pr.) and distributing the testa-tor's goods (31.77.21).
21. *Dig.* 31.34.4 (children); 33.1.13.1 (wife); 34.1.13.1; 34.1.18.1 (mother); 35.1.72.1 (children); 35.1.84 (children); 35.1.101.4 (daughter).
22. Burial: Philostratus *VS* 565; *CIL* 6.10229, 112 (with the necessary restora-tion by R. Syme, "The Testamentum Dasumii: Some Novelties," *Chiron* 15 [1985]: 41–63, at 59 = *RP* 5 [1988] at 541). Remain at tomb: *CIL* 6.10229; *Dig.* 34.1.18.5, cf. 33.2.34 pr.; Petronius *Sat.* 71.
23. *Dig.* 31.89.6; 32.39 pr.; 33.1.21.1; 35.2.25.1.

testator's memory. Thus a vast gulf lies between the very few *liberti* and *libertae* who were so close to the testator as to win nomination as heir, and the much greater number of former servants who were fondly and comfortably, but not extravagantly, looked after.

There is a sharp line between these freedmen and freedwomen manumitted by the testator *inter vivos* and those manumitted by will or by testamentary *fideicommissum*. Superficially the treatments accorded to each group posthumously appear similar, but there are major differences.

The great question is "How many slaves were freed by will?"—a question that has figured peripherally in modern debate over the frequency of manumission in general.[24] Clearly there was, in the principate of Augustus at least, some perception of abuse in the mass emancipation of slaves testamentarily. In an oft-quoted but hardly extravagant passage, Dionysius of Halicarnassus complained that "I at any rate know of some men who have allowed their slaves to be freed after their death, so that when dead they might be called good men and their funerals might be attended by a throng of mourners wearing liberty caps on their heads."[25] And a much-cited but little-known law of the period made some attack on the practice: the Lex Fufia Caninia of 2 B.C. placed precise limits on the proportional numbers of a slave *familia* that might be freed in any testament.[26] But does this Augustan interest reflect a real and widespread condition, or merely one which was perceived to be serious in the light of contemporary concerns, regardless of how common or uncommon it may have been?[27]

24. See especially G. Alföldy, "Die Freilassung von Sklaven und die Struktur der Sklaverei in der römischen Kaiserzeit," reprinted most recently, with substantial additions, in his *Die römische Gesellschaft: Ausgewählte Beiträge* (Stuttgart, 1986), 286–331, arguing that urban and suburban slaves had good prospects of manumission if they survived to the age of 30; rejected by W. V. Harris, "Towards a Study of the Roman Slave Trade," *MAAR* 36 (1980): 117–40; and T. E. J. Wiedemann, "The Regularity of Manumission at Rome," *CQ* 35 (1985): 162–75.
25. 4.24.6 (Loeb translation, E. Cary). Cf. Petronius *Sat.* 42.6: *planctus est optime—manumisit aliquot*. For newly freed slaves as pallbearers: Persius 3.105–6.
26. Kaser, *Privatrecht*, 297.
27. K. M. T. Atkinson, for instance, argued forcefully that the Lex Fufia Caninia was intended not so much to halt widespread manumission as to protect the economic interests of heirs: "The Purpose of the Manumission Laws of Augustus," *Irish Jurist* 1 (1966): 356–74.

To begin with the most remote of possibilities, slaves manumitted by the will were far less likely to be named heir than were existing *liberti* and *libertae*, indeed such an action should signal highly extraordinary circumstances. The slaves who were thus instituted may have had a sexual liaison with the testator, up to and including respectable concubinage.[28] The slave named as heir may have been an illegitimate child of the testator.[29] Or a slave might be named as heir by an insolvent testator, who could expect no heir to take up the inheritance.[30] Or, by extension, a slave might be an *heres necessarius*, a substitute heir named in the last place to take up the inheritance if no one else would or could—the reason normally cited for such an institution is again the avoidance of possible insolvency.[31] The appointment of a necessary heir as substitute is a mark of care by the conscientious testator for the future of the inheritance, and possibly of esteem for the slave concerned, but it is not a sign that the testator ever expected that slave to be heir. Thus, one cautious testator carefully spelled out that "if my brother Titius does not wish to be my heir or (a possibility I regard with horror) should die before he enters into the inheritance, or should have no male or female child born to him, then let Stichus and Pamphilus my slaves be free and my heirs in equal parts"; while the testament of "Dasumius" shows so many heirs in the first and second degrees that the chance of the slave Syneros, mentioned last, ever succeeding was virtually nonexistent.[32] In the remaining handful of cases where there is no sign that the slave was emotionally close to the testator or being used as a barrier against insolvency and intestacy, the will ended up under attack in court.[33]

In brief, the manumission and institution as heir of a slave, though attested, would have been a rare and unlikely event: if

---

28. Possibly slave *deliciae* at Pliny *HN* 34.11 (cf. *ILS* 1924); perhaps also Trimalchio? Soldiers' concubines probably at *BGU* 326 (cf. A. Watson, "Identity of Serapio") and *P. Select.* 14. On the nature of concubinage in practice: S. Treggiari, "Concubinae," *PBSR* 49 (1981): 59–81.

29. *Dig.* 36.1.80.2 and 3.

30. Heir to insolvent: *Dig.* 28.5.58; 28.5.61.

31. Justinian *Inst.* 2.19.1; *Dig.* 28.5.55; 28.6.18 pr.

32. *Dig.* 28.5.86; *CIL* 6.10229 + Eck, "Zum neuen Fragment."

33. *Dig.* 5.3.7.1 (*inofficiosum*); 36.1.46 pr. (*suspecta hereditas*); 48.10.24 (*falsum*). *Dig.* 28.5.8 is not a real incident.

such an heir were so close to the testator, he or she would normally have been freed in the testator's lifetime.

Turning to the much more common legacies, all consequent to the major benefaction of manumission, we find initially that slaves and freed often won favor in identical forms, as is to be expected.[34] Slaves, like freed, can be rewarded with the ownership of property—land, goods, and cash—or like freed they can receive pensions in the form of *alimenta*, annuities, or usufruct.[35] But beyond that the testator might also choose from a range of three other gifts, each of them prompted by the recent servile status of the recipient and each normally irrelevant to freedmen and freedwomen.

One possible benefaction, from the time that the tax was instituted under Augustus, was to instruct the heir to pay the 5 percent tax on manumissions out of the estate, thereby saving the new citizen an immediate and significant expense, and demonstrating both magnanimity and the concern expected of a good master.[36] Secondly, for some it may have been customary in death as in life to award freed slaves their old *peculia*, which was an actual gift of property.[37] And thirdly, it would be a thoughtful humanitarian gesture to assign to them as legacies the ownership of their own families, that is, their partners (*contubernales*) and their children, whom they themselves could then free.[38] How far any of these

---

34. Here, slave = slave freed posthumously; freedman or freedwoman = slave freed *inter vivos*.

35. Land: Petronius *Sat.* 71.2; *BGU* 326 (acreage + 1/3 of house); *PSI* 1040 (1/4 of house); *Dig.* 31.87.2 (*fundus*); 31.88.6 (*praediolum*); 31.88.12 (*fundus*); 32.41.3 (*fundus cum casa*); 32.97 (*praedia*); 33.7.7 (*taberna*); 34.3.28.7 (*fundus instructus*).

Goods: Petronius *Sat.* 71.2 (*lectum stratum*); *PSI* 1040 (garment); *Dig.* 31.88.3 (*instrumentum tabernae ferrariae*).

Cash: *Dig.* 31.88.13; 34.5.29; 35.1.40.3 (debt); 40.7.21; *CIL* 6.10229 (1000 den. to each of 7 + slaves).

Alimenta: *Dig.* 31.88.11 (monthly); 34.1.10.1; 34.1.18 pr. (monthly); 34.1.18.2 (*cibaria* + *vestiaria*); 34.1.20 pr. (as in life); 34.1.20.3 (*cibaria* + *vestiaria*); 34.5.29.

Annuity: *Dig.* 33.8.23.1; 34.1.20 pr.; 36.2.27.1.

Usufruct: *Dig.* 33.2.32 pr.; 33.2.36 pr.

36. Petronius *Sat.* 71.2; *CPL* 221; *CIL* 6.10229, 53–55.

37. *PSI* 1040; *Dig.* 32.97; 33.8.8.2; 33.8.19.1; 33.8.23 pr.; 33.8.23.2; 34.1.18.3 (returning 1/3); 40.1.6; 40.7.21 pr. (*sua omnia*). Cf. the *testamentum Alexandri* (116), which awards freedom to certain islands and assigns their property to them.

38. Petronius *Sat.* 71.2; *Dig.* 32.37.7 (*omnes suos*); 32.41.2 (*contubernales* and children); 34.1.20 pr. (*contubernales* and children); *CIL* 6.10229, 41, 44 (*contubernales* and children).

options was exercised is not known, but each was open to the testator who wished to exhibit particular concern for the well-being of his or her slaves.

At the same time, slaves manumitted by the will tended to be bound much more by conditions or requirements than were those already free: unlike the slave freed *inter vivos*, testamentarily freed slaves (*liberti/ae orcini/ae*) had escaped the legal obligation to show their gratitude to their former masters through respect, services, and the bequest of property. Now they had to pay for their freedom.

Such payment might come in the form of hard cash from the *peculium*, just as regular freedmen or freedwomen might "pay" for their liberty,[39] but it came more commonly in a form conditional on, or subject to, service to another. Thus, it could be left to the discretion of the new master: "if they have deserved well of you, I ask that you think them worthy of liberty"; "I wish him to be free if it pleases my wife"; "let those slaves who have caused no offense be free."[40] Alternatively, the testator could request that slaves not be allowed to serve another master, in effect thus instructing their new owner to free them either *inter vivos* or testamentarily.[41] Most often, manumission is requested by *fideicommissum* after a specified period—one, two, five, seven, and ten years of service or payment are stipulated—or at some future event: at the death of an heir, or the marriage of a daughter, or when children reach puberty or sixteen years of age.[42] This service to another after the testator's death thus benefited both slave and heir: the slave whose liberty was postponed or made conditional (*statuliber*) was in various ways better treated than ordinary slaves, while the heir enjoyed valuable *operae* which might otherwise be lost by the death of the manumissor.[43] A similar end could be achieved by simple *fideicommissum* to render *operae* to, or to stay with, a designated

39. *Dig.* 12.6.53; 40.7.14 pr.; 40.7.29.1; cf. 34.1.18.3 (*fideicommissum* to return 1/3 of *peculium*).

40. *Dig.* 40.4.20; 40.5.14; 40.4.51.1.

41. *Dig.* 40.5.12 pr.; 40.5.21; 40.5.41.1.

42. *Dig.* 19.1.43 (1 year); 32.30.2 (2); 40.5.23.4 (5); 40.7.40.2 (5); 40.7.14.1 (7); 40.5.41. pr. (10), cf. 12.6.67 pr. (10); 40.5.41.16 (marriage); 40.8.8 (death); 40.5.41.10 (at 16); 40.5.41.13 (at 16); 40.5.56 (at puberty).

43. *Statuliber*: W. W. Buckland and P. Stein, *A Text-book of Roman Law*[3] (Cambridge, 1963), 74–76.

person, or by the bequest of a pension conditional on remaining with that person.[44]

Other testators required just one last service before manumission: certain slaves were to be freed only when they had properly accounted to the heir for everything in the estate or that part of it which they controlled. Thus, in the testament of Antonius Silvanus, after all other legacies, comes: "As for my slave Cronio, after my death, if he has handled everything properly and handed it over to my above-named heir or procurator, then I wish him to be free and I wish that the 5 percent tax be paid for him from my property."[45] Among those so manumitted by the testator "Dasumius" are to be found a nurse, fishermen, scribes, an accountant, a valet, and a tutor; but the only servants whose employment is noted by the jurists in the Digest are those agents who controlled significant wealth and who might therefore be more implicated in potential legal problems.[46] Such an accounting clause was surely standard in wills—even the emperor Augustus had something similar—to the point that a testator might feel obliged explicitly to request that accounts *not* be required of the manumittee.[47]

This accounting clause leads to consideration of the central questions of testamentary manumission: who was freed, and how many were they? The answers are complementary. First, occupations in the Digest and two papyri include numerous agents and maidservants, as well as a treasurer, a banker, a steward, doctors, a stenographer, the grandson of a nurse, servants, a manservant, a blacksmith, and an otherwise unidentified foster child, plus several others, likewise unidentified, who were at least in a position to render accounts; while among the slaves freed by "Dasumius" are a valet, a steward, a stenographer, a school slave, *piscatores* (keepers of fishponds?), and a clothing keeper.[48] Such a list easily breaks

44. *Dig.* 38.1.42; *P. Oxy.* 2474; *Dig.* 34.1.18.2; 34.1.20.3. Cf. service at the testator's tomb: 40.4.44.

45. *CPL* 221.31–37.

46. Dasumius: *CIL* 6.10229. *Dig.*: 4.3.32; 33.8.23 pr.; 33.8.23.1; 34.3.12 (*actor*); 40.4.22 (*ratione argenti, quod sub eius cura esset reddita*); 40.4.53; 40.4.59.2; 40.5.18; 40.5.41.10; 40.5.41.11; 40.5.41.13; 40.5.41.16; 40.5.41.17 (*arcarius*); 40.7.21 pr.; 40.7.40.1; 40.7.40.3; 40.7.40.7 (*actores*); 40.7.40.8 (*actores* of *argentarius*).

47. *Dig.* 34.3.28.7. Augustus: Suetonius *Aug.* 101.4.

48. *Dig.* 32.97; 34.1.18.3; 34.3.12; 40.5.41.4; 40.7.40.3; 40.7.40.7 (*actores*); *PSI* 1040; *Dig.* 31.83; 31.88.13; 40.4.59 pr.; 40.5.40; 40.5.41 pr. (*ancillae*); 40.5.41.17

down into two groups, that is, personal servants, and agents or assistants in business matters; all but absent, then, are agricultural workers and managers, and manual laborers. At the same time, numbers are instructive. Where testamentary manumission is involved, well over two-thirds of our references in the Digest are to one or two slaves, while even allowing for lacunae in the inscription, the will of the dauntingly wealthy "Dasumius" mentions few more than a dozen slaves, each by name and occupation. Of the wills preserved on papyrus, only three troubled to liberate slaves: the rest, some of them substantially preserved, all of their authors wealthy enough to own slaves, are silent.[49]

From the evidence of wills alone, we should conclude that the large-scale testamentary manumissions scorned by Dionysius and curbed by Augustus were not very widespread, subsequently at least. Such slaves as were manumitted posthumously would normally be skilled and personally close to the master: the majority of slaves simply do not appear in wills. Where the nonmanumitted do turn up, it is invariably in the form of specified individuals or groups being bequeathed to specified heirs or legatees.[50] The silent majority, agricultural workers personally unknown to their masters, appear rarely and impersonally, as in the will of the testator who left eight rural slaves to his concubine, with instructions to the heirs to continue the same provisions that the slaves had always received.[51] Or again, they are implicit in the innocent general term of bequest of an agricultural property, *fundus instructus*—a farm with equipment. Yet it is perhaps not quite right to

---

(*arcarius*); 40.7.40.8 (*argentarius*); 40.7.21 (*dispensator*); 40.5.41 pr. (*medici*); 40.5.41.3 (*notarius*); 34.1.20 (grandson of *nutrix*); *P. Oxy.* 2474 (*oiketai*); *Dig.* 40.4.59 pr. (*pedisequus*); 31.88.3 (blacksmith with *taberna ferraria*); 40.5.38 (*alumna*). Dasumius: *CIL* 6.10229, 36–55. Trimalchio at *Sat.* 70–71 gives generous legacies to two household slaves, whom he invites to join the company at table. The codicil of the *filiusfamilias* (*CIL* 10.7452) directs his father to manumit an alumnus and a *minister* (*qui solus ex ministerio meo superavit*).

49. *CPL* 221; *P. Oxy.* 2474; *PSI* 1040. *BGU* 326 and *P. Select.* 14 presumably concern soldiers' concubines and heirs.

50. *P. Oxy.* 907; *CIL* 6.10229, 66–79 (legacy to a female relative, probably his daughter, of [among others] a chamberlain, a depiler, a cobbler, and a doctor); Dig. 28.5.38 pr.; 30.36; 32.41.4 (five boys under seven); 32.41.5; 32.41.10; 32.69.1; 32.91.2; 32.92.5; 33.5.21 (choice of ten); 33.7.20 pr.; 33.7.20.1; 33.7.20.2; 34.1.15.1; 34.1.17; 34.5.28; 40.12.35.

51. *Dig.* 34.1.15.1.

draw a simple distinction between the ideal of manumission and the practice which did not live up to it.[52] Rather, building on the distinction between urban and rural recognized by all, one should look to a genuine double standard. The ideal was restricted and applied to the personal universe of the individual testators: they rewarded the merit and industry which they observed by recognizing the common humanity, or rather civility, of certain of their slaves. This was largely irrelevant to the human property which worked their rustic farms, vineyards, or ranches. Occasionally a testator might also posthumously punish an unsatisfactory slave by requesting that he or she not be manumitted, but that at least marked personal feeling.[53] The mass of slaves would be passed over silently, as part of the estate, to the heirs.

The other group, outside of his family, whose support in his lifetime the testator felt obliged to recognize posthumously, was his friends. The term "friend" must be applied elastically, to cover not only intimates but associates, social superiors, inferiors, or clients, and even employees or hirelings such as doctors or professors: anyone unrelated to and not formerly owned by the testator, but close enough to deserve the *officium*, and honor, of remembrance. As usual there is a sharp division between heirs and legatees, and again particular patterns may be discerned.

The nomination of a complete outsider to the family as heir marks not only exceptional affection or gratitude but, almost invariably, childlessness. Two exceptions merely reinforce the obvious rule; sometimes a friend might be entrusted as heir with a *fideicommissum* to hand the inheritance over to the testator's child, in order to avoid legal restrictions; and sometimes a testator might disinherit his or her child in anger, to the profit of *extranei*.[54] But the central point here is that the roughly one-fifth of Roman testators who in the course of nature would be childless seem to

52. As does Wiedemann, "Regularity."
53. Notoriously "Dasumius," in emotional terms at *CIL* 6.10229, 80–82; but also at *Dig.* 35.1.67 (*si servum non manumiserit*) and 40.5.40.1 (*ne unquam manumitteretur*).
54. Fiduciary heirs: Cicero *Fin.* 2.58 (to daughter), 2.55 (to daughter); *Dig.* 36.1.48 (to son at 16); 36.1.61 pr. (to daughter). Cf. Cicero *Verr.* 2.1.123–24 (to brother); Pliny *Ep.* 10.75 (to municipality).
Disinheritance: Cicero *Cluent.* 135; Pliny *Ep.* 5.1; 10.104; *Dig.* 5.2.19. Cf. Philostratus *VS* 516–18.

have looked for heirs among their friends rather than their kin. Sometimes we find friends sharing with relatives, sometimes explicitly or implicitly preferred over kin, sometimes the only heirs mentioned (and in some of those cases clearly the sole heir in reality).[55] Most strikingly of all, however, we find friends sharing with other friends.

In clear contrast to the conservative strategies of those with children, and with the restrained treatment of freedmen and freedwomen, there is a strong tendency among some of the childless not to make one friend sole heir but to split up the patrimony once and for all among several. Literature offers numerous instances. Thus Cicero casually, and mainly in his correspondence, notes by name the six good men and true (*viri boni et honesti*), all unrelated to the testator or to each other, who were named heirs by Q. Turius, a businessman active in Africa; two of the heirs of an otherwise unknown Balbullius, Julius Caesar (who received 1/12) and his officer Q. Lepta (1/3); four of the heirs of a Brinnius, including Cicero, a freedman of the deceased, and two others; four of the heirs of the Campanian banker M. Cluvius, Cicero, Caesar, and two others; two of the heirs of a businessman operating in Greece, M'. Curius, Atticus (heir to 1/10) and Cicero (1/40); two of the heirs of the architect Cyrus, Cicero and Clodius; two of several coheirs of a Herennius, Cato and Piso; three of the coheirs in the allegedly forged will of Minucius Basilus; four of the heirs of a Scapula, all unrelated; the many *viri boni et honesti* heirs, with

---

55. Coheir with relatives: Valerius Maximus 7.7.2 (nephew); Cicero *Fam.* 13.29.34 (*propinquus*); Tacitus *Ann.* 1.8 (substituted with *propinqui*); Cicero *Cluent.* 135 (with son, but replacing disinherited son); Quintilian 8.5.19 (with wife); *Dig.* 5.2.19 (with daughter, one daughter disinherited); 36.1.82 (with mother and uncle); 44.2.30 (with nearest agnate).

Over relatives (excluding fiduciary heirs and disinheritances): Cicero *Cluent.* 135 (over *propinquus*); Valerius Maximus 7.8.3 (over important relatives); Cicero *Off.* 3.73–4 (nephew nominal heir); *Rhet. ad Herennium* 1.23 (over brother); Cicero *Phil.* 2.40–41 (over nephew); *Dig.* 17.1.62 pr. (over uncle and aunts). One of the polite form letters of *P. Bon.* 5 congratulates a friend on being judged worthy by their mutual friend (*dignum iudicavit*) to receive no small part of the inheritance, although numerous *propinqui* survived (*non exiguo numero propinquorum relicto*).

Only heir mentioned (with same exclusions): Cicero *Att.* 15.2.4; Philostratus *VS* 490 (probably sole heir); Livy 39.9.5–7 (sole heir); Cicero *Att.* 11.12.4; Cicero *Arch.* 11 (often named heir, but not by his relatives since he was the first citizen in his family); Valerius Maximus 7.7.6 (*gallus*, almost certainly sole heir); Plutarch *Sulla* (sole); Tacitus *Ann.* 2.48.1 (probably sole); Lucilius 419–21 Kr. (sole); Cicero *Fam.* 7.21; Valerius Maximus 7.9.3 (sole heir, an enemy).

his freedman, of P. Trebonius; and several others.[56] These random vignettes are supported by a series of similar items in the correspondence of Pliny, who found himself named part heir to Minicius Acilianus, Pomponia Galla (along with another senator and several knights), a Sabina (along with a Sabinus), and a Saturninus (along with the town of Comum).[57] The most interesting case, in that we know something of the portions involved, is that of the childless Vergil, who left one-half of his estate to his maternal half-brother (representing their mother's property?), one-fourth to his great patron Augustus, one-twelfth to his original patron Maecenas, and one twenty-fourth each to his friends Varius and Tucca.[58] Some of the heirs in these various cases will have been friends in the standard sense of the word; but some of them were clearly also in some sense patrons, and some business associates or even employees.[59] Most notably, the majority of soldiers chose as heirs their comrades. Here more than anywhere one senses the lack of interest in family who are not descendants, the absence of a feeling that a patrimony must be handed over, augmented but otherwise intact, to the next familial heir: the childless entrusted their memory to their friends.

Memory is the key to one practice attested primarily among the higher aristocracy, that of "testamentary adoption." Considerable controversy as to its exact legality has been sustained by the most notorious example of such an adoption, that of Octavian in the will of Julius Caesar. It is generally agreed that it has nothing to do with the formal legal modes of adoption (and as such is all but unknown to the jurists), but is simply the institution of an heir under a *condicio nominis ferendi*, a condition that the heir take the

---

56. *Fam.* 12.26.1–2; *Att.* 13.48.1; *Att.* 13.12.4, 13.4, 50.2; *Att.* 13.45 et al. (with Shackleton Bailey ad loc.); *Att.* 7.2.3; *Mil.* 48; *Att.* 13.6.2; *Off.* 3.78–74; *Att.* 12.38a.2, 12.40.2; *Verr.* 2.1.123–24. Cf. Caesennia, instituting her husband, a freedman, and a friend Aebutius to 1/72 (or 1/6 of a 1/12 share: *Caec.* 17–18); Felix, possibly naming Q. Cicero to 1/12 (*Q. Fr.* 3.7.8); Fufidius naming Cicero and others (*Att.* 11.2, 13, 15); a Nostius naming Cicero and at least one freedman (*Fam.* 13.46); a Precius, naming Cicero to a modest share (*Att.* 6.9.2).

57. *Ep.* 2.16.1; 5.1; 4.10; 5.7.

58. *Vita Vergili*. Cf. Fronto *Am.* 2.5: Fronto heir to 5/12 of the estate of an imperial procurator. *Dig.* 28.5.48.2 appears to have four unrelated heirs to different shares (1/6, 5/12, 5/24, 5/24).

59. Cf. *Dig.* 18.5.8 (a procurator heir); 28.5.60.1 (a partner coheir); 31.88.3 (blacksmith).

testator's name. As with regular adoption, where the adoptee did formally take over most of the adopting parent's name, in practice the heir was free to use as little of that name as he wished, and whatever elements suited him—indeed some, like the future emperor Tiberius, or Cicero's wild son-in-law Dolabella, are never recorded as bearing their new names—and above all there was no change in agnatic position, that is, the new heir did not enter the testator's family.[60]

Many instances of the practice have been cataloged, and many more may be surmised, but the purpose remains unassessed (and no ancient authority discusses it). Central is the distinction between the artificial and misleading term "testamentary adoption" and the legally correct *condicio nominis ferendi*. The purpose of adoption *inter vivos* was the perpetuation of the family, the acquisition of *potestas* over new *sui heredes*. This was not a paramount consideration in the so-called testamentary adoption: if it were, the testator would surely have formally adopted his heir during his lifetime. Indeed, there is no sign of serious interest in the nearest relative, agnatic or cognatic, as heir: very few of the heirs thus "adopted" are known to have stood in any relationship whatever to the testator.[61] Moreover, the testator "Dasumius" left as major heir a woman who was almost certainly his daughter, hence he did not even need the "testamentary adoption" which he also instituted.[62] Testators did not want such heirs to carry on their family, they wanted them to perpetuate their own name, precisely as the condition stipulated. That is to say, "testamentary adop-

---

60. See most recently: E. J. Weinrib, "The Family Connections of M. Livius Drusus Libo," *HSCP* 72 (1967): 247–78; Schmitthenner, *Oktavian*, with bibliography. D. R. Shackleton Bailey, *Two Studies in Roman Nomenclature* (State College, Pa. 1976), 92–99, offers much useful commentary, but his doubts as to the *communis opinio* seem ill founded. Attested instances may be just the tip of the iceberg: R. Syme, "Clues to Testamentary Adoption," in *Tituli* 4 (Rome, 1982) 1: 397–410 = *Roman Papers* (Oxford, 1988) 4:159–70. Shackleton Bailey's lingering fears that the adoption may have had a legal basis are dealt a serious blow by the fact that women were legally incapable of adoption, yet a certain Livia is recorded as "adopting" Dolabella testamentarily: Cicero *Att.* 7.8.3. A key legal text is the extract from Gaius at *Dig.* 36.1.65.10, quoting Julian: both praetor and heir seem to have considerable discretion in meeting the condition or not.

61. Notably: Octavian, Julius Caesar's great-nephew; M. Satrius, the nephew of Minucius Basilus (Cicero *Off.* 13.74); Atticus (Cicero *Att.* 3.20.1).

62. *CIL* 6.10229. Unless, as has been commonly suggested, the heir was his son-in-law: unlikely, cf. Champlin, "Miscellanea," 251–55.

tion" was concerned more with supporting the memory of the individual testator. It was born of the same mentality that repeatedly bound the bequest of a piece of land with the *fideicommissum* or *modus* that it not leave the name (*ne de nomine exeat*), or that occasionally might award a double share to one grandson "in honor of my name."[63] As such it should be considered as part of the testator's concern for commemoration,[64] and should confirm that childless testators had no necessary interest in perpetuating their family, natural or artificial.

For those testators who had children or who preferred to institute other relatives as heirs, there still remained the major duty of honoring their friends with legacies. Here the value was far less important than the honor for the *amicus legato honoratus*, who was thus rewarded for his "reverent and faithful" cultivation of the deceased by being remembered and praised (*amicus fidelissimus*) in the will.[65] Motives have been reviewed earlier, but modes deserve further attention. Of course, a friend could be recognized and thanked with anything in the standard run of legacies, from a *legatum partitionis*, through land and slaves, through personal belongings, to usufruct and various forms of pensions (the latter particularly appropriate for inferiors).[66] But extra honor could be added by naming special friends as substitute heirs, with little

---

63. *Dig.* 31.76.5.

64. See below, chapter 9.

65. Pliny *Ep.* 7.31.5–6; *Dig.* 33.1.10 pr. For the reasons, see above p. 13. The subject of posthumously honoring one's friends has been much studied: e.g., W. Kroll, *Die Kultur der Ciceronischen Zeit*, vol. 1, *Politik und Wirtschaft* (Leipzig, 1933) 110–11; Wistrand, *Arv och testamenten.*

66. *Legatum partitionis: Dig.* 34.3.26.

Land: *Dig.* 31.78.4; 32.7.27; 33.39.1; Josephus *AJ* 18.31.

Slaves: *Dig.* 40.5.41.3; Josephus *AJ* 18.156. The sale, gift, or bequest of slaves to the imperial family in the first century (and to some others) can be traced through the retention of *agnomina* from the names of their former families: H. Chantraine, *Freigelassene und Sklaven im Dienst der römischen Kaiser: Studien zu ihrer Nomenklatur* (Wiesbaden, 1967), 295–388; P. R. C. Weaver, *Familia Caesaris: A Social Study of the Emperor's Freedmen and Slaves* (Cambridge, 1972), 212–23.

Minor Legacies: *Dig.* 34.2.40.2 (*ornamenta universa* to *amica*); *Vita Persi* (books to teacher); *Vita Vergili* (the manuscript of the Aeneid); Pliny *Ep.* 2.20 (clothes); *BGU* 327 (clothes).

Usufruct: *P. Oxy.* 907.

Pension: *Dig.* 33.1.10 pr. (annuity + *habitatio* if help children's business); 33.1.10.1 (what was given in life to doctor to continue); 33.1.19.1 (annuity to *homo doctus*); 34.3.28 pr. (*alimenta* to *pupilli*).

Funerary *ollae* or *aediculae: CIL* 6.9405, cf. 12713; 10236; 21161.

intent that they ever inherit, but with the subsequent award of a legacy: Augustus, for one, nominated both relatives and friends in the third degree, for the glory of it.[67] Similarly, trusted friends were very often appointed, sometimes several at a time, to the burdensome honor of acting as tutor to the testator's children—friends often, rather than relatives, since they did not suffer the conflict of interests which might beset a potential heir on intestacy.[68]

Beyond such honors, two forms of legacy seem to have been regarded as particularly appropriate to friends. One is the simple donation of cash. The prime example appears in the recently published second- or third-century will of a veteran who, after caring for his wife and children, set down a list of friends with individual bequests to each (several of the names are lost): 1 silver talent to a friend (*philos*) who was a soldier; 200 Caesarian drachmae to a veteran; 600 Caesarian drachmae to a soldier; 200 Caesarian drachmae to a veteran; 200 Caesarian drachmae each to a standard bearer and a veteran ; and an uncertain sum to another pair of veterans and *philoi*.[69] Similarly, the cavalry trooper Antonius Silvanus left 50 silver denarii to a comrade (who would act as procurator of the estate) and 50 to his prefect;[70] while other papyri show such cash gifts to friends as 2000 silver drachmae, 10 silver Ptolemaic drachmae, two of 100 drachmae each to *colliberti*, and 100 silver drachmae to a friend.[71] Receipts from a military treasury apparently show legacies of 100 denarii being paid from the accounts of different testators to their legatees.[72] And literature, dealing with testators in a much higher stratum, produces cash legacies to *amici* of 30,000 sesterces, 50,000, 100,000, and

---

67. Tacitus *Ann.* 1.8; cf. Suetonius *Claudius* 4.7 (Claudius a tertiary substitute and legatee). Caesar included both Mark Antony and D. Brutus among his substitute heirs: Suetonius *Caes.* 83, Appian *BC* 2.143. "Dasumius" named at least seven friends or relatives among his secondary heirs, with a legacy to at least one of them and presumably to all: *CIL* 6.10229 + Eck, "Zum neuen Fragment." *Dig.* 31.89.2: if a substitute heir does not succeed, he and his wife are to receive 15 pounds of silver. Friends substituted at Cicero *De Orat.* 1.180 et al. (the *causa Curiana*); *Fam.* 13.61.
68. *HA Had.* 1.4; Pliny *Ep.* 2.1.8; Dio 48.44.5; Plutarch *Pomp.* 15.3; Suetonius *Caes.* 83 (for a posthumous child); Cicero *Verr.* 2.1.130; *Fam.* 13.61; *CPR* 6.2.76; *P. Mich.* inv. 2922; *P. Oxy.* 907; *Dig.* 3.3.70 (creditor).
69. *CPR* 6.2.76.
70. *CPL* 221.
71. *BGU* 327; *P. Haw.* 41; *P. Oxy.* 2857; *PSI* 738.
72. *P. Mich.* 435 + 440, elucidated at *RMR* 77.

(from an empress) the highly improbable (and in the event un-
paid) sum of 50 million.[73]

Similar, but far more interesting, is the legacy to friends, and
apparently to friends alone, of small amounts of gold and silver.
Thus, the poet Persius bequeathed to his teacher Chrysippus 2
pounds of silver along with a large amount of cash and 700 books;
and the Digest, while considering general questions relevant to
such bequests, speaks specifically for example of 15 pounds of
silver left to a substitute heir and his wife, 5 pounds of gold "to my
friend Titia, with whom I have lived without lying," and 3 pounds
of gold to a tutor.[74] The fragmentary testament of "Dasumius"
most clearly reveals the custom in practice, in A.D. 108. Here,
directly after the institution of his heirs, the testator turned to
bequeath (line 15) "to each of his friends written below" *auri
p(ondo) libras* (presumably 3, 4, or 5 pounds of gold—the figure has
dropped out) to some 10 or 12 people; and then *auri p. ii* to an
unknown number (line 18).[75] And he added at the end codicils
leaving an unknown number of pounds of (presumably) gold each
to the emperor Trajan, the consular Sosius Senecio, and others,
and 5 pounds of silver to a legatee who had already received
something in the will proper.[76] No ancient author discusses this
curious practice of bequeathing small amounts of precious
metals, an aristocratic if not ostentatious one (it certainly does not
appear in the papyri).

The custom is nonetheless significant, in that with it we come to
the subject of mementos, and perhaps to the outer boundary of
friendship. Three elements suggest this, the first being value. It is
clear that while by no means valueless, such individual legacies
were proportionally very small. The price of gold and silver fluc-

73. Cicero *Cluent.* 162; Pliny *Ep.* 10.75; Cicero *Att.* 2.20.6; Suetonius *Galba* 5.2;
cf. *Vita Persi* 50,000 or 100,000.

74. *Vita Persi; Dig.* 31.89.2; 34.2.35; 40.5.41.3. Cf. 34.2.6 pr., *auri pondo tot;*
34.2.9, *certum auri vel argento pondus;* and below, n. 80. Cf. Quintilian 7.6.11.

75. *CIL* 6.10229. Since the second group of legatees received 2 pounds of
gold, we should assume that the first, which included at least one (and presumably
all) of the secondary heirs, received more (so Eck, "Zum neuen Fragment," 290).
After the mention of two pounds of gold, the list of names continues for some 11
lines (18–28), but it is not clear whether in those lines the testator further reduced
the measure of his affection at intervals (in the parts now lost), to 1 pound of gold,
5 pounds of silver, etc.

76. 11.125–128. Otacilius Or...: 128, cf. 26.

tuated considerably, but high figures of HS 5500 for a pound of gold and HS 450 per pound of silver may be taken very roughly to represent second-century prices.[77] By that measure the individual bequests of gold and silver by "Dasumius" are dwarfed by his legacies of HS 600,000 to a relative by marriage (29), apparently 6 million to an aunt, and even 10,000 to a doctor. Particularly suggestive are the 2 pounds of silver left by Persius to Chrysippus, along with some HS 50,000 or 100,000 in cash and 700 books: cash value cannot have been a factor in choosing the legacy.

This leads to the second element, form. What precisely was handed over, bullion or crafted metal? A learned and influential appendix to Friedländer's *Sittengeschichte* maintained that gifts of gold and silver, even when described only by weight, always consisted of worked metal—plate and utensils (whose weight was indeed often engraved on them). The argument rested on inscriptions and numerous passages in Martial, with mention of the wills of Persius and "Dasumius."[78] Yet recourse to the appropriate chapter of the Digest, 34.2, "De auro argento [etc.] legatis," will quickly show that the initial impression is correct: such gifts came indeed in the form of bullion, however unlikely that might appear. Thus the jurists concern themselves with questions arising over the metal's being *factum* or *infectum*, worked or unworked, and worked metal in testaments would be either specified (as in "Dasumius' " "my largest gold platter," or "all my gold and silver statues") or categorized (as in "travel silver," or "bath silver").[79] Clearest is the testimony of Ulpian, who distinguishes weight as quantity from vessels, and several others work on the same assumption.[80] In short, wealthier Roman testators were quite capable of passing on appropriate keepsakes such as platters or spoons, if they wished; but they were equally capable of bequeathing small and quite unsentimental amounts of bullion.

77. Cf. Duncan-Jones, *Economy*, 126–27.

78. M. Bang, "Bezeichnung von Silbergerät nach dem Gewicht," in *Darstellungen aus der Sittengeschichte Roms*, 9/10th ed., L. Friedländer (Leipzig, 1921, 1922) 4: 301–3, with earlier bibliography.

79. *CIL* 6.10229, 67, 74; *Dig.* 34.2.40 pr., 1.

80. *Dig.* 34.2.19.1–2: *Proinde si certum pondus auri sit legatum vel argenti magis quantitas legata videtur, nec ex vasis tanget. Sed si argenti facto pondo centum sit legata, ex facto argento debebitur legatum.* Cf. 34.2.1.1 and 35 pr., cash value as substitute: 34.2.9, to be paid at current rate of value; 34.27 pr., *Quintus Mucius libro secundo iuris civilis ita definit argentum factum vas argenteum videri esse.*

Here the third and significant element appears, standardization: such gifts can be made absolutely equal, which means of course that they can also be varied. Some friendships are always closer than others, but the Romans were quite ready to categorize them formally. The most obvious (but by no means the only) manifestation of this was the order of reception (*admissio*) accorded to friends, a system particularly associated with the imperial court (*prima* and *secunda admissio*), but found among the aristocracy as early as the second century B.C.[81] "Dasumius'" grand listing of his friends is a direct corollary to this, a last, posthumous arranging of his friends by degree around him. This helps to explain Pliny's notable remark about Tacitus and himself, that in wills, unless one or other of the two was an intimate of the deceased, they both received "legacies of the same kind and value" (*eadem legata et quidem pariter*).[82] In other words, to the world, as Pliny would have us believe, so similar and closely connected were he and Tacitus that they received the same recognition, say 5 pounds of silver each, but never 5 to one and 3 to the other or gold to one and silver to the other. At a lower level, where men and women did not normally enjoy the use of gold and silver plate, standardized legacies in cash could play the same role in assessing and proclaiming the intimacy of the relationship.[83] Here then, with cash and bullion, the testator might recognize and rank individual social ties beyond the most intimate, with a token, nothing so personal as a keepsake, but something that could be converted into one.

For some, it was felt, the greatest obligation under the principate was to the emperor. Considerable ambiguity clouded an area where ties of friendship and grateful clientage shaded into questions of flattery and political loyalty. The emperors and our surviving authors were both much preoccupied with the proper be-

---

81. J. Crook, *Consilium Principis* (Cambridge, 1955), 22–23. Dining offered another hierarchical private occasion: cf. J. H. D'Arms, "Control, Companionship, and Clientela: Some Social Functions of the Roman Communal Meal," *Classical Views* 28 (1984): 327–48, at 344–48.

82. *Ep.* 7.20.6.

83. Thus 200 drachmae for each of three friends, more for two others (*CPR* 6.2.76); 50 denarii each to a friend and a superior officer, but 750 to a brother and substitute heir (*CPL* 221); 100 drachmae to each of two friends (*P. Oxy.* 2857).

havior of the good emperor, the *civilis princeps*, and the scandalous excesses of bad emperors—Tacitus reflected in Tacitean fashion on Domitian's not knowing that only a bad emperor would be instituted heir by a good father—and the subject of bequests to the emperor has been well studied.[84] Most of the material concerning the emperors as heirs and legatees was collected and analyzed by R. S. Rogers, who neatly distilled from it two major and two minor operating principles: that good emperors ought not to accept from testators who left children; that suspect wills were not to be upheld in order to profit from them; that bequests from persons unknown to the emperor ought not to be accepted; and that no legacy meant to harm another party ought to be accepted.[85] From another angle, J. Gaudemet studied the origins and development of the practice. The emperor was to many their most important *amicus*, one to whose favors, *beneficia*, they owed a great deal, and the emperor needed money. What more natural than that the gratitude of his freedmen, his chief centurions, his personal friends and associates should ultimately be conveyed in property? And then, by extension, that all citizens should render thanks for peace and prosperity to the father of his country?[86]

Most of this is quite true, and the emperors inherited vast sums from friends known and unknown alike: in his own will Augustus himself remarked that in the previous twenty years he had received some 1400 million sesterces in inheritances and legacies.[87] Even where direct evidence is lacking, a richly detailed mosaic picture of the emperor as heir, especially in the first century, can be pieced together from study of the names of slaves and landed estates in the imperial possession, both of which often retain the imprint of the name of a previous owner. Some of these may indeed have been acquired through gift or even confiscation; but

---

84. Tacitus *Agric.* 43.4. A good bibliography is provided in the excellent paper of E. Bund, "Erbrechtliche Geldquellen römischer Kaiser," in *Festschrift für Franz Wieacker zum 70. Geburtstag*, ed. O. Behrends et al. (Göttingen, 1978), 50–65, at 51–55. Add, in detail on one emperor, K. P. Müller-Eiselt, *Divus Pius constituit: Kaiserliches Erbrecht* (Kallmünz, 1982), 287–304.

85. R. S. Rogers, "The Roman Emperors as Heirs and Legatees," *TAPA* 78 (1947): 140–58.

86. J. Gaudemet, " 'Testamenta ingrata et pietas Augusti': Contribution à l'étude du sentiment impérial," *Studi in onore di Vincenzo Arangio-Ruiz* (Naples, 1953), 3: 115–37.

87. Suetonius *Aug.* 101.3.

that the scale of inheritance was vast is beyond doubt, witness the existence of freedmen and slaves in the imperial household with titles like *procurator hereditatum, a testamentis principis, a legatis,* or *a codicillis.*[88]

Nevertheless there is a sharp distinction to be drawn. Most strikingly, no surviving will on papyrus mentions the emperor (other than for dating purposes).[89] Nor do bequests to the emperor much interest the jurists in the Digest, either as raising questions of legal interest or as casual illustrations (no details of any case are reported).[90] On the other hand, of the testators explicitly attested as having left emperors as heirs or legatees, only two or three were not senators or knights, and all seem to have been personally known to him, while those testators deducible from the names of their slaves or their properties all likewise belong to the highest orders.[91] The existence of imperial servants charged with looking after legacies and inheritances, and of vast sums such as Augustus' 1400 millions, need not mean that large numbers of testators are involved. Far more likely is it that three clearly limited and overlapping groups of wealthy men and women left property to the emperors: people of the highest rank in society who were personal friends or acquaintances; clients, employees, soldiers, and any others who had won benefits from Caesar; and imperial freedmen and freedwomen, who in certain circumstances would automatically owe their patron a large part of their estate on death. It was inheritances from these people which quite properly interested the emperor and increased his wealth vastly. Thus, for instance, Tiberius was the sole testamentary heir of Cornelius Lentulus Augur in A.D. 25, and Nero was almost certainly the heir by will or intestacy of his father's freedman Narcissus

88. F. Millar, *The Emperor in the Roman World* (London, 1977), 153–63; O. Hirschfeld, *Die kaiserlichen Verwaltungsbeamten bis auf Diocletian*[2] (Berlin, 1905), 110ff.

89. The point is well made by Bund, "Erbrechtliche Geldquellen."

90. Their silence is remarked on by Gaudemet, "Testamenta ingrata," 115 n. 4. To his brief list of passing references add *Dig.* 5.2.8.2 (one could indeed bring the *querela inofficiosi testamenti* even when the emperor was an heir) and 28.1.31 (when a testator boasted that the emperor would be his heir, the estate would not be confiscated if he failed to fulfill his promise).

91. For a list see appendix V. The Claudius Polyaenus of Prusa who left the emperor Claudius his heir (Pliny *Ep.* 10.70) was presumably either an imperial freedman or a provincial notable enfranchised by the emperor.

in 54: with estates estimated at around HS 400 million apiece, these two men were the richest private citizens recorded under the principate.[92] Figures of such magnitude considerably change our perspective on the 1400 millions inherited by Augustus in his last two decades, which should represent not the posthumous loyalty of thousands of subjects, but the respect and gratitude of dozens of friends and servants, of whom Maecenas was by no means the poorest.[93]

The emperor was beyond the universe of the ordinary Roman testator; he was not a friend, and the principle that he did not accept bequests from persons unknown to him seems to have been largely observed on both sides: as Pliny said in the senate to Trajan, "You are instituted by friends and passed over by those who do not know you." [94] The proper way for a friend to treat him was as one treated a normal friend: "Dasumius," who undoubtedly moved in the highest circles, left the *civilis princeps*, Trajan, the appropriate gift of a few pounds of gold. The proper way for the subject to show gratitude and loyalty was in death the same as in life, to give something not to him but for him, by instructing an heir or legatee to dedicate in the testator's name a statue, or a building, or a foundation.[95] Thus, despite common modern assumptions, there was no general custom of leaving property to the emperor, outside of the normal circle, large in his case, of friends and clients.

Beyond the inner circle of the nuclear family, often overlapping with it, lay an outer circle of more or less affectionate social ties with individuals, from superiors (up to the emperor) down to slaves. A vast range of emotion is conceivable and visible, but that emotion is expressed in a strikingly limited range of modes; and again, while a range of motives is visible, such as expression of one's love, or reward for the love of another, one motive that runs

---

92. Seneca *Ben.* 2.27, with Suetonius *Tib.* 49.1; Dio 60.34: on which, Duncan-Jones, *Economy*, 343–44.

93. On Augustus, see Shatzman, *Senatorial Wealth*, 361–62.

94. *Pan.* 43.2: *Scriberis ab amicis, ab ignotis praeteriris.*

95. The forms and functions of such expressions of loyalty as statues and buildings, whether *inter vivos* or posthumous, have not been much investigated. On foundations, see below, chapter 8.

throughout, now more clearly, now less, is the implicit desire in some way to continue the relationship after death. Friends, freedmen, and slaves who become coheirs are both an exception to and an instance of the latter observation, since the affective tie here was exceptionally close and these people actually took over the legal personality, even the name where appropriate, of the testator. But legatees offer a less ambiguous illustration. Favored freedmen and freedwomen, for instance, carried on a patron-client relationship, the patron ensuring the client's welfare, often explicitly under the same terms as in life, the freedmen and freedwomen continuing to serve him or her (through cult and the care of the tomb) or the family.[96] Favored slaves freed in the will were treated in roughly the same manner, their manumssions surrounded with the same acts of grace as in life, their services assured even after death. And favored friends were honored in death as they were in life, with tutorships, substitute institutions, and individual legacies for the closest, standardized legacies of cash or bullion for the more remote, these in turn distinguishing the degree of intimacy by their cash value. The will thus fixed the testator's universe at death and in large part continued the social relationships of his or her lifetime. Nowhere is the intent of this clearer than here, where we turn from individual to communal relationships.

---

96. To *operae* and *obsequium* could be added *bona*, the bequest of property on death to the patron's family, a subject not covered here: the remarks of Fabre, *Libertus*, 301–15 are purely legal in nature, barely touching on real life.

# 8

## Community
### *Philanthropy—Forms—Purpose*

With bequests to special groups or to the larger community, we move outside the testator's personal universe into that of his society, away from personal gifts and keepsakes for individual relatives, friends, and servants, and toward public philanthropy for the group. Unlike other subjects of study, such as the family, the nature and function of ancient philanthropy has never suffered from lack of scholarly attention, triumphantly maintaining its centrality to classical history even as historians have reformulated their questions of it, now in terms of gift exchange, now in terms of the class struggle. This is inevitable, so intimately was it woven into the basic patterns of urban life, social, economic, political, and physical. And, equally to be expected, the habits of a lifetime continued after death, very much along the same lines.[1]

There is one general caveat, obvious but important. Public and competitive benefaction was the prerogative of the wealthy; gifts even to smaller groups in society demanded considerable spare cash. The greater part of humanity could not afford to be benefactors, or did not feel driven by the same pressures that induced more prominent citizens to endow a temple, a public banquet, or an alimentary scheme. Even among urban leaders around the Mediterranean world, only a small minority is known to have indulged in public benefactions. So too, after death, the huge significance of such gifts for the pleasure and well-being of the community, and for the power and prestige of the individual, must be kept in perspective. Nowhere in the papyri is there a hint of interest among testators either in their community or even in any smaller group: for them, the posthumous world consisted of

---

1. A good general introduction is offered by A. R. Hands, in *Charities and Social Aid in Greece and Rome* (London, 1968).

tightly circumscribed circles of family and friends. The Digest, which might show an interest in the complicated legal questions that could conceivably arise, includes fewer than twenty references to bequests to or for the community. And even the scores of inscriptions mentioning gifts or foundations are overwhelmed in number by those which record the simple epitaphs, or prescriptions regarding the disposition of their tombs, ordered by the wills of thousands of testators, with no thought to the needs of the community. Moreover, there is no need to assume that even those who could afford it felt the necessity of posthumous benefaction: the elaborate testament of "Dasumius," who moved in the very highest levels of society, is concerned exclusively with his private world. Relatively speaking, philanthropists alive or dead were a small minority, who presumably continued posthumously what they had practiced in life.[2]

What distinguishes posthumous benevolence to the group from bequests to individuals is the element of purpose. With family, friends, and servants, a bequest may or may not have had the strings of *fideicommissum*, condition, or *modus* attached, according to the strategies adopted by the testator; that is, more often than not a piece of land, a sum of money, or an annuity was the legatee's to do with as he or she wished. Not so with philanthropy to the wider circle, which was almost always directed to a purpose, explicit or implicit.

Thus, very rarely is a municipality actually instituted heir, with all the freedom which that implies, and the naming of a *collegium* or other small group is even more unusual. That was most easily accomplished by *fideicommissum*, but even if legal obstacles to the inheritance by a corporation were overcome, the moral consequences of passing over family and friends would have been hard to bear for most testators.[3] Thus, for all practical purposes, when we are dealing with a group we are dealing only with *legata*, not *hereditas*.

2. Pliny's benefactions are a case in point: *CIL* 5.5262, with Duncan-Jones, *Economy*, 27–31.

3. Municipalities: *Dig.* 3.5.25 (*fideicommissum*); 36.1.33 (*cautio*), cf. 36.1.59 pr. (*fideicommissum*); *ILS* 6228 (Tibur). Vulcatius Moschus, exiled to Massilia, left that city his heir: Tacitus *Ann.* 4.43. A Saturninus left Comum his heir to 1/4, later changing that to an even more favorable *praelegatum* of 1/4: Pliny *Ep.* 5.7.1, 3. At

Similarly, legacies to groups without specified purposes are very rare. Inscriptions invariably record a purpose. Therefore, in the few instances in the Digest where no purpose is mentioned, it should be assumed, not that none was stated, but rather that it was of no interest to the jurists.[4] The one real unrestricted legacy to a group is the literarily attested bequest of single cash donatives to the populace, presumably at the funeral; but these are very rare, extremely expensive, and above all confined to the leading men of the state, Julius Caesar, the emperors Augustus and Tiberius, and leading senators like Cornelius Balbus and Marcus Agrippa.[5] The salient observations about group legacies should therefore stand, that their use by the legatee was normally restricted. Philanthropy

---

*Dig.* 28.6.30, the colony of Leptis Magna is substituted to 3/4 in the third degree: not a likely heir, therefore, and surely compensated with a legacy. Acca Larentia and Timestheus both left the people of Rome their heirs, dubiously; several foreign kings in the days of the republic did likewise, but they were not Roman. On the legality of bequests to municipalities in general, see D. Johnston, "Munificence and *Municipia*: Bequests to Towns in Classical Roman Law," *JRS* 75 (1985): 105–25.

　　*Collegia*: J.-P. Waltzing collected the evidence then known in his *Étude historique sur les corporations professionelles chez les Romains depuis les origines jusqu'à la chute de l'empire d'Occident* (Louvain, 1895–1900) 2:458–63 and 4:706. He concluded, for the principate at least, that *collegia* appeared as heirs only under special dispensation from the law, if the testators were freedmen of the college, or if the inheritance were received by *fideicommissum*. Of the four inscriptions which he was able to cite, three concerned the *collegium fabrum* at Brixia (CIL 5.4122, 4394, 4433).

　　4. Thus, on municipalities, Johnston, "Munificence," 106, with note 22, citing *Dig.* 30.71.5, 31.88.8, 32.101 pr. (In fact, the first refers to vectigal land already owned by the community; the second, the bequest of another man's *chirographum*, is unique and clearly suffers from lack of context.) Johnston strongly supports his point by a comparison of the Digest with epigraphy in cases where property reverts to a municipality if a legatee fails to abide by a condition: where the Digest is silent, inscriptions show that the condition was expected to be transferred. At *Dig.* 32.38.6, a sum of money is left to the collegium of a temple: again, the testator must have at least stipulated whether it was to be distributed among the members or applied to the group's purposes.

　　5. Augustus left large sums to the people of Rome and to his *tribules*, and individual donatives to soldiers in the praetorian guards, the urban cohorts, and the legions; Tiberius, as in so much else, imitated him with bequests to the Vestal Virgins, the soldiers, and the people (Suetonius *Aug.* 101, *Tib.* 76; Dio 59.12). Cornelius Balbus left 100 sesterces to each citizen (Dio 48.32.2); Caesar left 300 sesterces and his *horti*; Agrippa allegedly left 400 sestereces, his *horti*, and his baths (Dio 54.29.4). On the same scale are the one-time funeral distribution of an anonymous magnate at Mons Fereter (*CIL* 11.6481) of 400 sesterces each to the decurions whom he had not otherwise named in his testament, 300 to the *seviri* and Augustales, and 200 to the *plebs*: these and the range of his other benefactions suggest that he was a senator. (The distributions of Atticus, at Philostratus *VS* 548, and of Constantine, at Eusebius *VC* 4.63, are annual donatives or *sportulae*, and smaller.)

was rarely a gift without strings; it remains to be seen what the testator intended.

Broadly speaking, legacies to groups took one of two forms; outright gift or endowment, corresponding more or less to single and recurrent acts of generosity.[6]

The more commonly attested singular legacies normally concerned public works. A testator sets aside a specific sum of money for—or commands an heir or legatee to see to—the construction, embellishment, restoration of, or addition to, one from a range of structures intended for the physical use and the spiritual or aesthetic pleasure of fellow citizens or comrades. Favored are the public buildings and other works essential to urban communal life: temples, altars, theaters, amphitheaters, baths, libraries, porticoes, aqueducts, arches, roads.[7] Julius Caesar's bequest of his transtiberine gardens for the recreation of the people of Rome falls into the same area of benefaction.[8] On a smaller scale, but sharing the purpose in part at least of public amenity or civic inspiration, is the widespread bequest of statues, statuettes, and busts, images of the gods, the emperor, the testator, and sometimes the testator's friends or relatives—often raised in or near one of the aforementioned public works.[9] And along with public

6. The two could of course go together, as when a donor gave money both for baths and their upkeep, e.g., Pliny the Younger (*CIL* 5.5262).

7. The following examples do not constitute an exhaustive list of such bequests, they merely indicate the forms attested; all were likewise possible as benefactions *inter vivos*. Most will be found in the invaluable lists of Italian and African costs compiled by Duncan-Jones, *Economy*, 89–119, with 378, and 156–237, with 379–380. A great mass of Asian material is gathered by T. R. S. Broughton at *ESAR* 4 (1938): 715–97. Temple: *CIL* 8.15576, 18227, 26498; *ILAf* 527; *AE* 1933.233; *CIL*10.415, 531, 6309; 11.6110. Theater: Suetonius, *Tib.* 31.1. Amphitheater: *CIL* 11.1527. Bath: *CIL* 5.5262 (plus upkeep: Pliny the Younger); 11.5939; 13.3162, 5417 (*ad marmorandum balneum*). Library: *IK* 17.2 (Ephesus) 5113; *ILS* 9362. Portico: *Dig.* 34.2.6.2 (*publica*); *CIL* 12.1357 (*ante thermas*). Aqueduct: *Dig.* 22.6.9.5; *CIL* 13.596. Arch: *ILAlg* 1.3040; *AE* 1925.23–24 + 1949.40 (with statues), 1967.536 (with statues). Road: *Dig.* 31.30; *CIL* 2.3167 (revised). Undefined or unknown *opera publica*: Pliny *Ep.* 10.75; *CIL* 3.10095, 5.8664; *IK* 23.1 (Smyrna) 424.

8. Suetonius *Caes.* 83. Imitated by Agrippa (Dio 54.29.4).

9. E.g.: Gods: *ILAlg* 1.177 (Apollo, in forum), 3040; *CIL* 8.4582; *AE* 1925.23–24 + 1949.40 (statues on arch); *CIL* 2.21 (Aesculapius, *ob merita splendidissimi ordinis*). Emperor: *AE* 1941.105, 1978.286, 1974.691; *CIL* 11.1924; *MAMA* 6.91; *IGLS* 1312. Self: *CIL* 8.11202; *ILS* 6468. Friend/relative: *CIL* 6.1451 (friend); *CIL* 9.2456 (husband); *CIL* 6.1460 (father).

works go public services. Thus, money or bullion could also be left for specific civic purposes, such as buying grain for the people, subsidizing public use of the baths, or relieving a tax burden in hard times; or slaves could be left to care for a particular building.[10]

Recurrent legacies—foundations, endowments—must have been far less common than outright gifts: they were presumably more complicated and time-consuming to administer; the capital required to produce significant interest would be considerable; and many testators must have observed how even the most careful of schemes fell apart in time. Nevertheless, foundations flourished in the palmy days of the later first, second, and early third centuries; and scores of them were carefully recorded on stone by the donor, by his or her agent, or by the grateful recipient. These detailed descriptions necessarily covered all aspects of the act, from the donor's situation and intentions, to the nature, capital, and administration of the foundation, to the elaborate precautions often taken to protect its proper functioning. It is this wealth of information that has attracted considerable modern attention, an attention quite out of proportion to the actual importance of foundations within the larger framework of ancient philanthropy. Yet it is just this detail that gives us insight into the thinking behind the benefaction, the largely unspoken hopes and assumptions which are quite absent from the bald dedication of a bath or a theater. Foundations therefore require closer attention.[11]

10. *CIL* 3.6998, *Dig.* 32.35.3; *CIL* 2.3664, 5.8664; *Dig.* 34.1.17; 40.12.35.
11. A comprehensive modern treatment is still lacking. The only general work on both Greek and Roman foundations remains B. Laum's *Stiftungen in der griechischen und römischen Antike* (Leipzig, 1914), a work more used and abused than read. Laum's second volume, *Urkunden*, offers texts and translations of some 381 foundation documents (232 Greek, 149 Latin), which are not always accurate and to which many more recent examples could be added. But his first volume, *Darstellung*, offers a straightforward and still fundamental classification and analysis of the material. A. Mannzmann, *Griechische Stiftungsurkunden: Studie zu Inhalt und Rechtsform* (Münster, 1962), offers a close legal study. Standard essays are those by G. Le Bras, "Les fondations privées du Haut-Empire," in *Studi in onore di Salvatore Riccobono* (Palermo, 1936), 3: 23–67; E. F. Bruck, "Foundations for the Deceased in Roman Law, Religion, and Political Thought," in *Scritti in onore di Contardo Ferrini* (Milan, 1949) 4: 1–42 (German version in *Über römisches Recht im Rahmen der Kulturgeschichte* [Berlin, 1954], 46–100); and F. de Visscher, "Les fondations privées en droit romain classique," *RIDA*³ 2 (1955); 197–218. Among more recent works, particulary valuable are: Andreau, "Fondations"; C. P. Jones, "A Deed of Foundation from the Territory of Ephesos," *JRS* 73 (1983): 116–25; M. Wörrle, *Stadt und Fest in kaiserzeitlichen Kleinasien* (Munich, 1988).

The essence of foundations is elusive, not least because Greek and Latin lack words to describe the general concept, that is, the establishment and administration of a fund whose revenues are to be applied, often at stated periods, to a particular purpose. Scholars have tried to impose categories on a wide variety of forms. Thus B. Laum, in his standard discussion, distinguished among "sacral," "agonal," and "social" foundations, but most others appear to recognize two main types, funerary/private and social/public; or (slightly different) reflexive (primarily for the donor and close family) and nonreflexive (for third parties).[12] These are roughly accurate, and observe or assume a difference not just in purpose but in size and nature as well. Yet at the same time, most students would allow that the two types could be to some degree mixed, or at least that the borders between them might be blurred.[13]

There is some disagreement as to the underlying purpose of foundations, between what might be called "religious" and "social" purposes. G. Le Bras, in the fundamental paper on foundations of the high empire, saw their main purpose as religious, to ensure the cult of the dead; but he also observed that the religious was strongly reinforced by the social, as individuals were forced to turn to society to ensure the continuance of family rites when their families could no longer be trusted.[14] This notion was carefully developed by E. F. Bruck in a paper which connected the rise of foundations with the decay of family religion in the late republic: by contracting with society through the foundation, the dead ensured their cult and remembrance at a time when scepticism was growing and conventional piety in decline. But recently J. Andreau has forcefully attacked Bruck (and others) on several fronts. To put the matter briefly, Andreau would distinguish sharply between reflexive foundations for commemorative purposes and nonreflexive for social ends, and in a valuable study he uses them to illuminate social relations in early imperial Italy.[15]

12. Laum, *Stiftungen*, 60–115, with a valuable analysis of the evidence; Amelotti, *Testamento*, 139, Jones, "Deed," 116; Andreau, "Fondations," 180.
13. Vehemently denied by Andreau, "Fondations," 161: see below. The foundation of Flavius Praxias of Acmonia (Jones, "Deed," 116) undercuts the public/private distinction.
14. Le Bras, "Fondations," 28–32.
15. Bruck, "Fondations," 1–46; Andreau, "Fondations," 159–61.

Andreau believes, it appears, that one should separate psychological impulses (belief in immortality, desire for posthumous cult, taste for glory) from social ends, and that the latter predominate —indeed, even if psychological motives were necessary, they would explain nothing about the precise judicial and social forms taken by a foundation in a particular society.

Yet F. de Visscher, the modern legal authority on Roman foundations, concluded some time ago:

> If one can attribute to our foundations ends which are now of a social nature and now of a cultic nature, I hasten to add that this distinction could in no fashion serve as a basis for a classification of foundations. Most often, dispositions of a social nature, in favor of the living, are joined to prescriptions of a cultic nature....Both pursue, in sum, the same end, which is to perpetuate the memory of the founder.[16]

Andreau protests that social and funerary foundations are almost always separate, but he misses the point. As regards testamentary decisions at least, de Visscher touches the heart of the matter.

Rather than categorize as public/private or social/funerary, and rather than debate the founders' almost always unexpressed intention, one might start by inquiring what foundations actually paid for.[17] Despite the great variety of individual circumstances and geographical and chronological differences, most foundations and certainly all testamentary foundations directed their endowment to one of a very limited number of purposes. The most expensive and rarest was the *alimenta*, the scheme for making regular payments of subsistence allowances to a fixed number of local citizens. Far more common are the continuation after death of more standard philanthropic activities. Two were normally restricted to specified groups (local decurions, Augustales, or fellow members of a *collegium*): cash handouts (*sportulae/dianomai*); and food in the form of a communal meal, ranging from a banquet to a snack of cake and honeywine. Others were normally for the benefit of everyone: games of all kinds and sizes, gladiatorial, circus, theatrical; the distribution of oil; and occasionally the maintenance or administration of public buildings, as in the subsidy of

16. Visscher, "Fondations," 201, as quoted by Andreau, "Fondations."
17. Cf. Duncan-Jones, *Economy*, 80–81, 136–38.

admission to the baths or of their heating and upkeep.[18] And, finally, money was assigned to serving the cult of the dead by providing, at certain times of the year, any or all of: libations (*profusiones*), sacrifices, dinners (*cena, epulum*), or roses or violets to decorate the tomb.

One social pattern is easily observed. The larger and wealthier the foundation, the higher in rank the donor tends to be (senators, knights, and local magistrates or decurions), and the greater the likelihood that the beneficiaries are either the citizen body or its leading representatives, the decurions and (sometimes) the Augustales, members of the guild of leading freedmen. The more modest foundations are established by people of lower rank (the Augustales or ordinary citizens, freeborn or freed) and almost always for a more restricted group, which was most often a *collegium* of fellow workers or fellow worshippers.[19] Thus, not unreasonably, we can see two outer circles in the universe of the individual: beyond the circle of friends, and overlapping with it, lies one of peers and colleagues, be they fellow decurions or fellow members of a *collegium*; and beyond that, acknowledged posthumously only by the wealthiest, lies the community to be patronized as a whole.

The important question here concerns "the nature of the return" for the donor.[20] From the point of view of most testators, the fundamental motive for leaving a will did not apply. Whatever one's *officium* might be in life, the posthumous duty to leave a will embraced only family and friends. Moreover, overt posthumous expressions of affection or patriotism—"to my dearest fellow citizens," or "to my beloved native city,"—are extremely rare.[21] On the other hand, from the benefactors' point of view, the honors and

18. Free admission: *Dig.* 32.35.3, *CIL* 11.720. Heating and/or upkeep: *CIL* 5.5262, *NdS* (1928): 283.
19. Thus, in detail and with tables, Andreau "Fondations," 164–179, on Italy. His results could be duplicated elsewhere in the West. The overwhelming majority of smaller foundations were observably directed to the cult of the dead: e.g., Laum, *Stiftungen*, 87.
20. Cf. Hands, *Charities*, 49–61.
21. *Dig.* 32.35.3 (*municipibus meis amantissimis*); *FIRA* 55b (*municipes carissimi*); *Dig.* 32.101 pr. (*tei glukutatei mou patridi*); *FIRA* 53 (*patria mea amantissima*). *Patria* without qualification at *Dig.* 33.1.21.3, 34.2.6.2, 36.1.59 pr.; at *CIL* 2.4511, *colon(is) Barcinonens(ibus)...[apud q]uos natus sum.*

distinctions which had stimulated or rewarded their benevolence in life were of virtually no interest after death.²² Moreover, there is, rather curiously, no sign that Roman testators sought honors or exemptions for their survivors, rewards that were often sought by living benefactors.²³ What then did they seek?

Ordinary testators and living philanthropists each acted from a variety of motives; but for the philanthropic testator benefiting a considerable number of fellow human beings, some of them perhaps unknown, there is one motive that is omnipresent, threading unobtrusively through every kind of foundation, sometimes ignored by modern scholarship, sometimes noticed but appreciated too briefly. Any testator might be moved by a number of impulses: some might be most concerned with their posthumous cult, some with the altruistic provision of relief or entertainment to their fellows; but all were impelled by a desire for remembrance. We can seldom say that this was surely the prime consideration for any single person, but we can claim that it was the most important for Roman testators as a group.

Memory was a fundamental part of the cult of the dead, more important indeed than any belief in a personal afterlife. And provisions for the cult normally took the form of what might be called private foundations or trusts, administered by the *liberti* and *libertae* of the deceased: sacrifice, dining, and decorating the tomb or statue of the testator were standard procedures; and the foundations established for colleagues of the dead were essentially the same as the far more common trusts imposed upon their freedmen and freedwomen. Hence, in terms of both form and purpose, the cult of the dead belongs properly in the next chapter. What is important here is the calendar of the dead.

Four times in the year stand out as important to the deceased: the *Parentalia* in February, running from the 13th to the *Feralia* on the 21st and the *Cara Cognatio* on the 22nd, a period for fond remembrance and sacrifice to the dead; the *dies violae* (or *violationis*

---

22. There is the occasional demand for a public statue (*ILS* 6468, cf. *CIL* 9.449?), but these will normally have been arranged earlier.
23. Hands, *Charities*, 55, with references. The nearest approach (apparently unique) is the condition attached by a Spanish testator to his gift of games, that if any of his freedmen or freedwomen, or their slaves, won the honor of the sevirate they should be excused from the attendant *munera*: *CIL* 2.4514 (Barcino).

or *violaris*) in March and the *dies rosae* (or *rosationis*) in May, when the tomb was appropriately adorned; and the *natalicia*, the birthday of the deceased.[24] One or two other appropriate days might appear,[25] but almost all benefactors, when they named a day, ordered that their rites be celebrated on one or two of these four.[26] Testators are no different. Thus, at Rome, Turius Lollianus set aside sums, the interest on which was to pay for sacrifices on his birthday and the *parentalia*; M. Naevius Restitutus of Pisa granted the interest on 4000 denarii to be spent by the guild of Pisan naval builders on the celebration of the *parentalia* and the *rosaria* at his tomb; Iunia Libertas requested that, if other arrangements lapsed, the republic of Ostia spend 100 sesterces of the income of a sepulchral property for sacrifice on the days of *parentalia*, *rosa*, and *viola*.[27]

The days of the dead direct attention to the common element in all but one of the other important forms of foundation: timing. Whether distributing *sportulae* to decurions and Augustales, or providing them with a meal, whether presenting games or distributing oil, it was the common practice of Roman testators to specify a day or days each year or every few years when the benefaction was to occur. In theory such a day might be chosen at random, or to reflect the civic or religious or agricultural calendar, or to recall historic events; but in practice the great majority chose their birthday or the birthday of a near relative.[28] So, for example, the

24. All are found together in the acephalous testamentary instructions to freed slaves (*CIL* 6.10248 = *ILS* 8366), and the deed of gift of Flavius Syntrophus (*CIL* 6.10239 = *FIRA* 94). Cf. *ILS* 7213.

25. E.g., *CIL* 3.3893, roses on 1 June, the day of the goddess Carna; or *Suppl. Ital.* 181, a *profusio* and *epulum* on 12 May, a day lying between celebrations of the festival of the dead, the Lemuria, on 9, 11, and 13 May.

26. E.g., (both alive and dead), *CIL* 3.707 (*rosalia*), 11042 (*rosalia*); 5.2046 (*rusarum* [sic]), 2090 (*rosalia*), 4016 (*rosalia* and *parentalia* for self, wife, and children), 4410 (*rosalia*), 4440 (*natalicia, parentalia*), 5272 (*parentalia, rosalia, natalis*), 5907 (*parentalia*), 7450 (*rosa* for parents and self).

27. *FIRA* 45; *ILS* 7258; *AE* 1940.94.

28. *CIL* 2.1174 (*alimenta*), 3415 (*ludi*), 4511 (distribution to decurions and Augustales every five years); 6.9626 (cash); 8.9052 (games and *sportulae*), 11201 (dinner and *sportulae* to decurions and *curiae*), 12422 (*sportulae* to decurions, oil to citizens), 24017 (dinner), 25428 (games and *sportulae* to decurions), 26275 (games and *sportulae* to decurions); 9.5376 (*sportulae* to decurions); 11.3890 (*sportulae* to decurions), 4789 (dinner to town), 6520 (oil to *collegium*); 14.2827 (snack to two towns); *NdS* (1928): 283 (*sportulae* to decurions and Augustales); *ILS* 6468 (*sportulae* to decurions [also dinner], Augustales, citizens); *I. Cret.* 4.300 (*sportulae*).

Spanish senator who distributed 400 denarii to each decurion of
Barcino for his birthday and 300 to each Augustalis; or the Mau-
retanian veteran and decurion who funded annual civic games
and *sportulae* on his birthday and that of his wife; or the Italian
woman who distributed cakes and wine each year on her birthday
to the citizens of Minturnae and Casinum.[29] Moreover, when the
birthday of the deceased or a near relative is not in question, the
nearest thing will do—the birthday of a patron or of the emperor.[30]
Directly or indirectly, the emphasis is firmly on the donor, and
participants in the foundation are meant to remember him or her
on the most significant of days.

Undoubtedly the name of the donor would be prominently
mentioned on the birthday, at the distribution of oil or the provision of a meal; indeed it would be hard to avoid in those cases
where the beneficiaries met (as so often) at the tomb for the cult of
the dead, or before the donor's statue, or at the public building
which the donor had paid for.[31] Games would of course bear the
donor's name, *certamina sub nomine eius*.[32] And the beneficiaries of
alimentary schemes would also bear the name of their original
benefactor, as in *ingenui Iuncini* or *Variani alumni*.[33] Some of those
schemes also bore explicit witness to their memorial nature: so
with the Spanish lady of senatorial rank who added to an existing
scheme two payments to be made on the birthdays of (probably)
her husband and herself; or the woman from Tarracina in Italy
who bequeathed a million sesterces for the *alimenta* of a hundred
boys and a hundred girls "in memory of her son Macer."[34]

The one common element in all the forms of foundation is thus
the survival of the testator in the memory of the community; an

29. *CIL* 2.4511; 8.9052; 14.2827. See further Laum, *Stiftungen*, 77, 78–79,
108–111.
30. Patron: Laum, *Stiftungen*, 35, *CIL* 3.6998. Emperor: *I. Cret.* 4.300, *CIL*
14.2795; cf. 5.7637 (dedication of a statue of the emperor), *ILAf.* 527 (dedication
of statue of the Genius Augusti).
31. Statue: *ILS* 6468, *CIL* 5.5272 (not testamentary), 8.9052. Public building:
9.1618, 11.126 (neither testamentary). Even at the funeral pyre, *rogum*: 11.5047.
32. *Dig.* 33.1.21.3, cf. 33.1.24, *certamen Chrysanthianum* at Sardis. At 33.1.6, the
heirs preside over the games.
33. *CIL* 2.1174; Fronto *Ad Am.* 1.14.1. Duncan-Jones, *Economy*, 228 and 319 for
examples.
34. *CIL* 2.1174 (Hispalis); *FIRA* 55d. The senatorial lady of 14.4450 (Ostia)
apparently left a large fund to cover the *alimenta* of 100 girls, games in memory of
an Aemilia Agrippina (her mother?) in April or May each year, and a dinner for
the decurions thrice annually.

element shared with all manner of single gifts, the public works and amenities, each of which would bear the name of the benefactor prominently displayed on an explanatory inscription, a *titulus*—there is no Greek or Latin expression for "anonymous donor." This is not to say that the cult of the dead lacked religious sentiment, or that philanthropy lacked feelings of patriotism and loyalty. It is however to agree with de Visscher, that foundations (and indeed outright gifts) essentially shared the same goal, the perpetuation of the memory of the donor.

How can we test this? Perhaps by looking at those rare cases where a testator explicitly discusses the act of generosity: are concern for the soul or the community, or for anything else, prominent? In one case, the jurist Modestinus, apparently paraphrasing a will, speaks of the legacy left to a city "so that from the revenues a game might be held each year in that city to preserve the memory of the deceased."[35] Or again, the heavily damaged inscription of the veteran and decurion of Auzia (Mauretania), L. Cassius Restutus, quotes from the twenty-sixth paragraph of his will careful instructions for annual circus games and annual *sportulae* to the decurions on his birthday and that of his wife, the *sportulae* to be distributed before the third hour of the day, at the base of their freshly cleaned, perfumed, crowned, and illuminated statues. Then, in a section difficult to reconstruct and soon breaking off, Restutus seems to have expressed his belief that their memory would thus be kept alive (?) "by you and your descendants" with most joyful (hearts? praises?).[36]

A statue base from Praeneste, dated to 385, slightly after our period, is even more informative, since it offers a rare insight into two quite different views of the same act of benefaction: those of the donor and those of the recipient. The grandiose dedicatory resolution by the town dwells on the donor's love for and piety toward all the citizens, and on his remembering their *honorificentia* (honor for him) by leaving a certain property to all those citizens whom he so loved, and so forth. But the actual passage from the will, that of a senator of Rome, shows a very different tone and intention.

35. *Dig.* 33.2.16.
36. *CIL* 8.9052.

To all the citizens of Praeneste I wish [the said property] to be given, so that in memory of me they may cherish my spirit every year without hesitation, and so that they may erect a statue in my name in the forum and write on it this very extract from my will, and let them not have the power to sell [the property], so that if ever they wish to alienate it, the state treasury may take it over.

Self-centered, hardheaded, and not a hint of the affection which his fellow citizens chose to see.[37]

Manius Megonius Leo of Petelia, in southern Italy, was more tactful, but no less firm.[38] In a paragraph again quoted verbatim from the will, he promised that if a pedestrian statue of him with stone foundation and marble base were erected in the upper forum, like that set up to him by the Augustales near the one set up by his fellow citizens (!), he would fund appropriate distributions of cash to the decurions at a feast and to the citizens on his birthday and at the Parentalia. Then follows a direct plea to the best of fellow citizens, *optimi municipes*, in the name of the emperor (Antoninus Pius), that they hold to his intentions forever and inscribe the whole paragraph on the statue base, "so that it might be better known to our descendants, or that it might also serve to remind those who would be munificent to their *patria*." In a companion text, from the base set up by the Augustales, Leo directed that the income from a certain property go to subvent the furnishings at their banquets, and that the wine from another property be enjoyed by them—in both cases to encourage men to serve as Augustales willingly, by providing an example and by relieving expenses. Then another direct plea, here to the Augustales, that they continue to observe his wishes forever, and so that their body might more easily know his will the whole relevant paragraph is to be inscribed on the spot. In both instances, civic duty is apparent, the need to set an example for other benefactors, and to encourage civic-minded freedmen. But even more important is the fundamental insistence that the deeds be known, which is to say remembered.

The last and clearest possible insight into the intentions of a donor are the dispositions made while living by a woman of Gy-

37. *FIRA* 54 = *CIL* 14.2934.
38. *ILS* 6468–6469.

theion in Laconia, the Phainia Aromation referred to earlier.[39] After elaborate instructions for the acquisition of money to supply oil at the gymnasium forever to citizens, noncitizens, and even (on six days in the year) slaves, and after a precise statement of the procedure to be followed in case of a default by the magistrates, she proceeded to request that this record of her philanthropy be set up on three pillars, one in the agora in front of her house, one in the Kaisareion, and one in the gymnasium itself, so that her philanthropy would be clear and well-known to both citizens and foreigners forever (lines 41–48). "For I wish to be immortal by arranging such a just and most sympathetic trust" (56–58). Here there can be no doubt that philanthropy, however well-intentioned, was the means, not the end. The arrangement was strictly *quid pro quo.*

Most testators did not reach outward beyond their circles of friends and servants to groups in society or to the community at large. The cost of such public benefactions, whether gift or endowment, was more than most could or would want to bear, and even in the wealthy there was no sense that the duty of leaving a will embraced patriotism or philanthropy. For those who did indulge in public benefaction the motives will certainly have varied. Some undoubtedly thought of the good of their soul, the glory of their family, or the well-being of their fellow citizens. But the one motive which runs implicitly through all such gifts, and which sometimes turns up explicitly in the donors' last wills, is the desire to be remembered on earth after they were gone. In that they joined everyone else who left a will.

39. *IG* 5.1.1208, improved at *SEG* 13.258.

# 9

## Memory
### *Funeral—Tomb—Cult*

Customarily, near the end of the will, after the institution of heirs, the assignment of legacies and *fideicommissa*, and the manumission of slaves, and normally just before the formal *mancipatio*, witnessing, and dating of the document, some testators turned to their final business, that is, to instructions for their funeral, for the construction of their tomb or other monument, and for the maintenance of the tomb and their cult.[1] The physical location of these instructions is no accident. The testator's distribution of largesse was not quite the last exchange in a gift-giving relationship. The last *officium* belongs rather to the beneficiaries—the heirs, legatees, and freed slaves—who in return are to care for the testator's physical remains and his or her memory. The question then arises: what precisely, at the last, did testators require in return, and why?

Concern for the afterlife is ubiquitous, and exceptions are rare and cautionary. Some might wish to avoid the bother of a funeral: Seneca, possibly to avert trouble for his family, asked that he be cremated without any funeral solemnity, just as Atticus had requested that he be buried without funeral pomp (he was interred in a family tomb).[2] More troubling were those philosophers like Maecenas who did not care to be buried at all: let nature bury his remains.[3] A case like that came to the attention of the jurist Modestinus, when a man was instituted heir on the condition that he throw the testator's remains into the sea. He entered on the estate but did not comply with the condition. Could he be expelled?

---

1. Cf. Amelotti, *Testamento*, 155–61. The *collegia funeratica* performed precisely the same services for many who did not (normally: see above, p. 55) leave a will: F. Ausbüttel, *Untersuchungen zu den Verein im Westen des römischen Reiches* (Kallmünz, 1982), 59–71, with bibliography.

2. Tacitus *Ann.* 15.64.5; Nepos *Att.* 22.4.

3. Seneca *Ben.* 92.35.

Modestinus replied that an heir was to be praised rather than accused who did not throw the remains into the sea, as the testator had wished, but gave them over to the tomb "mindful of the human condition"; indeed, one should rather first inquire into the sanity of the man who could impose such a condition.[4] Of course it was imperative in the ancient world that people should be buried, but for some much more was necessary. The great Frontinus, writer, soldier, administrator, and three times consul, forbade (probably in his will) the erection of a monument. It was a waste of money since, if his life had been worthy, his memory would endure. Pliny found this inverse snobbery ostentatious: memorials—tombs with bodies inside and inscriptions outside—were the correct thing.[5] Most testators would agree without question.

The first concern of testators was for the proper treatment of their bodies after they lost control of them. If all were carried out properly, they could expect (with more or less elaboration) that their eyes would be shut for the last time, that their bodies would be washed, anointed, and dressed for lying in state, and that in due course they would be carried in procession to a place of inhumation (possibly temporary, if a tomb was not yet prepared) or of cremation; all of this accompanied by ritualized expressions of grief.[6] How did they ensure that this would indeed be carried out properly?

Normally the heir would be in charge of the funeral; such was the assumption of most testators and the explicit understanding of the law.[7] Yet sometimes the task might be assigned specifically to one of several coheirs, or to a legatee.[8] The key point, however,

4. *Dig.* 28.7.27, *memoria humanae condicionis.*
5. *Ep.* 9.19.6.
6. J. M. C. Toynbee synthesized the primary written and artistic evidence in her *Death and Burial in the Roman World* (London, 1971), 43–61, including reliefs which depict a lying-in-state (pl. 9) and a funeral procession (pl. 11). Cf. H. Blumner, *Die römische Privataltertümer* (Munich, 1911), 482–511, on death, funeral, and monuments. Alongside Polybius' famous account of the funeral of a *nobilis* at 6.53, Hopkins (*Death and Renewal*, 219) drew attention to Lucian's depiction of a young girl's obsequies at *On Grief* (*De luctu*) 12–15. Add also the detailed observations of Propertius at 2.13b, which T. Birt read as his testamentary instructions: "De Properti Poetae Testamento," *RhM* 51 (1896): 492–505.
7. Specifically Ulpian, at *Dig.* 11.7, esp. 11.7.12.4. Cf. *Dig.* 34.4.30.2.
8. E.g.: *BGU* 1655, sons/heirs to bury, if not then daughter/legatee; *BGU* 1662, daughter to bury, sons (presumably heirs) to reimburse her; *P. Select.* 14, daughter/

is that instructions for the funeral were, with the single known exception of Augustus' separate roll of directions, notably brief if they were included at all. Thus, inserted into long and elaborate orders for the construction and maintenance of his monument, "Dasumius" devotes a single sentence to his obsequies: his body is to be entrusted to his great friend Ursus Servianus and the bier is to be carried by Servianus' freedmen. Similarly, the long extract from the testament of an anonymous Gaul of roughly the same period, which is likewise minutely concerned with the tomb, simply demands that funeral and tomb be cared for by the testator's heir and grandson, two friends, and a freedman, adding a detailed list of various possessions to be placed in the tomb.[9] A testator in the Digest, after ensuring that if he died abroad a certain man would be paid to bring his body back home, directed his heirs to care for his body wherever he may have died, and to place it in the tomb of his sons in Campania.[10] Among the testators of the papyri, Longinus Castor has but one sentence, entrusting the laying out and burial of his body to the care and piety of his heirs. Antonius Silvanus and several others have nothing to say of burial at all.[11]

In truth, testators were not much interested in their funerals: others could take care of that. Ritual was prescribed by custom, while expenses came out of the estate if not otherwise assigned, as appropriate to the wealth and dignity of the deceased.[12] An heir or legatee could be given the task of supervision, but if nothing was said the heir would assume it automatically. Beyond naming a supervisor, those testators who cared to express concern dealt with one of two items, how much the funeral would cost and where precisely it would end. Each of these was really part of care for the tomb: the arrival, not the journey, was what mattered.

Whereas few gave much thought to their funeral, some testators devoted immense care to their monument. In the words of

---

legatee to bury, heirs to reimburse; *Dig.* 32.42 wife heir to 1/12, to receive body for burial in a certain *fundus* and erect monument for a certain sum.

9. *CIL* 6.10229.111–12; 13.5708.16–25 (cf. *Dig.* 34.2.40.2: a woman buried with specified jewelry). Freedmen: Herodes Atticus assigned his to bury him at his Marathon estate (Philostratus *VS* 565).

10. *Dig.* 34.4.30.2. The *testamentum Alexandri* directs Ptolemy to transport the body to Alexandria.

11. *BGU* 326; *CPL* 221.

12. *Dig.* 11.7.12.5

the philosopher Trimalchio, "It's wrong, I think, that a man should concern himself with the house where he lives his life but give no thought to the home he'll have forever."[13] Many will have been silent in their wills because, like Trimalchio or Augustus, they had arranged for their tomb while still alive; but those who had not shown that forethought must leave the tomb to the care of their heirs, and certain concerns recur.

First, some might have to designate exactly where they wished to be buried—"make me a monument in the Vatican, at the Circus, next to the monument of Ulpius Narcissus"—or with whom.[14] Second, some wanted their monument to be constructed speedily. In the days of Augustus, Cestius' modishly Egyptian pyramid at Rome was completed within 330 days of his death, as prescribed in his testament, while a century later "Dasumius" apparently imposed a time limit for the erection of his monument. Another heir had inscribed on a tomb in A.D. 233 that she had completed and dedicated it within the time prescribed by the testament; one late republican testator ordered his sons to complete the monument within a certain number of days on pain of disinheritance.[15]

And third, frequently, testators might dictate how much money should be spent on their funerals and tombs together, sometimes naming a minimum figure to prevent the heir from skimping.[16] Such costs, testamentarily directed or not, are often recorded on the epitaph, perhaps reflecting to some extent the relative size of estates. A study of North African monument costs has compiled a list with 52 entries, which run from 96 sesterces to over 80,000, most of them in the range between a few hundred and 2000 sesterces.[17] Certainly many if not most of these expenditures were

13. Petronius *Sat.* 71.6, translated by W. Arrowsmith.

14. *AE* 1945.136. Herodes Atticus specified Marathon; Mark Antony Alexandria, at the side of Cleopatra; Aurelius Chaeremon near the tomb of his wife (Philostratus *VS* 565; Plutarch *Ant.* 58; *P. Oxy.* 2348).

15. *CIL* 6.1374; 10229.113–14; *ILS* 8096 (Auzia, Mauretania); *Dig.* 28.5.45.

16. It is normally not possible to distinguish among costs of funeral, site, monument and incidentals—so S. Mrozek, *Prix et rémunerations dans l'Occident romain (31 av. n.è–250 de n.è)* (Gdansk, 1975), 53—e.g., *CIL* 8.3079 (Lambaesis), *in funus et monimentum HS II mil.*, cf. *ILS* 2795.

17. Duncan-Jones, *Economy*, 99–101. At *Dig.* 32.42, Scaevola discusses a testator who wanted up to 40,000 sesterces spent on his tomb, yet whose whole estate came to less than 180,000. At the other extreme, in the admittedly fictional testament of Metrodorus, funeral and tomb are assigned about 5 percent of the estate, 1/10 of

explicitly directed by the testator in the will.[18]

The most elaborate of all testamentary prescriptions for the tomb itself is that of an anonymous Gaul from the tribe of the Lingones, written some time in the late first or early second century.[19] It prescribes a shrine (*cella*) with an open bay (*exedra*) in which was to be placed a seated statue of the deceased in the best marble or bronze, at least five feet high. At the foot of the exedra was to be a couch with two benches of stone on each side of it. These were to be equipped with specified coverings—pillows, robes, and tunics—on the days on which the chapel opened, for dining and sacrifice. Standing before the exedra was to be an altar of the best Luna marble, containing the bones of the deceased. The chapel door was likewise to be of Luna marble, easy to open and close, and the exterior of the building was to bear an inscription with the names of the magistrates in whose year of office it was begun (presumably the year of the testator's death), and the age at which the testator died. The chapel itself was to be placed amid orchards and a lake, and detailed provisions were set down for its upkeep, for the exclusion of intruders from it, and for sacrifices there for the deceased.

The blueprint of the *testamentum Lingonis* combines the two cardinal elements of tombs: the representation of the living and the celebration of the dead. The first unites here both plastic and written portraits of the testator, that is, a statue and an inscription. Thousands of such commemorations in reality are best summed up and satirized by the overwhelmingly baroque exemplar of Trimalchio's tomb, arranged *inter vivos*: a statue of himself with a puppy at his feet, flowers, perfume, and the fights of the gladiator Petraites depicted around him; an elaborate allegorical frieze depicting his life as merchant, *sevir*, and benefactor; a statue of his

---

this for funeral, 9/10 for tomb. Lists and discussions of monument prices at Friedländer, *Sittengeschichte* 4:304–09, Mrozek, *Prix*, 52–56, and Duncan-Jones, *Economy*, 79–80 and 127–31.

18. E.g., *BGU* 1662 (400 silver drachmae); 1695 (200 Augustan denarii); *P. Oxy.* 2857 (100 dr. minimum); *P. Select.* 14 (800 dr. minimum); *CIL* 2.1359 (700 den.); 6.1828 (HS 20); 1848 (HS 100,000); 2164 and 2165 (50,000); 10245 (50,000); *AE* 1945.136 (6000); *CIL* 8.2764 (12,000); 22944 (*ad funus eius erogatus* 400); *ILS* 8096 (16,000).

19. *CIL* 13.5708. Consult also *FIRA* 49 and J. J. Hatt, *La Tombe gallo-romaine* (Paris, 1951), 65–84.

wife with dove in hand and puppy at feet, a little boy, jars of wine, and a sundial; an elaborate descriptive and philosophical account of his life inscribed and attached to the tomb (the standard *titulus*); and an orchard and vineyard around it.[20] An exaggeration, perhaps, but no busier than some of the more elaborate surviving monuments, such as the tomb of the Haterii.

The other component of the tomb so well displayed in the *testamentum Lingonis* is the preparation for the reception of the living when they visit to celebrate and sacrifice to the dead. Again, numerous examples, including careful diagrams of the area with each fruit tree noted, survive. One of the most detailed comes from the testament of the wife of a freedman of the emperor Trajan, providing for a building in the *ager Nomentanus* near Rome with atrium, a chamber next the sarcophagus, another chamber with two small shrines, a compluvium, a triclinium, a solarium, and a porticus: all the comforts of home.[21]

Most Romans, in life or in their wills, would not have personally prescribed such detail for their final resting place, through lack of need (if a tomb already existed), of interest, or of money. Silence would be more common, or such blunt injunctions as "build me a monument worthy of my youth," or "build me something like the tomb of P. Septimius Demetrius in the Via Salaria," or (in jest) "I want a monument built with an inscription in gold letters."[22] But what was supremely important, from the most magnificent of tombs down to the simplest of jars, was an inscription, the appropriate *titulus* ranging in scope from the *Res Gestae* of the emperor Augustus down to the briefest mention of a name. Hence the thousands of often modest inscriptions with recording formulae such as *testamento poni iussit*, *testamento fieri iussit*, or *ex testamento*, abbreviated or written out in full, or monitory formulae such as "this tomb does not go to the heir" (*hoc monumentum heredes non sequetur*) and variations on it. These are ubiquitous, on plain stones, marble plaques, sarcophagi, statue bases, altars, tombs;

20. Petronius *Sat.* 71.
21. *AE* 1977.31.
22. *CIL* 10.7452 (codicil of a son-in-power); *Dig.* 35.1.27 (cf. *ILS* 8074, from Lamiggigi, Numidia: while still alive a man arranges for "a monument of the shape and size of the monument of Obstoria Bellica and Petronius Verecundus"); *Testamentum Porcelli.*

and their purpose is clear. Burial and cult were important to society, memory was what mattered to the individual. Ulpian summed up the common conception: a monument exists for the sake of preserving memory.[23] That is one reason why tombs jostle for space close to the roads just outside the walls of an ancient city, their *tituli* demanding, often in so many words, that the traveler stop and read them.[24] But there were more active ways of preserving memory.

Several testators took careful thought not only for their monument but for its future, in two connected ways. First, the physical upkeep of the tomb, if there was a tomb, had to be provided for, along with the celebration of regular cult acts. Hence plans might be devised to ensure curatorship, the most elaborate example being again that of the anonymous Gaul: two freedmen were to supervise and maintain the building, the orchard and the lake; three gardeners and their apprentices were to be employed, and provision was made for substitutes should any of them die or leave; and 60 modii of wheat and 30 denarii of clothing were assigned annually to the gardeners. More bluntly, Trimalchio assigns the *custodia* of his tomb to one of his freedmen "so that people won't run up and shit on my tomb." Sometimes it was apparently assumed that a curator would live at the tomb and off its revenue.[25] Thus, explicitly, one testator in the Digest, after assigning *cibaria et vestiaria* to some *liberti*, ordered them to remain wherever his body was, so that in the absence of his daughters they might celebrate his memory each year at the sarcophagus. Another made a legacy dependent on residence at the tomb.[26] Inscriptions confirm, showing freedmen curators obtaining a livelihood from the tomb while using the income of the *fundus* to

23. *Dig.* 11.7.2.6.
24. Cf. the anonymous *De Sepulchris* in F. Blume et al., *Die Schriften der römischen Feldmesser*, Vol. 1, *Texte und Zeichnungen* (Berlin, 1848), 271: *Nam monumentum plurimis est constitutum rationibus. Est unum quod ad itinera publica propter testimonium perennitatis est constitutum.*
25. Petronius *Sat.* 71; *FIRA* 49. On the economic function and value of the tomb-garden, see N. Purcell, "Tomb and Suburb," in *Römische Gräberstrassen: Selbstdarstellung—Status—Standard*, ed. H. von Hesberg and P. Zanker, Bayerische Akademie der Wissenschaften, Philosophisch-Historische Klasse, Abhandlungen, n.f. 96 (Munich, 1987) 25–41, at 35–36.
26. *Dig.* 34.1.18.5; 35.1.71.2 (or that he take up residence in that city).

maintain it and themselves.[27] The custodians were backed up by sanctions against incursion, in the form of penalties for the damage of tomb or *titulus*, or at law with the action for violating a tomb. And, like the anonymous Gaul and "Dasumius," care was sometimes taken that the curatorship be continued as long as possible, through often complex procedures for substituting curators.[28]

Physical maintenance and protection by such custodians were only the first step; the integrity of the tomb must be ensured. Hence there survives a great number of prohibitions, often supported by fines, against the alienation, gift, sale, pledge or division of the tomb.[29] At the same time, the burial of unauthorized outsiders is constantly being prohibited: "this tomb does not receive strangers."[30] The common purpose is to preserve the integrity of the tomb as the testator conceived it, preventing dispersion or intrusion by assigning it to certain people.

Even then, perpetual curatorship and threatening prohibitions are not very satisfactory hedges against an uncertain future. Many testators felt the need for something more positive and more compelling, and that was achieved by testators actually offering burial to their freedmen and freedwomen in their monuments. Thus scores of times one finds this formula, or variations on it: "They built this monument both for themselves and for their freedmen and freedwomen and for their descendants."[31] This widely used bargain was simple but extremely effective. The freedmen and freedwomen were in essence afforded a private burial club, no small comfort in an uncertain world. It thus became in their interest to maintain the tomb of their master or mistress, who with luck could count on future generations: the social and economic dependence of freedmen on their patron was

27. *CIL* 3.656, *fundus* assigned to *liberti* and descendants, with its *reditus* to care for tomb and them; 14493, vineyards assigned to *curatores sepulchri*; 13.1734, *custodia* and *habitatio* conjoined; *ILS* 1798, *custodia monumenti inhabitandi ne quis interdicere vellit.*

28. Dasumius: *CIL* 6.10229.95ff. Cf. *ILS* 8342, *nam curatores substituam uti vescantur ex horum hortorum reditu natale meo et per rosam in perpetuo*; 8378 (the most worthy substitutes are chosen by vote).

29. A good selection of inscriptions at *FIRA* 81 and 82.

30. *ILS* 8265.

31. E.g., *ILS* 8220: *fecerunt et sibi et libertis libertabusq. suis posterisq. eorum.* Dozens of examples in *ILS* alone: 7929, 7932, 7933b, 8015, 8089, 8090, 8092, 8149, 8210, 8215, 8216, 8217, 8219, 8220, 8224, 8225, 8227, 8228, etc., through to 8389. On this *sepulchrum familiare*, see above all Kaser, "Grabrecht," 37–51.

a much more certain foundation for the monument and the memory than was the piety of an independent heir.[32] And in most cases
assurance was made as sure as possible by including in the monument all the freedmen and freedwomen of the family. Hence a
striking number of cases where ungrateful freedmen and freedwomen are excluded by name from the tomb because of their
crimes, injuries, or ingratitude: one needed to be assured of the
survivors' *pietas*.[33]

Quite often a *modus*, a restriction determining the conduct of
the beneficiary, is attached to the gift or legacy of the tomb or
places in it, to make its purpose very clear: normally "that it not
leave my name," *ne de nomine meo exeat*, or some variant thereof.[34]
Occasionally, the word *familia* is substituted for *nomen*, but it clearly refers to the same favored freedmen and freedwomen.[35] The
efficacy of such a bargain is strikingly illustrated by a large and
complicated text on marble from the vicinity of the Porta Capena
at Rome, wherein four men and a woman record in 13 B.C. that
they have built a monument with crematorium (*monumentum cum
ustrina*) and bequeathed it to those freedmen and freedwomen
who shall be named in their wills *ut de nomine non exeat*. Despite
sales of portions, cooptations of beneficiaries into the group,
negligence, and restorations (all recorded on the same stone),
almost 125 years later, in A.D. 110, three of the four original
families are still recorded as involved in the management of the
monument.[36]

32. Hence the common formula on epitaphs, *H(oc) M(onumentum) H(eredem)
E(xterum) N(on) S(equetur)*, on which see Kaser, "Grabrecht," 42, and below.
33. E.g., the testament of "Dasumius," *CIL* 6.10229, 92, *prae[t]erquam Hymno
pess[ime de me merito...]; ILS* 8156=*IGUR* 3.1245, *excepto M. Antonio Athenione...
ideo quia me pos* [sic] *multas iniurias parentem sibi amnegaverit* [sic]; *ILS* 8115, *excepta
Secundina liberta, impia adversus Caecilium Felicem patronum suum*; *ILS* 8285, *excepto
Hermete lib...propter delicia sua*; *AE* 1979.94, *excepto Hilaro liberto meo abominando*.
Without further specifics: *CIL* 14.1437; Thylander, *Inscriptions d'Ostie* A 222; *ILS*
8283, 8284. Along the same lines is *CIL* 6.12649, which after discussing arrangements for the maintenance of the cult at the tomb by *libertis libertabusque posterisq.
eorum*, turns to bequeath a nail and a rope to the freedman Atimetus, by whose
treachery the testator lost his daughter. Easily the most upsetting is *ILS* 8286
(Rome), whose author gives the right of burial to a man and two women and their
freedmen, "because the rest of my own freedmen did not deserve it, nor did my
daughter" (*ceteri et liberti propii* [sic] *meriti non fustis* [sic] *neque filia mea*).
34. *ILS* 8226, 8231, 8266, 8274, 8275, 8277, 8282. The name(s) may even be
spelled out: 8262, 8278, 8351. *Ex origine nostra*: 8221/2.
35. *ILS* 8230, 8274.
36. *CIL* 6.10243.

Here a slight digression is necessary. The legal and historical study of perpetuities in general has been placed on a new level by the recent work of D. Johnston.[37] Working from the Digest, Johnston has carefully distinguished between two important and very different kinds of legal prohibitions against alienation: those directed to family, normally children, and those directed to freedmen and freedwomen. To simplify some conclusions of an exhaustive study: in one type of prohibition, surviving relatives of the testator were forbidden to alienate a property *inter vivos*, though they were free to do as they wished testamentarily; in the other, freedmen and freedwomen were prohibited from alienating the property from the *nomen*, and their disposition of it by will was restricted. The trust to children was not much of a perpetuity, since it lasted for only one generation and was even then open to attack. The trust to freedmen and freedwomen might be accompanied by some form of *alimenta* for them, but that was a secondary and possibly conflicting concern: the main purpose was to perpetuate the *nomen* of the testator in connection with a property.

In the case of near family, the trusts concerned were always directed to individuals, and they affected only one generation.[38] Above all, they emphasized the family, with exhortations such as "Do not alienate this property, and leave it in the family" to a son, or "The house is not to be alienated, but to be left in the family" to a brother.[39] Here sentiment was surely the main element in the decision; the property reserved was property particularly identified with the family, and ancestral acres always held a special place in the Roman heart—witness Cicero on the special quality of his estate at Arpinum, or Pliny who would part with any but his maternal and paternal estates to the daughter of his mentor, and whose maternal estates were treating him badly yet still delighted him because they were his mother's. [40]

37. "Prohibitions and Perpetuities"; "Trusts and Tombs," *ZPE* 72 (1988): 81–87; *Roman Law of Trusts*, 76–107 (chapter 4, "The Dead Hand: Perpetuities and Settlements").

38. References in the Digest are: 30.114.15; 31.69.3; 31.77.11; 31.78.3; 31.88.15; 32.38 pr.; 32.38.3; 32.38.4; 32.38.7; 32.93 pr.; 35.2.54.

39. *Dig.* 30.114.15; 31.69.3.

40. Cicero *Leg.* 2.1.3–5; Pliny *Ep.* 7.11.5, 2.15.2. Cf. *Dig.* 32.38.7, a mother directing her sons not to alienate any lands from her *bona*. On sentiment and property, see my discussion and works cited in "The *Suburbium* of Rome," *AJAH* 7 (1982): 103 with n. 40.

The situation with former slaves is markedly different: where family trusts stressed family, these trusts emphasized the name; they were always directed to a group, not an individual, and they were clearly intended to last, being directed to *liberti* and *libertae*, and their descendants.[41] Exhortations by the testator accordingly run to "Let it not leave the name of my family," or "I forbid the Cornelian estate to leave the name of my family." Here we meet a problem, a gap between the inscriptions and the Digest. As Johnston has proven, despite considerable similarities, family settlements of property (Digest) and of family tombs (inscriptions) were at law two quite separate entities, the first effected through *fideicommissa*, the second as *legata sub modo*. Hence, the much-repeated argument is ill founded which attempts to find the origin of family trusts in testators' anxiety for the maintenance of their tombs.

But what then was the purpose of the family settlements recorded in the Digest? Johnston makes the obviously correct suggestion that the testator's memory was to be perpetuated with his *nomen*. But should we leave it at that? The similarities with the inscriptional provisions for the family tomb have always struck observers: the restriction to the testator's family name, the prominence of *groups* of freedmen and freedwomen, the accrual of shares in the property to survivors.[42] But surely in many if not all of the *fideicommissa* there is also a funerary intent not noted by Johnston. In all but three cases only one property is concerned, to be shared among all the former slaves of the testator: did that property have any special significance for him? One of the single properties we know was very small, a small estate to be shared among fifteen freedmen and freedwomen, a small estate with a hut, that is, surely a burial plot with provision for celebration of the dead.[43] And one legal text specifically states a motive: the

41. *Dig.* 31.77.15; 31.77.27; 31.77.28; 31.87.2; 31.88.6; 31.88.14; 32.38.1; 32.38.2; 32.38.5; 32.94; 33.1.18 pr.; 35.1.108.

42. Individual *libertilae*: *Dig.* 33.7.20.1; 32.94 (three); 35.2.25.1; 38.2.26; cf. 31.77.10 (whoever wants it). *Libertis libertabusque*: *Dig.* 31.77.13; 31.77.28; 31.88.6; 32.35.2; 32.38.5; 32.41.1; 32.93.2; 33.1.9; 33.1.18 pr.; 33.2.34 pr.; 33.2.35; 33.7.3; 34.1.4 pr.; 34.1.16.1. *Ne de nomine exeat*: *Dig.* 31.88.6; 32.38.1; 32.94; 35.1.108.1. *Ne alienarent*: *Dig.* 31.77.15; 31.77.27; 31.77.28; 31.87.2; 31.88.14; 32.38.5; 33.1.18 pr. Shares accrue: *Dig.* 33.2.34 pr.; 33.7.3.

43. *Dig.* 32.38.5. Cf. another *praediolum* at 31.88.6.

testator bequeathed by *fideicommissum* to his *liberti libertaeque* the property in which he wished to be buried, and when the last survivor of them died the property was to devolve upon the city of Arles.[44] Whether *fideicommissum* or *modus*, the intent of the family settlements recorded by the Digest was surely the same as that recorded on inscriptions: not just any property was to be kept in the family but, more often than not, specifically that property on which the testator's tomb was situated. That is, in both cases the testator's name and memory were closely bound up with the tomb.

One testator spoke for all, *inter vivos*: the property was not to pass from his name or his family, so that his memory might be sacrificed to as long as possible.[45]

Ancient views of the afterlife, of the survival of the soul after bodily death, have been extensively studied, and are as varied as human hopes and fears can make them.[46] That there was indeed an "ancient, deep-seated belief" in the soul's survival is apparent both in the literature and in the cult of the dead in all of its manifestations.[47] But if we set to one side the literary and philosophical literature which is our source for views of the afterlife, the thrust of the epigraphical evidence is starkly different. Among the manifold views of the afterlife attested or implied by inscriptions, nihilism is easily the most common: "I was not, I was, I am not, I don't care." A full study of sentiments in ancient epitaphs observed that while the afterlife centered on the cult of the dead, there existed no real doctrine, and it concluded that "the belief of the ancients...in immortality was not widespread, nor clear, nor very strong."[48]

In their wills, testators summed up their personal universes and prepared them for death. Hence, they made arrangements

44. *Dig.* 33.2.34 pr.

45. *ILS* 8274 (Rome): *ita ut ne de nomine suo aut familia exeat ut possit memoriae suae quam diutissime sacrificari.*

46. Two old but very useful surveys: F. Cumont, *After Life in Roman Paganism* (New Haven, 1922), and C. Pascal, *Le credenze d'oltretomba* (Pavia, 1912, reprinted as *L'oltretomba dei pagani*, Genoa, 1981).

47. Toynbee, *Death and Burial*, 33–39. For a brief survey, Hopkins, *Death and Renewal*, 226–232.

48. R. Lattimore, *Themes in Greek and Latin Epitaphs* (Urbana, 1942), 342 (such belief appearing mainly in lamentation and consolation); cf. along the same lines, H. Häusle, *Das Denkmal als Garant des Nachruhms*, Vol. 75 of *Zetemata* (Munich, 1980).

for elaborate tombs or simple epitaphs, or they left such matters to their heirs. Where they did take some thought, most directed it to the physical monument, but in their wills they showed neither concern for their souls, nor certainty or curiosity about the afterlife. The only future lay in this world.

The formal cult of the dead is not explicitly important to testators. A few dozen inscriptions (out of thousands of epitaphs) record foundations of one sort or another, set up to care for the *parentalia*, the *rosalia*, and so forth, but no papyrus mentions them and there is almost no concern evidenced in literature or the Digest; where such cults do occur in wills, they are public or semipublic events, not small family celebrations. Other testators left these matters to the piety of their heirs or their freedmen and freedwomen, not considering them important enough to mention. It is easy to assert that the Romans believed that the Manes, the ancestral shades, hung around the tomb, waiting to feed on offerings of food and drink; but there is no sign that any individual testator ever imagined himself in that position.[49] The only overt allusion to soul or afterlife in any will appears to be the following, from the broken epitaph of a Spanish testator, who (roughly translated) charges his heirs to offer up unmixed wine to his ashes: "let my intoxicated soul (*meus ebrius papilio*) flutter about, let herbs and flowers cover my bones, if anyone should stand near the epitaph in my name let him say 'that which the eager flame did not steal, that which has turned itself into a spark after the body has dissolved, rest in peace.' "[50] Eccentric, humorous, illiterate, or all three, but not to be taken as the norm.

Why then trouble with feasts, libations, sacrifices, flowers, if not for one's posthumous well-being? The normal sentiment seems to have been, regardless of one's personal beliefs on the

49. Lucian scorns the uselessness of pouring wine on graves and bedecking them with flowers: *De Luctu* 9, *Nigrinus* 30. Numerous inscriptions deplore and deride the cult of the dead, most notoriously *ILS* 8156 = *IGUR* 3.1245.

50. *CIL* 2.2146 (Obulco: I follow here the restorations of Buecheler at *CLE* 1851, rather than those of Mommsen *ad loc.*): *Heredibus mando etiam cinere ut m[era vina ferant,] volitet meus ebrius papilio, ipsa ossa tegant he[rbae et flores, hic ut] si quis titulum ad mei nominis astiterit, dicat [quod non rapuit] avidus ignis, quod corpore resoluto se vertit in fa[villam, bene quiescere.]* The conception of the soul as a butterfly emerging from the chrysalis of the body appears also on *CIL* 6.26011, (*litteris valde rudibus*) = *CLE* 1063 (Rome): *papilio volita(n)s.* Otherwise it is very rare in antiquity: *PW* s.v. "papilio" 3.

hereafter, that the survivors should have a good time eating and drinking (on whatever scale), put a generous portion on the grave, and then remember the deceased; the dead might be watching in the vicinity of grave or statue, but the ceremony essentially concerned the living, who watched over, and remembered, them.[51] The concern of the testator is always with memory, to the exclusion of all else. In the end, as throughout, the will is a document of the living, and memory is the final reward for the good and careful testator.

51. E. F. Bruck, "Foundations," 10–18.

# Conclusion

To every generalization an exception may be found and, no matter how formulaic, all Roman wills differed. But if one could sketch a typical or ideal Roman testator, certain characteristics would stand out. Since men were four times more likely to leave wills than women, this fanciful testator will be called, misleadingly but conveniently, "he."

First, he was initially impelled by a convergence of the expectations of society and his own inclinations. His will was granted a privileged status as the vessel of the truth and as the last judgment, one in which he appropriately honored those whom he and others deemed worthy, and exposed the unworthy. This privilege was unthinkable without a concomitant duty: if he had something worth leaving, the testator had a duty to family, friends, and society both to make a will and to do it properly. In return he gained a multiple sense not only of satisfaction but of security, present and future.

He was a person of substantial status and property, and mere youth or lack of family did not prevent him from answering duty's call. Accordingly, he wrote his will as early in life as possible, and supplemented or revised it frequently; the document was emphatically his own invention, written by himself or dictated to another; and he was careful to summon witnesses who would take an interest, but not too close an interest, in it. Given this very personal nature of the document, and its importance, others might understandably feel considerable concern for the integrity of its making, a concern particularly manifested in society's terror, greatly exaggerated, of the machinations of forgers and captators.

Overwhelmingly, the testator's concern was his immediate family and how to care for them. He was deeply conscious that his children were his natural heirs. If he disinherited them, it was seldom in anger, but normally as a strategy to hold together the family or the estate while providing for everyone. Far more often he instituted them his primary heirs, either all equally or sons before daughters, but both before everyone else. His wife, whatever their affectionate life might have been, he placed close behind his children and before all others, caring for her but firmly separating her from the bulk of the patrimony. Surviving parents, brothers and sisters, and their children he might also remember, but there his sense of family duty and affection stopped.

Beyond the immediate family, the testator singled out two close groups of nonrelatives for recognition, servants and friends. He might name a loyal freedman or an intimate friend heir, particularly if he had no surviving family; but normally he would remember such outsiders with legacies of different values and significance, ranking them far behind family. His freedmen and freedwomen would most appropriately receive some form of pension or land, closely bound to his heirs or his own remains by conditions or trusts; he would recognize a few favored slaves by manumitting them and leaving them similar legacies, but would bind them with even further obligations. Close friends, from emperor to client, he could remember with appropriate bequests; but he would perhaps more commonly feel obliged to leave mementos of cash or bullion, each nicely calibrated to the degree of intimacy.

Here the sense of duty ceases. The testator has appropriately remembered and cared for everyone who mattered, and their relationship is fixed for eternity. But what is implicit in these actions he also had the option of making explicit, that is, the preservation of his memory. If he were rich, he might leave a legacy (almost never an inheritance) to a group or a community, most commonly a public building or a recurrent public service, winning their continued remembrance through reminders of his philanthropy. Much more likely, he might leave either brief or elaborate instructions for his funeral or (far more important) for the erection and possibly for the upkeep and preservation of a monument—his intention being again to secure his memory on earth, not his personal afterlife.

These then were the motives of the ideal Roman testator.

A unique curiosity is a testament in the form of a mathematical puzzle in verse. Attributed to a certain Metrodorus, who is gener-

Table 1.    Distribution under the Fictional Testament of Metrodorus

| Recipient | Portion of the Estate | Amount | Percentage of Estate |
|---|---|---|---|
| *Heirs* | | | |
| Son | ⅕ | 132 talents | |
| Wife | 1/12 | 55 | |
| Four sons of dead son | 1/11 each | 240 | |
| Two brothers | 1/11 each | 120 | |
| Mother | 1/11 | 60 | |
| Total to heirs | | 607 talents | 91.9% |
| *Legatees* | | | |
| Cousins | | 12 talents | |
| Friend | | 5 | |
| Total to legatees | | 17 talents | 2.6% |
| *Manumissions* | | | |
| (six slaves) | | 25 minae | |
| | | 20 | |
| | | 50 | |
| | | 10 | |
| | | 8 | |
| | | 7 | |
| Total to slaves | | 120 minae | |
| | | = 2 talents | 0.3% |
| *Funeral* | | | |
| Tomb and sacrifice to Zeus | | 30 talents | |
| Pyre, cakes, grave-clothes | | 2 | |
| Gift to corpse | | 2 | |
| Total funeral expenses | | 34 talents | 5.2% |
| Total estate | | 660 talents | 100.0% |

ally assigned to the age of Constantine, it appears among thirty-one such epigrammatic puzzles preserved in the fourteenth book of the *Anthologia Palatina*.[1] The puzzle is straightforward, and the shares and sums involved are to be worked out as shown in Table 1. Nowhere do we have both a complete will and a complete accounting of an actual estate. How realistic is this fantasy?

Assuming that the testator (or versifier) has calculated the values of the shares of the entire estate, before the legacies and funeral costs have been deducted, then he has divided his property as follows. The heirs together receive the overwhelming bulk,

1. Text, translation, and notes can be found in the Loeb and Budé editions of the Greek Anthology.

roughly 92 percent of it. The descendants, a son and four grand-children (five *sui heredes*?), together take more than half of the estate (372 talents out of 660: about 56 percent). The wife takes exactly one share, the standard one-twelfth. The division among son, grandsons, wife, brothers, and mother strikingly recalls the contemporary, early fourth-century, distribution of his property by the centurion Valerius Aion among his daughter, brothers, sisters, and wife.[2]

The legatees (cousins, friend, and slaves) take roughly 3 per-cent of the total value. The largest single legacy—6 talents each, if there are only two cousins, otherwise the 5 talents assigned to the friend Eubulus—is about 10 percent of the smallest share received by an heir, and no single legacy exceeds 1 percent of the total value of the estate.[3] Cousins are notably ranked here as legatees, far behind closer kin.

The value of the freed slaves themselves is unknown, but the total of legacies to them comes to no more than 0.3 percent of the estate. In a nicely authentic touch, there appears to be a family among the freed slaves: Syrus, Synete, and Synetus son of Syrus.

There are no legacies to the emperor, to any group, or to the community at large.

Funeral and tomb take approximately 5 percent of the total, accounting for about twice the amount left in legacies. Nine-tenths of this sum goes to the tomb and the presumably recurrent sacrifice, only one-tenth to the funeral itself.[4]

In brief, on all counts this fiction conforms remarkably to our general picture of the historical Roman will.

2. *P. Col.* 188.

3. On that scale, the testator "Dasumius," who may have afforded one legacy of HS 6 million (*CIL* 6.10229.87), would have left an estate worth upwards of 600 million—not impossible on the scale of private wealth in the high empire, cf. Duncan-Jones, *Economy*, 343–44.

4. There are of course, in the nature of the piece, no musings on the afterlife.

# Appendix I
# Wills Attested in Literature

| | |
|---|---|
| Acerronia Polla | Tac. *Ann.* 14.6.2 |
| Aebutia | Val. Max. 7.8.2 |
| Aebutius | Liv. 39.9.2. |
| P. Aelius | Cic. *Cluent.* 162 |
| P. Aelius Hadrianus | *HA Hadr.* 1.4 |
| Aemilia Pudentilla | Apul. *Apol.* 99.3, 100.2, 5 |
| Aemilia Tertia | Pol. 31.26 |
| L. Aemilius Paullus | Plut. *Paul.* 39; Pol. 31.28 |
| M. Aemilius Scaurus | Val. Max. 4.4.11 |
| Alexio | Cic. *Att.* 15.2.4 |
| M. Annaeus Mela | Tac. *Ann.* 16.17.6, 7 |
| L. Annaeus Seneca | Tac. *Ann.* 15.62.1, 64.5–6 |
| M. Anneius Carseolanus | Val. Max. 7.7.2 |
| P. Annius Asellus | Cic. *Verr.* 2.1.104–14 |
| L. Annius Bassus | Plin. *Ep.* 7.31.5–6 |
| M. Annius Verus | *HA Marcus* 4.7 cf. 7.4 |
| P. Anteius Rufus | Tac. *Ann.* 16.14.5 |
| T. Antistius | Cic. *Fam.* 13.29.3–4 |
| L. Antistius Vetus | Tac. *Ann.* 16.11.2 |
| Antoninus Pius (imp.) | *HA Pius* 12.8 |
| M. Antonius | Plut. *Ant.* 58.4–8; Suet. *Aug.* 17.1; Dio 50.3.3–4, 51.15.7 |
| Apuleius | Apul. *Apol.* 23.1 |
| Arrianus | App. *BC* 4.41 |
| Asudius Curianus | Plin. *Ep.* 5.1.1, 11 |
| Asuvius | Cic. *Cluent.* 37 (forged) |
| Attius | Plin. *Ep.* 6.33.2, 6 |
| Attius? | Plin. *Ep.* 6.33.6 |
| Augustus (imp.) | Suet. *Aug.* 101.1–4, *Tib.* 23, 50.1, 51.1, 57.2, *Claud.* 1.5, 4.7, *Nero* 4.1; Tac. *Ann.* 1.8.1–3; Dio 53.31.1, 56.32.1–4, 57.14.1–2, 18.11; *RG* 20.3; Charisius 132 B |
| Aurelia | Plin. *Ep.* 2.20.9–11 |
| N. Aurius | Cic. *Cluent.* 21 |

| | |
|---|---|
| Balbullius | Cic. *Att.* 13.48.1 |
| T. Barrus | Val. Max. 7.8.8 |
| Brinnius | Cic. *Att.* 13.12.4, 13.4, 13.50.2 |
| | |
| Q. Caecilius | Val. Max. 7.8.5; Cic. *Att.* 3.20.1–2; Nepos *Att.* 5.1–2, 13.2, 14.2, 22.4 |
| L. Caecilius Cilo | Plin. *Ep.* 2.1.8; *CIL* 5.5279 |
| C. Caecilius Isidorus | Plin. *HN* 33.135 |
| Q. Caecilius Metellus Nepos | Val. Max. 7.8.3 |
| Caesennia | Cic. *Caec.* 17, 18 |
| Cn. Calpurnius Piso | Tac. *Ann.* 3.16.5–7, 17.8, 18.1 |
| C. Calpurnius Piso | Tac. *Ann.* 15.59.8 |
| L. Calpurnius Piso Frugi | Plin. *HN* 33.38 |
| L. Calpurnius Piso (Caesar) | Tac. *Hist.* 1.48 |
| Calva | Cic. *Att.* 15.3.1 |
| Cassius | Scribonius Largus *Comp.* 120 |
| P. Catienus | Plin. *HN* 7.122 |
| Censorius Niger | Fronto *Ant. Pium* 3, 4, 7 (= *Am.* 2.5) |
| Claudius (imp.) | Suet. *Claud.* 44.1; Dio 61.1.2 |
| Clodius Aesopus | Plin. *HN* 9.122 |
| Ti. Claudius Atticus Herodes | Philos. *VS* 2.1 (549); Fronto *M. Caes.* 3.3 |
| Ti. Claudius Atticus Herodes | Philos. *VS* 2.1 (558, 565) |
| Ti. Claudius Nero | Dio 48.44.5; *Fouilles de Xanthos* 7 (1981): 38 |
| Claudius Polyaenus | Plin. *Ep.* 10.70.2, 4 |
| M. Cluvius | Cic. *Att.* 13.45.3, 13.46.3–5, 13.37a, 14.9.1, 14.10.3, 16.6.3, cf. 16.2.1 |
| Constantinus (imp.) | Eus. *VC* 4.63; Socr. *HE* 1.39, cf. Soz. *HE* 2.34; Phot. *Bibl.* 473a; et al. |
| M. Coponius ("causa Curiana") | Cic. *Caec.* 53, 67, 69, *De Orat.* 1.180, 2.24, 2.140–41, *Brut.* 144–45, *Top.* 44, cf. *Inv.* 2.122 |
| Corfidius | Plin. *HN* 7.176–77 |
| L. Cornelius Balbus | Dio 48.32.2 |
| L. Cornelius Cinna | Sen. *Clem.* 1.9 |
| L. Cornelius Lentulus Augur | Suet. *Tib.* 49.1; Sen. *Ben.* 2.27.1 |
| Cornelius Scipio | Plin. *HN* 35.8 |
| P. Cornelius Scipio Aemilianus | Plin. *HN* 33.141; Plut. *Mor.* 199 F; Aelian *VH* 11.9; Pol. 18.35 |
| P. Cornelius Scipio Africanus | Pol. 31.27 |
| L. Cornelius Sulla | Plut. *Sulla* 38.2, *Pomp.* 15.3; App. *BC* 1.105; Cic. *Sulla* 54, *Vat.* 32; cf. Dio 37.51.4 |

| | |
|---|---|
| M'. Curius | Cic. *Att.* 7.2.3, cf. 7.3.9 |
| T. Curtilius Mancia | Plin. *Ep.* 8.18.4 |
| Cyrus | Cic. *Mil.* 48 |
| | |
| Dinaea | Cic. *Cluent.* 22, 41 |
| Diodotus | Cic. *Att.* 2.20.6 |
| Domitia | Suet. *Nero* 34.5 |
| Domitia Lucilla | *HA Marcus* 4.7 |
| Cn. Domitius Afer | Plin. *Ep.* 8.18.5; Quint. 6.3.92 |
| L. Domitius Ahenobarbus | Suet. *Nero* 6.3 |
| Domitius Balbus | Tac. *Ann.* 14.40–41, *Hist.* 2.86 |
| Cn. Domitius Lucanus | Plin. *Ep.* 8.18 |
| Cn. Domitius Tullus | Plin. *Ep.* 8.18 |
| | |
| Cn. Egnatius | Cic. *Cluent.* 135 |
| | |
| Q. Fadius Gallus | Cic. *Fin.* 2.55 |
| L. Faenius Rufus | Tac. *Ann.* 15.68.2 |
| C. Fannius | Plin. *Ep.* 5.5.2 |
| Favorinus | Philos. *VS* 1.8 (490) |
| Hispala Faecenia | Liv. 39.9.5–7 |
| Felix | Cic. *Q. Fr.* 3.7.8 |
| Flavius Scaevinus | Tac. *Ann.* 15.54.1–3, 55.3–5 |
| Fufidius | Cic. *Att.* 11.2.1, 11.13, 11.15 |
| C. Fufius Geminus | Dio 58.4.5 |
| M. Fulcinii | Cic. *Caec.* 10–12 |
| L. Fulcinius Trio | Tac. *Ann.* 6.38; Dio 58.25.2 |
| T. Furius Sabinus Aquila Timestheus | *HA Gord.* 28.1 |
| | |
| Gaius [Caligula] (imp.) | Suet. *Gaius* 24.1 |
| Galba (imp.) | Suet. *Galba* 17 |
| Galeo | Cic. *Att.* 11.12.4 |
| M. Gallius | Suet. *Tib.* 6.3 |
| Gegania | Plin. *HN* 34.11–12; cf. *ILS* 1924 |
| Geminius Victor | Cyprian *Ep.* 1.1.1 |
| | |
| Hadrianus (imp.) | *HA Hadr.* 24.11; Philos. *VS* 1.25 (534) |
| St. Helena (Aug.) | Eusebius *VC* 3.46 |
| Herennius | Cic. *Att.* 13.6.2 |
| Q. Horatius Flaccus | nuncupativum: *Vita Horati* |
| Q. Hortensius Hortalus | Cic. *Att.* 7.3.9; Plut. *Cato Min.* 52.5–7 |
| | |
| Istummenius? Mundus | Cic. *Att.* 15.26.5 |
| (Iulia) Berenice | Jos. *AJ* 18.156 |
| (Iulia) Salome | Jos. *AJ* 18.31, *BJ* 2.167 |
| Cn. Iulius Agricola | Tac. *Agric.* 43.4 |

| | |
|---|---|
| C. Iulius Caesar | Suet. *Caes.* 83.1–3, *Aug.* 7.2; App. *BC* 2.135, 136, 143, 3.16, 19, 22; Dio 44.35.2–3; Plut. *Cic.* 43.8, *Brutus* 20.3, 22.1, 3, *Ant.* 16.10, *Caesar* 64, *Mor.* 206 F; Tac. *Ann.* 2.41.1; Plin. *HN* 35.21; Florus 2.15; Eutrop. 7.1; Liv. *Per.* 116; Oros. 6.18.1; Vell. 2.59.1; Nic. Dam. *Aug.* 13, 17, 20, 30; Cic. *Att.* 14.10.3, *Phil.* 2.71; *RG* 15.1; *Fasti Ostienses, sub anno* 44 |
| Sex. Iulius Frontinus | Plin. *Ep.* 9.19 |
| (Iulius) Herodes (rex) | Jos. *AJ* 17.53, 78, 146, 147, 188–91, 195, 199, 221, 226, 317ff. |
| Iulius Largus | Plin. *Ep.* 10.75.1–2 |
| P. Iulius Lupus | *HA Pius* 1.6, 9 |
| C. Iulius Tiro | Plin. *Ep.* 6.31.7–12; cf. *CIL* 2.3661, *AE* 1975.849 |
| Iunia Tertia | Tac. *Ann.* 3.76 |
| P. Iunius | Cic. *Verr.* 2.1.130–53 |
| A. Licinius Archias | Cic. *Arch.* 11 |
| L. Licinius Crassus | Plin. *HN* 1.4; Cic. *Brut.* 212 |
| L. Licinius Lucullus | Macr. *Sat.* 3.15.6; Cic. *Att.* 13.6.2 |
| Livia | Cic. *Att.* 7.8.3 |
| Livia (Iulia Aug.) | Suet. *Tib.* 51.2, *Gaius* 16.3, *Galba* 5.2; Dio 58.2.3a |
| Lustricius Bruttianus | Plin. *Ep.* 6.22.3 |
| C. Maecenas | *Vita Horati;* Dio 55.7.5; Sen. *Ep.* 92.35 |
| Cn. Magius | Cic. *Cluent.* 21, 33 |
| Manlius | Cic. *Fam.* 13.30 |
| Q. Marcius Rex | Cic. *Att.* 1.16.10 |
| T. Marius Siculus | Val. Max. 7.8.6; *CIL* 11.6058 |
| Mindia Matidia | Fronto *Ant. Imp.* 2.1–2, *Am.* 1.14 |
| M. Mindius | Cic. *Fam.* 13.26.2, 28.2 |
| Minucius? Acilianus | Plin. *Ep.* 2.16.1 |
| L. Minucius Basilus | Cic. *Off.* 3.73–74; Val. Max. 9.4.1; Cic. *Verr.* 2.1.115 |
| Naevius Anius | Val. Max. 7.7.6 |
| Natalis | Sen. *Ep.* 87.16 |
| Nicopolis | Plut. *Sulla* 2.7–8 |
| Nostius | Cic. *Fam.* 13.46 |
| Numisius | Sen. *Contr.* 9.5.15 |

| | |
|---|---|
| L. Octavius Naso | Cic. *Q. Fr.* 1.2.10, 11 |
| C. Oppianicus | Cic. *Cluent.* 31 |
| Otho (imp.) | Suet. *Otho* 10.2 |
| | |
| Sex. Pacuvius | Dio 53.20.4 |
| Pantuleius | Tac. *Ann.* 2.48.1 |
| Papiria | Pol. 31.28 |
| M. Papirius | Cic. *Dom.* 49 |
| Passienus Crispus | Suet. *Nero* 6.3; cf. Jer. *Chron.* Ol. cciv; *Schol. ad Iuv.* 4.81 |
| A. Persius Flaccus | *Vita Persi* |
| Petronia | Suet. *Vit.* 6 |
| C. Petronius | Tac. *Ann.* 16.19.5; Plin. *HN* 37.20 |
| T. Pinnius | Cic. *Fam.* 13.61 |
| C. Plinius Secundus | Plin. *HN* pref. 20 |
| C. Plotius | Cic. *Fin.* 2.58 |
| Pompeius | Val. Max. 7.8.4 |
| Sex. Pompeius | Sen. *Tranq. Anim.* 11.10 |
| Sex. Pompeius Falco | *HA Pert.* 10.4 |
| Pompeius? Macula | Cic. *Fam.* 6.19.1 |
| Cn. Pompeius Magnus | Dio 48.36.5 |
| Pompeius Reginus | Val. Max. 7.8.4 |
| Pomponia Galla | Plin. *Ep.* 5.1 |
| T. Pomponius Atticus | Nepos *Att.* 22.4 |
| M. Popillius | Val. Max. 7.8.9 |
| Porcius Cato | Plut. *Cato Min.* 6.7 |
| Postumius | Cic. *Sest.* 111 |
| Precius | Cic. *Att.* 6.9.2, 7.1.9, *Fam.* 14.5.2; cf. *Att.* 12.24.3; *CIL* 10.5678 |
| Publicius Malleolus | *Rhet. ad Her.* 1.23, cf. Cic. *Inv.* 2.149 |
| C. Publicius Malleolus | Cic. *Verr.* 2.1.90 ff. |
| | |
| XL Martyres | ed. Knopf-Krüger-Ruhbach 116–19; Musurillo 28 |
| C. Quinctius | Cic. *Quinct.* 14, 15, 38–39 |
| | |
| L. Rubrius | Cic. *Phil.* 2.40, 41, 62, 74, 103 |
| Rustius Caepio | Suet. *Dom.* 9.2 |
| | |
| Sabina | Plin. *Ep.* 4.10.1–4 |
| Saturninus | Plin. *Ep.* 5.7.1, 3 |
| Ap. Saufeius | Cic. *Att.* 6.1.10 |
| (T. Quinctius?) Scapula | Cic. *Att.* 12.38a.2, 40.4 |
| L. Seius Strabo | Plin. *HN* 36.197 |
| L. Sempronius Atratinus | Jer. *Chron.* Ol. clxxxviii |
| Sempronius Tuditanus | Val. Max. 7.8.1 |

| | |
|---|---|
| Septicia | Val. Max. 7.7.4 |
| Q. Sertorius | App. *BC* 1.114 |
| Q. Servilius Caepio | Plut. *Cato Min.* 11.4 |
| Sicinius | Apul. *Apol.* 23.6, 68.6, 71.6 |
| Sicinius Pontianus | Apul. *Apol.* 96.4 |
| C. Sulpicius Olympus | Cic. *Verr.* 2.1.125–28 |
| | |
| L. Tarius Rufus | Sen. *Clem.* 1.15.4, 6 |
| Terentia | Cic. *Att.* 11.16.5, 25.3, 23.3, 24.2, 22.2 |
| Terentius | Val. Max. 7.7.5 |
| Tettius | Val. Max. 7.7.3 |
| Tiberius (imp.) | Suet. *Tib.* 76, *Gaius* 14.1, 16.3, *Claud.* 6; Dio 59.1.2 – 2.2, 55.9.8 |
| P. Trebonius | Cic. *Verr.* 2.1.123–24 |
| Q. Tullius | Lucil. 419–21 Kr. |
| M. Tullius Cicero | Cic. *Att.* 12.18a.2 |
| Q. Turius | Cic. *Fam.* 12.26.1–2 |
| Turpilia | Cic. *Fam.* 7.21 |
| L. Turselius | Cic. *Phil.* 2.41, 62, 103 |
| | |
| L. Valerius 'Heptachordo' | Val. Max. 7.8.7 |
| Valerius Paulinus | Plin. *Ep.* 10.104 |
| Valerius Varus | Plin. *Ep.* 6.8.4 |
| Vedius Pollio | Dio 54.23.5–6, cf. Ovid. *Fasti* 6.637–48 |
| Velleius Blaesus | Plin. *Ep.* 2.20.7–8 |
| C. Vennonius | Cic. *Fam.* 13.72.2 |
| Verania | Plin. *Ep.* 2.20.1–6, cf. *AE* 1982.75, Mart. 1.12 |
| Q. Veranius | Tac. *Ann.* 14.29.1 |
| P. Vergilius Maro | *Vita Vergili* 37, 40; Plin. *HN* 7.114; Gell. *NA* 17.10; Mart. 11.50 |
| L. Verginius Rufus | Plin. *Ep.* 6.10.4–5, 9.19.1 |
| Vespasianus (imp.) | Suet. *Dom.* 2.3 |
| Vibienus | Val. Max. 7.7.7 |
| T. Vinius | Tac. *Hist.* 1.48 |
| M. Vipsanius Agrippa | Frontinus *Aq.* 2.98–99, 116; Dio 54.29.4–5 |
| Ummidia Quadratilla | Plin. *Ep.* 7.24.2, 3, 7, 8 |
| Urbinia | Quint. 4.1.11, 7.2.4, 26; cf. 8.3.32, 9.3.13; Tac. *Dial.* 38.2; Charisius 98 B |
| | |
| Vulcatius Moschus | Tac. *Ann.* 4.43.8 |

ANONYMI/AE

Apul. *Apol.* 2.10–11 (male)
Caes. *BC* 2.18.2
Cic. *Att.* 2.1.5
Cic. *Brut.* 1.6.4
Cic. *Fam.* 7.2.1
Fronto *M. Caes.* 1.6
Fronto *Ver. Imp.* 2.7.5
Nic. Dam. *Hist.* 110 = Athen. *Deip.*
  153 F – 154 A
Plin. *Ep.* 2.4.1–2 (male)
Plin. *Ep.* 4.2.2 (female)
Plin. *Ep.* 4.22.1
Plin. *Ep.* 7.6.8 (male)
Plin. *Ep.* 7.11
Plut. *Sulla* 2.8 (female)
Quint. 8.5.17, 19 (male)
Quint. 9.2.934–35 (male)
Sen. *Ep.* 50.2
Suet. *Tib.* 31.1
Suet. *Tib.* 44.2
Suet. *Vit.* 14.3 (male)
Tac. *Ann.* 13.43.6 (2 females)
(Possibly also: Cic. *Att.* 1.6; *Att.*
  14.7; *Cluent.* 32; Philos. *VS* 1.21;
  *Schol. ad. Iuv.* 1.158)

CODICILLI

M. Annaeus Lucanus                  *Vita Lucani*

SOME FICTIONAL WILLS             (See also Horace, Persius, Martial,
                                 Juvenal, Lucian)

Ancus Marcius                       Liv. 1.34.12
Demaratus                           Liv. 1.34.2–3
Acca Larentia                       Gell. *NA* 7.7.6; Plut. *Mor.* 273 B
Tarrutius                           Plut. *Rom.* 5

Hermocrates                         Lucilius, *Anth. Gr.* 11.171
Anonymus                            Metrodorus, *Anth. Gr.* 14.123

Trimalchio                          Petronius *Sat.* 71ff.
Pansa                               Petr. 47
Anonymi                             Petr. 53
C. Pompeius                         Petr. 76

Eumolpus                              Petr. 141

Anonymus                              Phaedrus 4.5

M. Grunnius Corocotta                 In: F. Buecheler, ed., *Petroni*
                                      *Saturae*[8] (1963), 346–47

Alexander (rex)                       In: P. H. Thomas, ed., *Incerti*
                                      *auctoris rerum gestarum Alexandri*
                                      *Magni cum libro de morte*
                                      *testamentoque Alexandri*[2] (1966)
                                      43–49

Jupiter                               Tert. *Apol.* 15.1
Fabricius Veiento                     "Codicilli": Tac. *Ann.* 14.50
Terentius Varro                       "Testamentum": Buecheler *Petroni*
                                      *Saturae* 321

Licinnius, Sulpicius, et al.          *P. Bon.* 5 (= *C. Pap. Lat.* 279) is a
                                      unique, bilingual formulary for
                                      letters of etiquette, which includes
                                      three letters of condolence to
                                      those who have received
                                      inadequate legacies, and six of
                                      congratulations on receiving
                                      inheritances.

# Appendix II
## Papyri

Abbreviations are those of J. F. Oates, R. S. Bagnall, W. H. Willis, and K. A. Worp, *Checklist of Editions of Greek Papyri and Ostraca*³ (1985): I substitute arabic for roman numbers. For revisions, see the *Berichtigungsliste der griechischen Papyrusurkunden aus Aegypten*, vol. 1 (1922) – (latest) vol. 7 (1986).

\* = actual will, translation, copy, or extract.

| PAPYRI | (Later, better, or standard publications and major revisions) |
|---|---|
| *BGU* 1.326\* | *Chrest. Mitt.* 316, *Sel. Pap.* 85, *FIRA* 50: Longinus Castor |
| 1.327 | *Chrest. Mitt.* 61, *FIRA* 65: Fabullius Macer |
| 1.340 | Iulius Chaeremonianus |
| 1.361 | *Chrest. Mitt.* 92, *FIRA* 57 (male) |
| 2.388 | *Chrest. Mitt.* 91 + W. Schubart ap. G. Plaumann, *Der Idioslogos* (Berlin, 1919) 54–56: Sempronius Gemellus |
| 2.600\* | + Kreller 30f.: Cornelius Rufus |
| 3.613 | *Chrest. Mitt.* 89: Antistius Gemellus |
| 4.1113 | *Chrest. Mitt.* 169, *FIRA* 31: Pomponius |
| 7.1655\* | |
| 7.1662 | Valerius Turbo |
| 7.1695\* | *C. Pap. Lat.* 223; better, Amelotti App. 7: Safinnius Herminus |
| 7.1696\* | *C. Pap. Lat.* 224 |
| 13.2244\* | (Male) |
| *C. Pap. Lat.* 214 | *FIRA* 60: Flavia Valeria |
| 215 | Lucretia Diodora |
| 221\* | *FIRA* 47: Antonius Silvanus |
| *C.P.R.* 1.78 | |
| 6.2.76\* | Iulius |
| *P. Berl.* inv. 7124\* | *C. Pap. Lat.* 220, Amelotti 6; better, *Ch.L.A.* 10.412: Sempronius Priscus |
| inv. 13887\* | *Ch.L.A.* 10.427: Hostilius Clemens |

195

| | |
|---|---|
| *P. Cair. Goodsp.* 29 | Amatius Priscus |
| *P. Catt.* r.4.1–15 | *FIRA* 19b: Iulius Martialis |
| v. | *Chrest. Mitt.* 88.I.21ff.: Valerius(?) Apolinarius |
| *P. Col.* 7.188* | + R. S. Bagnall and K. A. Worp, *CE* 59 (1984): |
| | 307–10 (*P. Col.* inv. 331): Valerius Aion |
| *P. Coll. Youtie* 64* | Better, A. Bowman and J. Thomas, *BASP* 14 |
| | (1977): 59–64: Ignatius Rufinus |
| *P. Freib.* 2.8 & 9 | *SB* 6291, 6292: Iulius Gemellus |
| *P. Giss.* 1.35* | |
| *P. Hamb.* 1.70 | *Sel. Pap.* 59, *FIRA* 29: Flavia Ptolema |
| 1.73* | |
| *P. Haw.* 41 | Better, J. G. Milne, *Archiv* 5 (1913): 380f.: |
| | Maecenas Gratus |
| *P. Laur.* 1.4* | (=*Pap. Flor.* 1.4) |
| *P. Lips.* 9 | *Chrest. Mitt.* 211: Aurelius Tithoetion |
| 29* | *Chrest. Mitt.* 318, Amelotti, *Testamento romano*, |
| | 15: Aurelia Eustorgis |
| 30* | *Chrest. Wil.* 500, Laum 205 |
| *P. Lond.* 2.171b | *Chrest. Mitt.* 309, Amelotti, *Testamento romano*, |
| | 16: Serenus |
| 3.898 | |
| inv. 2529 + 2504 | Lucretius Minor |
| (unpubl.)* | |
| *P. Mich* 4.435 + 440 | *C. Pap. Lat.* 219 + 190; Better, R. Fink, *Roman* |
| | *Military Records on Papyrus* (1971), 77, *Ch.L.A.* |
| | 5.277 |
| 4.437* | Better, *C. Pap. Lat.* 225 |
| 4.439* | Better, *C. Pap. Lat.* 222, *Ch.L.A.* 5.278 (male) |
| 4.446 | Better, *C. Pap. Lat.* 226 (male) |
| inv. 2922 | *SB* 7558, *FIRA* 30: + H. Youtie *ZPE* 13 (1974): |
| | 241–48: Antistius Gemellus |
| *P.N.Y.U.* inv. 2.15* | Amelotti 19 |
| *P. Oxy.* 6.907* | *Chrest. Mitt.* 317, *FIRA* 51: Aurelius |
| | Hermogenes |
| 6.990* | Aurelia Aias |
| 9.1208 | Aurelius Pausiris |
| 12.1502 | |
| 14.1649* | (Female) |
| 22.2348* | Amelotti 11: Aurelius Chaeremon |
| 27.2474* | Amelotti 17 |
| 38.2857* | Claudius Alexander |
| 43.3103 | Aurelius Morus |
| 52.3692* | Iulius Diogenes |
| *P. Princ.* 2.38* | Aurelia Serenilla |
| *P. Ross.–Georg.* 2.18, | |
| nr. lxxvi | |

| | |
|---|---|
| 2.26 | Amelotti 8 |
| *P. Ryl.* 2.109 | Amelotti 12: Aurelius Hermias |
| *P. Select.* 14* | = *Pap. Lugd.–Bat.* 13.14: Iulius Diogenes |
| *PSI* 3.293 | |
| 6.690 | Flavia Titanias |
| 6.696* | |
| 7.738 | Valerius Primigenes |
| 8.940 | Claudius Flamma |
| 9.1027 | *C. Pap. Lat.* 213, *FIRA* 59: Herennius Valens |
| 9.1040* | *FIRA* 10: Psennamun Harpocrates |
| 10.1101 | Amelotti 14: Aurelia Tasarap... |
| 13.1325* | Sabinia Apollonarion |
| *P. Stras.* 1.41 | *Chrest. Mitt.* 93: Aurelius Heron |
| + *P. Lips.* 32 | |
| 4.277* | Aurelius |
| *P. Vindob. Gr.* | *AC* 20 (1951): 418–19: Dioskurus |
| inv. 25819 | (female) |
| *P. Wisc.* 1.14 | = *Pap. Lugd.–Bat.* 16.14: Valens |
| *P. Yale* inv. 1547* | Better, *Ch.L.A.* 9.399 |
| *Stud. Pal.* 20.29 | |
| 20.35* | Amelotti 13 |
| | |
| *P. Hamb.* 1.72 | *C. Pap. Lat.* 174, Amelotti 10, *Ch.L.A.* 11.496: formula |
| *P. Mich.* 4.453 | *C. Pap. Lat.* 227: a will? |
| *P. Oxy.* 3609? | |
| *P. Bon.* 5 | Cf. above, on literary wills |

New material arrives constantly: e.g., the valuable *P. Oxy.* 3741, 3756, and 3758 (all fourth century).

# Appendix III
## Select Inscriptions

This is only a choice from the thousands of inscriptions mentioning wills. For further references of interest, see *Dizionario Epigraphico* s.v. "codicilli," "fideicommissum," "heres," "legatum."

| LATIN | (Later, better, or standard editions) |
|---|---|
| *CIL* 2.1174 | *FIRA* 55a, D'Ors 424ff.: Fabia Hadrianilla |
| 2.1359 | *ILS* 5498, D'Ors 406ff.: Iunius Iunianus |
| 2.2146 | *CLE ad* 1851: Porcius |
| 2.3167 | D'Ors 408: Iulius Celsus |
| 2.3415 | |
| 2.3664 + p. 961 | *ILS* 6960, Laum 111, D'Ors 419 |
| 2.4511 | D'Ors 422ff., *Inscripciones romanas de Barcelona* 32: Minicius Natalis |
| 2.4514 | *ILS* 6957, D'Ors 420ff., Amelotti, *Testamento romano,* 3: Caecilius Optatus |
| 2.656 | Opimius Felix |
| 3.6998 = 13652 | *ILS* 7196, *FIRA* 53, Laum 121, *MAMA* 5.202: Aelius Onesimus |
| 3.14493 | Laum 117, *I. Dacia* 2.187 |
| 5.3072 | *ILS* 8339 |
| 5.4488 | Valerius |
| 5.5262 | *ILS* 2927: Plinius Secundus |
| 5.7637 | *ILS* 5065 |
| *Suppl. Ital.* 181 | Laum 65a: Antonius Valens |
| 6.1374, 1375 | *ILS* 917, 917a: Cestius |
| 6.1527 | *ILS* 8393, better E. Wistrand, *Laudatio Turiae:* "Turia" |
| 6.9405 | *ILS* 7238: Mamilius Felix |
| 6.10229 | *FIRA* 48 + W. Eck, *ZPE* 30 (1978): 277–95: "Dasumius" |
| 6.10230 | *ILS* 8394, *FIRA* 70: Murdia |
| 6.10236 | Calupius? Daulicius? Paetus |
| 6.10239? | *FIRA* 94: Flavius Syntrophus |

| | |
|---|---|
| 6.10245 | Priscus Gamianus |
| 6.10248 | *ILS* 8366 |
| 6.12133 | *ILS* 8365: Apisius Capitolinus |
| 6.12649 | |
| *AE* 1945.136 | *FIRA* 56bis, Amelotti 4: Popilius Heracla |
| *AE* 1952.36 | Manlia Felicitas |
| 8.1641 | *ILS* 6818, *FIRA* 55b: Licinius Papirianus |
| 8.1858, 1859 | *ILAlg.* 2.3040, 3041: Cornelius Egrilianus |
| 8.9052 | Cassius Restutus (*sic*) |
| 9.449 | Minatia...la |
| 9.1670 | |
| 9.1938 | |
| *Suppl. Ital.* 4.50 | |
| 10.114 etc. | *ILS* 6468–71, Laum 33, 33a, Amelotti, *Testamento romano*, 2: Megonius Leo |
| 10.5056 | *ILS* 977, *FIRA* 55c: Helvius Basila |
| 10.6328 | *ILS* 6278, *FIRA* 55d: Caelia Macrina |
| (10.7452 | *ILS* 8377, *FIRA* 56: *codicilli*) |
| 11.419 | *ILS* 6663, *FIRA* 118: Septimius Liberalis |
| 11.1436 | *ILS* 7258, *I. It.* 7.1.19: Naevius Restitutus |
| 11.3551 | *Tituli* 6 (1987): 316–24 |
| 11.4593 | Amelotti, *Testamento romano*, 5 |
| 11.6481 | |
| 11.6520 | *ILS* 6647, Laum 46: Caetrania Severina |
| 12.1587 | |
| 12.3861 | *ILS* 8378 |
| 13.5708 | *ILS* 8379, *FIRA* 49, Hatt 66ff.: Iulius Fabia? Agrippina? |
| 14.4450 | |
| *AE* 1940.94 | Amelotti, *Testamento romano*, 1: Iunia Libertas |
| *AE* 1977.31 | Claudia Saturnina |

| GREEK | (Later, better, or standard editions) |
|---|---|
| Laum 35 | N. Vulic, *Spomenik* 71 (1931): 186: Vettius Philo |
| *IG* 5.1.1208 | Laum 9, better *SEG* 13.258 |
| *Hesperia* 30 (1961): 236, 403 | |
| *SEG* 29.127, 35–47 | Stratolaus |
| *IK* 17.2 (Ephesos) 5113 | Iulius Aquila Polemaeanus |
| *IGRR* 4.1168 | Laum 72: Evaristus |
| *IGRR* 4.661, 660 | Laum 173, better, F. Cumont, *Musées royales du cinquantenaire, Bruxelles: Catalogue des sculptures et inscriptions antiques*² (Brussels, 1913), 150–55, nr. 133, *SEG* 13.542: Flavius Praxias |

*SEG* 1980.1392(?)          Epikrates
*IG* 12 Suppl. 364          + Dunant-Pouilloux (1958) 76, nr.
                            185: Caninius Rebilus
*IGRR* 1.1509               *I. Cret.* 4.300: Flavius Xenon
*AE* 1960.326               *FIRA* 85bis: Pompeius Epaphras
*IG* 14.956                 Laum 213, better *IGUR* 246: Claudius
                            Apollonius and Claudius Rufus

# Appendix IV
## *Captatio* and Related Improprieties


| | |
|---|---|
| Plautus | *Miles* 705–15 |
| Cicero | *Par.* 39, 43 |
| | *Off.* 3.74 |
| Horace | *Epist.* 1.1.77–79 |
| | *Serm.* 2.5 |
| Longinus | 44.9 |
| Ovid | *Ars* 2.271–72, 329–32 |
| Seneca II | *Brev. vit.* 7.7 |
| | *Ben.* 1.14.3; 4.20.3; 6.38.4 |
| | *Cons. ad Marciam* 19.2 |
| | *Const. sap.* 6.1; 9.2 |
| | *Ep.* 19.4; 95.43 |
| | *Ira* 3.34.2 |
| Petronius | *Sat.* 116–17; 124–25; 140–41 |
| Pliny I | *HN* 14.5; 20.160 |
| Statius | *Silv.* 4.7.33–40 |
| Martial | 1.10; 2.26; 2.32; 2.40; 3.52; 4.56; 5.18; 5.39; 6.27; 6.62; 6.63; 7.66; 8.27; 8.38; 9.9; 9.48; 9.88; 9.100; 10.8; 11.44; 11.55; 11.83; 12.10; 12.40; 12.56; 12.73; 12.90 |
| Pliny II | *Ep.* 2.20; 4.2; 4.15.3; 5.1.3; 7.24.7; 8.18.1–3, 7–10 |
| | *Pan.* 43.5 |
| Epictetus | 4.1.148 |
| Tacitus | *Germ.* 20.5 |
| | *Dial.* 6.2 |
| | *Hist.* 1.73 |
| | *Ann.* 3.25.2; 13.42.7; 13.52.2; 14.40.3 |
| Juvenal | 1.37–41; 3.128–30, 161, 220–22; 4.18–19; 5.98, 137–40; 6.38, 548–50; 10.201–2; 10.236–39; 12.98–101, 111–14; 16.51–54 |

| Plutarch | *Mor.* 497 A–C |
| Lucian | *Dial. mort.* 15(5), 16(6), 17(7), 18(8), 19(9), 21(11) |
| | *Rhet. praec.* 24 |
| | *Timon* 21–23 |
| Aelian | Fr. 83 H |

# Appendix V
## Emperors as Heirs and Legatees

(Emperors' wills attested: Augustus, Tiberius, Caligula, Claudius, Hadrian, Antoninus Pius, Constantine [Constantius II, Theodosius]).

Bibliography: Rogers, "Roman Emperors"; Guademet, "Testamenta ingrata"; Millar, *Emperor;* Bund "Erbrechtliche Geldquellen"; Petronius *Sat.* 76.

Augustus: Dio 56.32.3; Suetonius *Aug.* 59, 66.4, 101.3
Cornelius Cinna (*ex asse*); Horace; Julius Caesar (3/4); Herod; Maecenas; Pacuvius; Sempronius Atratinus; Tarius Rufus; Vedius Pollio; Vergil (1/4); Agrippa

Tiberius: Dio 57.17.8, 58.16.2; Suetonius *Tib.* 15.2, 44.2; Tacitus *Ann.* 2.48.2
Cornelius Lentulus (*ex asse*); Cassius (leg.); Fufius Geminus (1/2); Livia (Iulia Aug.); Pantuleius; Seius

Caligula: Dio 59.15; Suetonius *Gaius* 38.2
Domitius Ahenobarbus (2/3); Sex. Pompeius

Claudius: Dio 60.6. 3, 17.7
Claudius Polyaenus

Nero: Suetonius *Nero* 32.2; Dio 62.11.2
(Annaeus Mela;) Antistius Vetus; Calpurnius Piso; Domitia; ? Prasutagus

Vitellius: Suetonius *Vit.* 14.2

Domitian: Pliny *Pan.* 43; Suetonius *Dom.* 9.2, 12.2; Tacitus *Dial.* 13.7
Julius Agricola

Trajan: Pliny *Pan.* 43; *CIL* 6.10229, 126.

Hadrian: *HA Hadr.* 18.5

Antoninus Pius: *HA Pius* 8.5; *Dig.* 31.56, 49.14.22.2 (cf. Gaudemet 115)

Marcus Aurelius: *HA Marcus* 7.1, 11.8
Matidia

Commodus: *HA Comm.* 5.14, 19.5

Pertinax: *HA Pert.* 7.3; *Inst.* 2.17.8

Caracalla: Dio 77.12.5

Severus Alexander: *CJ* 6.23.3

EMPRESSES

Livia
  Herod, Salome

Antonia
  Berenice

Agrippina
  Acceronia

Faustina
  Matidia

# Bibliography

Amelotti, M. *Il testamento romano attraverso la prassi documentale.* Vol. 1, *Le forme classiche di testamento.* Studi e testi di papirologia 1. Florence, 1966.

———."Il testamento romano classico alla luce di nuovi documenti." In *Estudios de derecho romano en honor de Alvaro d'Ors.* 1: 151–59. Pamplona, 1987.

Andreau, J. "Fondations privées et rapports sociaux en Italie romaine (Ier–IIIe s. ap. J-C)." *Ktema* 2 (1977): 157–209.

Astolfi, R. *Studi sull'oggetto del legato in diritto romano.* Padua, 1964–1979.

———. *Lex Iulia et Papia.* 2d ed. Padua, 1986.

Berger, A. *An Encyclopedic Dictionary of Roman Law.* Philadelphia, 1953.

Biondi, B. *Successioni testamentarie e donazioni.* 2d ed. Milan, 1955.

Birt, T. "De Properti poetae testamento." *Rheinisches Museum* 51 (1986): 492–505.

Borgolte, M. *"Felix est homo ille, qui amicos bonos relinquit:* Zur sozialen Gestaltungskraft letztwilliger Verfügungen am Beispiel Bischof Bertram von Le Mans (616)." In *Festschrift für Berent Schwineköper,* edited by H. Maurer and H. Petzold, 5–18. Sigmaringen, 1982.

———. "Freigelassene im Dienst der Memoria. Kulttradition und Kultwandel zwischen Antike und Mittelalter." *Frühmittelalterliche Studien* 17 (1983): 234–50.

Bossu, C. "M' Megonius from Petelia (Regio III): A Private Benefactor from the Local Aristocracy." *Zeitschrift für Papyrologie und Epigraphik* 45 (1982): 155–65.

Boyer, G. "Le droit successoral romain dans les oeuvres de Polybe." *Revue Internationale des Droits de l'Antiquité*[2] 4 (1950): 169–87. (Reprinted in *Mélanges* 1: 264–98. Paris, 1962.)

Boyer, L. "La fonction sociale des legs d'après la jurisprudence classique." *Revue historique de droit français et étranger*[4] 43 (1965): 333–408.

Browder, E. L. "Recent Patterns of Testate Succession in the United States and Europe." *Michigan Law Review* 67 (1968/69): 1303–60.

Bruck, E. F. "Cicero vs. the Scaevolas. Re: Law of Inheritance and Decay of Roman Religion (*De legibus,* II, 19–21)." *Seminar* 2 (1945): 1–20. (Reprinted as "Cicero gegen die Scaevolae in Sachen: Erbrecht und Verfall der römischen Religion," in *Über römisches Recht im Rahmen der Kulturgeschichte,* 24–45. Berlin, 1954.)

———. "Foundations for the Deceased in Roman Law, Religion, and Political Thought." In *Scritti in onore di Contardo Ferrini* 4: 1–42. Milan, 1949. (Reprinted as "Die Stiftungen für die Toten in Recht, Religion und politischem Denken der Römer." In *Über römisches Recht im Rahmen der Kulturgeschichte*, 46–100. Berlin, 1954.)

Brunt, P. A. *Italian Manpower*. Oxford, 1971.

———. "Two Great Roman Landowners." *Latomus* 34 (1975): 619–35.

———. *The Fall of the Roman Republic and Related Essays*. Oxford, 1988.

Bryant, C. D., and W. E. Snizek. "The Last Will and Testament: A Neglected Document in Sociological Research." *Sociology and Social Research* 59 (1974/75): 219–30.

Bund, E. "Erbrechtliche Geldquellen römischer Kaiser." In *Festschrift für Franz Wieacker zum 70. Geburtstag*, edited by O. Behrends et al., 50–65. Göttingen, 1978.

Bürge, H. "Cum in familia nubas: Zur wirtschaftlichen und sozialen Bedeutung der familia libertorum." *Zeitschrift der Savigny-Stiftung für Rechtsgeschichte (Romanistische Abteilung)* 105 (1988): 312–33.

Champlin, E. "Miscellanea testamentaria I–III." *Zeitschrift für Papyrologie und Epigraphik* 62 (1986): 247–55.

———. "Miscellanea testamentaria IV–VII." *Zeitschrift für Papyrologie und Epigraphik* 69 (1987): 197–206.

———. "The Testament of the Piglet." *Phoenix* 41 (1987): 174–83.

———. "*Creditur vulgo testamenta hominum speculum esse morum:* Why the Romans Made Wills." *Classical Philology* 84 (1989): 198–215.

———. "The Testament of Augustus." *Rheinisches Museum* 132 (1989): 154–65.

Cichorius, C. "Ein neuer Historiker und die Anfänge von Livius." In *Römische Studien*, 261–69. Leipzig, 1922.

*Collectio bibliographica operum ad ius Romanum pertinentium*. Brussels, 1949–78.

Corbier, M. "Idéologie et pratique de l'héritage (Ier s. av. J-C – IIe s. ap. J-C)." *Index* 13 (1985): 501–28.

Crook, J. "A Legal Point about Mark Antony's Will." *Journal of Roman Studies* 47 (1957): 36–38.

———. "Intestacy in Roman Society." *Proceedings of the Cambridge Philological Society* 199 (1973): 38–44.

———. "Women in Roman Succession." In *The Family in Ancient Rome*, edited by B. Rawson, 58–82. Ithaca, N.Y., 1986.

Daube, D. "The Predominance of Intestacy at Rome." *Tulane Law Review* 39 (1964/65): 253–62.

———. *Roman Law: Linguistic, Social, and Philosophical Aspects*. Edinburgh, 1969.

Deen, J. W. "Patterns of Testation: Four Tidewater Counties in Colonial Virginia." *American Journal of Legal History* 16 (1972): 154–76.

Dixon, S. "*Infirmitas sexus:* Womanly Weakness in Roman Law." *Tijdschrift voor Rechtsgeschiednis* 52 (1984): 343–71.

——. "Breaking the Law to Do the Right Thing: The Gradual Erosion of the Lex Voconia in Ancient Rome." *Adelaide Law Review* 9 (1985): 519–34.

——. "Polybius on Roman Women and Property." *American Journal of Philology* 106 (1985): 147–70.

Dumont, F. "Le testament d'Antoine." In *Droits de l'antiquité et sociologie juridique: Mélanges Henri Lévy-Bruhl*, 85–104. Paris, 1959.

Duncan-Jones, R. P. *The Economy of the Roman Empire: Quantitative Studies.* 2d ed. Cambridge, 1982.

Dunham, A. "The Method, Process, and Frequency of Wealth Transmission at Death." *University of Chicago Law Review* 30 (1962/63): 241–85.

Eck, W. "Zum neuen Fragment des sogenannten Testamentum Dasumii." *Zeitschrift für Papyrologie und Epigraphik* 30 (1978): 277–95.

Epstein, S. *Wills and Wealth in Medieval Genoa: 1150–1250.* Cambridge, Mass., 1984.

Fabre, G. *Libertus: Recherches sur les rapports patron-affranchi à la fin de la république romaine.* Rome, 1981.

France, R. S. "Wills." *History* 50 (1965): 36–39.

Friedländer, L. *Darstellungen aus der Sittengeschichte Roms.* 10th ed. Leipzig, 1922.

Friedman, L. M. "Patterns of Testation in the Nineteenth Century: A Study of Essex County (New Jersey) Wills." *American Journal of Legal History* 8 (1964): 34–53.

Gardner, J. F. *Women in Roman Law and Society.* London, 1986.

——. "Another Family and an Inheritance: Claudius Brasidas and His Ex-wife's Will." *Liverpool Classical Monthly* 12 (1987): 52–54.

Gaudemet, J. " 'Testamenta ingrata et pietas Augusti': Contribution à l'étude du sentiment impérial." In *Studi in onore di Vincenzo Arangio-Ruiz*, 3: 115–37. Naples, 1953.

Geary, P. J. *Aristocracy in Provence: The Rhône Valley at the Dawn of the Carolingian Age.* Stuttgart, 1985.

Genzmer, E. "La genèse du fideicommis comme institution juridique." *Revue historique de droit français et étranger*[4] 40 (1962): 319–50.

Gilliam, J. F. "The Minimum Subject to the *vicensima hereditatium*." *American Journal of Philology* 73 (1952): 397–405.

Goody, J. "Strategies of Heirship." In *Production and Reproduction: A Comparative Study of the Domestic Domain*, 86–98. Cambridge, 1976.

——. *The Development of Family and Marriage in Europe.* Cambridge, 1983.

Gottfried, R. S. *Epidemic Disease in Fifteenth Century England: The Medieval Response and the Demographic Consequences.* New Brunswick, N.J., 1978.

Grosso, G. *I legati nel diritto romano.* 2d ed. Turin, 1962.

Guarino, A. "Pauli de iure codicillorum liber singularis." *Zeitschrift der Savigny-Stiftung für Rechtsgeschichte (Romanistische Abteilung)* 62 (1942): 209–54.

Hands, A. R. *Charities and Social Aid in Greece and Rome.* London, 1968.

Harries, J. " 'Treasure in Heaven': Property and Inheritance among Senators of Late Rome." In *Marriage and Property*, edited by E. M. Craik, 54–70. Aberdeen, 1984.

Hatt, J. J. *La tombe gallo-romain*. Paris, 1951. (Reprinted 1986.)

Häusle, H. *Das Denkmal als Garant des Nachruhms*. Munich, 1980.

Henne, H. "A propos du testament de César." In *Droits de l'antiquité et sociologie juridique: Mélanges Henri Lévy-Bruhl*, 141–51. Paris, 1959.

Heurgon, J. "Les éléments italiques dans la satire romaine." *Wissensch. Zeitschr. der Universität Rostock* 15 (1966): 431–39. (Reprinted in *Scripta Varia*, 67–87. Brussels, 1986.)

Hirschfeld, O. *Die kaiserliche Verwaltungsbeamten bis auf Diocletian*. 2d ed. Berlin, 1905.

Hobson, D. "Women as Property Owners in Roman Egypt." *Transactions and Proceedings of the American Philological Association* 113 (1983): 311–21.

Hohl, E. "Zu den Testamenten des Augustus." *Klio* 30 (1937): 323–42.

Hopkins, K. "Brother-Sister Marriage in Roman Egypt." *Comparative Studies in Society and History* 22 (1980).

———. *Death and Renewal: Sociological Studies in Roman History*. Vol. 2. Cambridge, 1983.

Horsfall, N. "Some Problems in the 'Laudatio Turiae.' " *Bulletin of the Institute of Classical Studies of the University of London* 30 (1983): 85–98.

Howell, C. "Peasant Inheritance Customs in the Midlands." In *Family and Inheritance: Rural Society in Western Europe, 1200–1800*, edited by J. Goody et al., 112–55. Cambridge, 1980.

Humbert, M. *Le remariage à Rome: Étude d'histoire juridique et sociale*. Milan, 1972.

Humphreys, S. C. "Death and Time." In *Mortality and Immortality: The Anthropology and Archaeology of Death*, edited by S. C. Humphreys and H. King. London, 1981. (Reprinted in *The Family, Women, and Death: Comparative Studies*, 144–64. London, 1983.)

*Index: Operum ad ius romanum pertinentium quae ab anno mcmxl ad annum mcmlxx edita sunt index*. 1978–82.

Johnson, J. R. "The Authenticity and Validity of Antony's Will." *L'Antiquité Classique* 47 (1978): 494–503.

Johnston, D. "Munificence and *municipia*: Bequests to Towns in Classical Roman Law." *Journal of Roman Studies* 75 (1985): 105–25.

———. "Prohibitions and Perpetuities: Family Settlements in Roman Law." *Zeitschrift der Savigny-Stiftung für Rechtsgeschichte (Romanistische Abteilung)* 102 (1985): 220–90.

———. *The Roman Law of Trusts*. Oxford, 1988.

———. "Trusts and Tombs." *Zeitschrift für Papyrologie und Epigraphik* 72 (1988): 81–87.

———. "Successive Rights and Successful Remedies: Life Interests in Roman Law." In *New Perspectives in the Roman Law of Property: Essays for Barry Nicholas*, edited by P. Birks, 153–67. Oxford, 1989.

Kaser, M. *Das römische Privatrecht.* Vol. 1, *Das altrömische, das vorklassische und klassische Recht.* 2d ed. Munich, 1971.

——. "Zum römischen Grabrecht." *Zeitschrift der Savigny-Stiftung für Rechtsgeschichte (Romanistische Abteilung)* 95 (1978): 15–92.

Keenan, J. G. "Tacitus, Roman Wills and Political Freedom." *Bulletin of the American Society of Papyrologists* 24 (1987): 1–8.

Kelly, J. M. "The *Centumviri.*" Chap. 1 in *Studies in the Civil Judicature of the Roman Republic.* Oxford, 1976.

Kreller, H. *Erbrechtliche Untersuchungen auf Grund der graeco-aegyptischen Papyrusurkunden.* Leipzig, 1919.

Kroll, W. *Die Kultur der Ciceronischen Zeit.* Vol. 1, *Politik und Wirtschaft.* Leipzig, 1933.

Kuryłowicz, M. "Heres fiduciarius: Bemerkungen zum römischen Erbrecht in den lateinischen Grabinschriften." *Zeitschrift für Papyrologie und Epigraphik* 60 (1985): 189–98.

La Pira, G. *La successione ereditaria intestata e contro il testamento in diritto romano.* Milan, 1930.

Lattimore, R. *Themes in Greek and Latin Epitaphs.* Urbana, Ill., 1942.

Le Bras, G. "Les fondations privées du Haut-Empire." *Studi in onore di Salvatore Riccobono* 3: 23–67. Palermo, 1936.

Lenel, O. *Palingenesia Iuris Civilis.* Leipzig, 1889, 1960.

Levick, B. "Atrox fortuna." *Classical Review* 22 (1972): 309–11.

Lussana, A. "Osservazioni sulle testimonianze di munificenza privata della Gallia Cisalpina nelle iscrizioni Latine." *Epigraphica* 12 (1950): 116–23.

——. "Munificenza privata nell'Africa romana." *Epigraphica* 14 (1952): 100–113.

——. "Contributo agli studi sulla munificenza privata in alcune regioni dell'Impero." *Epigraphica* 18 (1956): 77–93.

Maine, H. *Ancient Law.* New York, 1864.

Mansbach, A. R. *Captatio: Myth and Reality.* Diss., Princeton University, 1982.

Mannzmann, A. *Griechische Stiftungsurkunden: Studie zu Inhalt und Rechtsform.* Münster, 1962.

Marino, F. "Il falso testamentario nel diritto romano." *Zeitschrift der Savigny-Stiftung für Rechtsgeschichte (Romanistische Abteilung)* 105 (1988): 634–63.

Marshall, A. J. "The Case of Valeria: An Inheritance Dispute in Roman Asia." *Classical Quarterly* 25 (1975): 82–87.

Martini, R. "Sulla presenza dei 'signatores' all'apertura del testamento." In *Studi in onore di Giuseppe Grosso* 1: 483–95. Turin, 1968.

Migliardi Zingale, L. "Note a nuovi documenti testamentari romani." *Anagennesis* 2 (1982): 109–29.

Millar, F. *The Emperor in the Roman World.* London, 1977.

Mitchell, S. "Sestullii: A Roman Family in Phrygia." *Anatolian Studies* 29 (1979): 13–22.

Mohler, S. L. "Cicero's Legacies." *Transactions and Proceedings of the American Philological Association* 63 (1932): 73–87.

Montevecchi, O. "Ricerche di sociologia nei documenti dell'Egitto greco-romano: I. I testamenti." *Aegyptus* 15 (1935): 67–121.

Moreau, P. "Patrimoines et successions à Larinum au Ier siècle av. J.-C." *Revue historique de droit français et étranger* 66 (1986): 169–89.

el-Mosallamy, A. H. S. "Revocation of Wills in Roman Egypt." *Aegyptus* 50 (1970): 59–73.

Mrozek, S. "Quelques remarques sur les inscriptions relatives aux distributions privées d'argent et de la nourriture dans les municipes italiens aux Ier, IIe, et IIIe siècles d.n.e." *Epigraphica* 30 (1968): 156–71.

———. "Les bénéficiaires des distributions privées d'argent et de nourriture dans les villes italiennes à l'époque du Haut-Empire." *Epigraphica* 34 (1972): 30–54.

Nielsen, H. S. "*Alumnus:* A Term of Relation Denoting Quasi-adoption." *Classica et Mediaevalia* 38 (1987): 141–88.

Nisoli, E. *Die Testamentseröffnung im römischen Recht.* Diss., Bern, 1949.

Nonn, U. "Merowingische Testamente: Studien zum Fortleben einer römischen Urkundenform im Frankreich." *Archiv für Diplomatik* 18 (1972): 1–129.

Norden, F. *Apulejus von Madaura und das römische Privatrecht.* Leipzig and Berlin, 1912.

Pavis d'Escurac, H. "Pline le Jeune et la transmission des patrimoines." *Ktema* 3 (1978): 275–88.

Pomeroy, S. "Women in Roman Egypt." In *Reflections of Women in Antiquity,* edited by H. Foley, 303–22. New York, 1981.

Préaux, C. "Sur les fondations dans l'Egypte gréco-romain." *Revue Internationale des Droits de l'Antiquité*[3] 3 (1956): 145–72.

Purcell, N. "Tomb and Suburb." In *Römische Gräberstrassen. Selbstdarstellung—Status—Standard,* edited by H. von Hesberg and P. Zanker, 25–41. *Bayerische Akademie der Wissenschaften, Philosophisch-Historische Klasse, Abhandlungen,* n.f. 96. Munich, 1987.

Rawson, B., ed. *The Family in Ancient Rome.* Ithaca, N.Y., 1986.

Renier, E. *Étude sur l'histoire de la querela inofficiosi en droit romain.* Liège, 1942.

Rogers, R. S. "The Roman Emperors as Heirs and Legatees." *Transactions and Proceedings of the American Philological Association* 78 (1947): 140–58.

Rosenthal, J. T. *The Purchase of Paradise: Gift Giving and the Aristocracy, 1307–1485.* London, 1972.

Rossi, A. M. "Ricerche sulle multe sepolcri romane." *Rivista storica dell' Antichità* 5 (1975): 111–59.

Saller, R. P. *Personal Patronage under the Early Empire.* Cambridge, 1982.

———. "Roman Dowry and the Devolution of Property in the Principate." *Classical Quarterly* 34 (1984): 195–205.

———. *Patria potestas* and the Stereotype of the Roman Family." *Continuity and Change* 1 (1986): 7–22.

——. "Men's Age at Marriage and Its Consequences in the Roman Family." *Classical Philology* 82 (1987): 21–34.

——. "*Pietas*, Obligation, and Authority in the Roman Family." In *Alte Geschichte und Wissenschaft: Festschrift für Karl Christ zum 65. Geburtstag*, edited by P. Kneissl and V. Losemann, 393–410. Darmstadt, 1988.

——. "Roman Heirship Strategies: In Principle and in Practice." Forthcoming.

Saller, R. P., and B. D. Shaw. "Tombstones and Roman Family Relations in the Principate: Civilians, Soldiers, and Slaves." *Journal of Roman Studies* 74 (1984): 124–56.

Sallmann, K. "Satirische Technik in Horaz's Erbsleichersatire." *Hermes* 98 (1970): 178–203.

Schmitthenner, W. *Oktavian und das Testament Cäsars*. 2d ed. Munich, 1973.

Schmitt-Pantel, P. "Évergetisme et mémoire du mort: A propos des fondations de banquets publics dans les cités grecques à l'époque hellénistique et romaine." In *La mort, les morts dans les sociétés anciennes*, edited by G. Gnoli and J.-P. Vernant, 177–88. Cambridge, 1982.

Schulz, F. *History of Roman Legal Science*. 2d ed. Oxford, 1953.

Scialoia, V. "Il testamento di Vergilio." *Athenaeum* 8 (1930): 168–73. (Reprinted in *Scritti giuridici* 2: 303–6. Rome, 1934.)

Shatzman, I. *Senatorial Wealth and Roman Politics*. Brussels, 1975.

Shaw, B. D. "The Age of Roman Girls at Marriage: Some Reconsiderations." *Journal of Roman Studies* 77 (1987): 30–46.

——. "The Family in Late Antiquity: The Experience of Augustine." *Past and Present* 115 (1987): 3–51.

Sheehan, M. M. *The Will in Medieval England from the Conversion of the Anglo-Saxons to the End of the Thirteenth Century*. Toronto, 1963.

Spawforth, A. J. S. "Balbilla, the Euryclids and Memorials for a Greek Magnate." *Papers of the British School at Athens* 73 (1978): 249–60.

Syme, R. "Clues to Testamentary Adoption." *Tituli* 4 (Rome, 1982) 1: 397–410.

——. "The Testamentum Dasumii: Some Novelties." *Chiron* 15 (1985): 41–63.

Taubenschlag, R. *The Law of Greco-Roman Egypt in the Light of the Papyri (332 B.C. – 640 A.D.)*. 2d ed. Warsaw, 1955.

Tellegen, J. W. "*Captatio* and *crimen*." *Revue Internationale des Droits de l'Antiquité*[3] 26 (1979): 387–96.

——. *The Roman Law of Succession in Pliny the Younger*. Vol. 1. Zutphen, 1982.

Toynbee, J. M. C. *Death and Burial in the Roman World*. London, 1971.

Tracy, V. A. "*Aut captantur aut captant*." *Latomus* 39 (1980): 399–402.

Veyne, P. "La famille et l'amour sous le haut-empire romain." *Annales. Economies, Sociétés, Civilizations* 33 (1978): 35–63.

Vidal, H. "Le dépôt in aede." *Revue historique de droit français et étranger*[4] 43 (1965): 545–87.

Visky, K. "Tracce di diritto ereditario romano nelle iscrizioni della Pannonia." *Iura* 13 (1962): 110–32.

de Visscher, F. "Les fondations privées en droit romain classique." *Revue Internationale des Droits de l'Antiquité*[3] 2 (1955): 197–218. (Reprinted in *Études de droit romain public et privé*, 189–207. Milan, 1966.)

——. *Le droit des tombeaux romains.* Milan, 1963.

——. "La carrière et le testament d'un préfet du prétoire de Tibère." *Bulletin de la Classe des Lettres de l'Académie Royale de Belgique* (1957): 168–79. (Revised version in *Études de droit romain public et privé*, 71–87. Milan, 1966.)

*Vocabularium Codicis Iustiniani.* Prague, 1923–25.

*Vocabularium Iurisprudentiae Romanae.* Berlin, 1903– .

Voci, P. *Diritto ereditario romano.* 2d ed. Milan, 1963–67.

Wallace-Hadrill, A. "Family and Inheritance in the Augustan Marriage Laws." *Proceedings of the Cambridge Philological Society* 207 (1981): 58–80.

Waltzing, J.-P. *Étude historique sur les corporations professionelles chez les Romains depuis les origines jusqu'à la chute de l'empire d'Occident.* Louvain, 1895–1900.

Watson, A. "The Identity of Sarapio, Socrates, Longus, and Nilus in the Will of C. Longinus Castor." *Irish Jurist* 1 (1966): 313–15.

——. *The Law of Persons in the Late Roman Republic.* Oxford, 1967.

——. *The Law of Succession in the Late Roman Republic.* Oxford, 1971.

Wenger, L. *Die Quellen des römischen Rechts.* Vienna, 1953.

Wieacker, F. "Hausgenossenschaft und Erbeinsetzung: Über die Anfänge des römischen Testaments." In *Festschrift der Leipziger Juristen Fakultät für Dr. Heinrich Siber zum 10 April 1940*, 1–57. Leipzig, 1941.

——. "The *causa curiana* and Contemporary Roman Jurisprudence." *Irish Jurist* 2 (1967): 151–64.

Wiedemann, T. E. J. "The Regularity of Manumission at Rome." *Classical Quarterly* 35 (1985): 162–75.

Wistrand, E. *Arv och testamenten i romarnas sociala liv.* Vol. 22 of *Studia graeca et latina Gothoburgensia.* Göteborg, 1966. (With a synopsis in German, pp. 28–30.)

——. *The So-called Laudatio Turiae.* Vol. 34 of *Studia graeca et latina Gothoburgensia.* Göteborg, 1976.

von Woess, F. *Das römische Erbrecht und die Erbanwärter: Ein Beitrag zur Kenntnis des römischen Rechtslebens vor und nach der Constitutio Antoniniana.* Berlin, 1911.

Wörrle, M. *Stadt und Fest in kaiserzeitlichen Kleinasien: Studien zu einer agonistischen Stiftung aus Oinoanda.* Munich, 1988.

Wrightson, K. "Kinship in an English Village: Terling, Essex, 1500–1700." In *Land, Kinship, and Life-cycle*, edited by R. M. Smith, 313–32. Cambridge, 1984.

Wrigley, E. A. "Fertility Strategy for the Individual and the Group." In *Historical Studies of Changing Fertility*, edited by C. Tilly, 134–54. Princeton, 1978.

# Index

Designer:    Barbara Jellow
Compositor:    Metro Typography
Text:    10/13 Baskerville
Display:    Baskerville
Printer:    BookCrafters
Binder:    BookCrafters